SPEED >

SPEED

*Facing Our Addiction
to Fast and Faster—
and Overcoming Our
Fear of Slowing Down*

STEPHANIE BROWN, PhD

BERKLEY BOOKS, NEW YORK

THE BERKLEY PUBLISHING GROUP
Published by the Penguin Group
Penguin Group (USA) LLC
375 Hudson Street, New York, New York 10014

USA • Canada • UK • Ireland • Australia • New Zealand • India • South Africa • China

penguin.com

A Penguin Random House Company

This book is an original publication of The Berkley Publishing Group.

Library of Congress Cataloging-in-Publication Data

Brown, Stephanie, (date–)
Speed : facing our addiction to fast and faster—and overcoming
our fear of slowing down / Stephanie Brown.
pages cm
ISBN 978-0-425-26473-7 (pbk.)
1. Compulsive behavior.   2. Speed—Psychological aspects.   3. Technological innovations—
Psychological aspects.   4. Progress—Psychological aspects.   5. Change (Psychology).
6. Slow life movement.   I. Title.
RC533.B756 2014
616.85'84—dc23
2013032750

PUBLISHING HISTORY
Berkley trade paperback edition / January 2014

PRINTED IN THE UNITED STATES OF AMERICA

10   9   8   7   6   5   4   3   2   1

Cover image: Abstract blue © Style_TTT / Shutterstock.
Cover design by Diana Kolsky.
Text design by Tiffany Estreicher.

For Haddie and Cammie:
May you always savor the joys of quiet
time in a slow-enough world

ACKNOWLEDGMENTS

Thank you. Thank you to so many colleagues, friends, clients, and family for years of support on this massive project. In contrast to the subject of *Speed*—this crazy, fast pace of life so many of us now think of as normal—the conception, writing, and revising of this book have gone on and on for many years. This book has been SLOW to find itself, and I trust it will be better for it.

The idea of a culture out of control needed time to develop. People heard it, began to read about it, and to watch themselves. More and more joined me in support. Three made this book happen. First, writer Joan O'C. Hamilton has given me hands-on help with editing, support, and advice through a long, difficult process. Networker extraordinaire, she connected me with agent Jillian Manus, who believed in the idea and the book. She found Denise Silvestro at Penguin, who agreed: speed is a serious problem that isn't going away. Denise has given me a tutorial in popular writing, for which I am grateful, as well as unquestioning support for the idea of cultural speed as an addiction, and the process of recovery as a model for societal change.

Many others offered direct help and sustaining support. With great skill, Yvonne Pearson worked closely with me on the first draft of the manuscript, taking my leave-nothing-out first pass and trimming it down to cohesive, submission-ready form.

Next came friends who read the manuscript and/or offered support from early on. Barbara Tyler, Anne Hillman, Paul Goldstein, Laurel Leone, JoAnn Stultz, Gloria Van Bree, and Dave Mandelbrot seemed to never tire of the saga of *Speed*, and offered wise advice about the book and publishing.

My Addiction Institute associates offered the same endless support, always asking, "What about *Speed*?" Long-standing colleagues Tom Gorham and Patrick MacAfee offered me speaking opportunities early on, as did Santa Clara University, while cheerleaders Cathy Calliotte, Ed and Esther Bourg, Lenora Yuen and John Peters, Thomas and Kären Nagy, Cynthia Scheutz and Jim Perkins, Ellyn Bader and Peter Pearson, Barbara and Ric Almond, and Joyce Schmid never lagged in spirit. Mary Jaiswal, Alison Reichenthal, William Reichenthal, Courtney Hughes, and Irene McGhee gave great examples. Computer guru Jon Wu jumps in to save the day.

My childhood friends Robin, Linda, and Patricia have followed the writing for years. It's safe to say everyone will be glad to see *Speed* finally arrive!

Last, but always first, I thank my husband, Bob Harris, for his support, examples, and humor; our daughter Makenzie; son-in-law Anthony; and our granddaughters, Campbell and Hadley, who have filled our lives with love, meaning, and purpose, ever reminding us that our cherished bonds grow deeper as we slow down, listen, and talk together.

Stephanie Brown
August 2013

CONTENTS

PART 1

Speed: A Cultural
Addiction to a
Fast Pace of Life

Prologue

"Help! I need to go faster, I can't go any faster, and I can't stop or even slow down!" This is the cry I began to hear more than fifteen years ago as people started to realize that the world of technology, with its promise of limitless speed and a guarantee of boundless riches and success, had trapped them in a virulent downward spiral of addiction.

"I can't do it all, but I can't stop trying. I wake up earlier and earlier to steal time to catch up, to pay attention to the kids, to pack their lunches, to get them off to school without shouting, to answer email from last week, to call the East Coast ahead of the rush of my day, to endure a slowed-down drive through traffic to get to the board meeting while I'm wondering how I'll cook dinner and make parent-teacher night. I think I can do it all, but the sad truth is I can't." This was from Maria, a successful woman of the twenty-first century, and her lament is all too common.

I have spent most of my professional life working with

individuals grappling with the idea of limits. The very essence of addiction to anything—drugs, alcohol, sex, work—is the unwinnable struggle between the desire to keep using or doing something that provides some kind of instant gratification and the reality that there are limits to how long such behavior can go on without severe, even lethal consequences.

This is a book about a new kind of addiction that I believe has taken hold in our culture. The bad news is that it is pervasive, cheap, and not yet widely accepted as the serious problem I believe it is. The good news is it is treatable, and everything we have learned about other addictions applies here.

I call it the addiction to speed. Obviously, I'm not talking about the drug methamphetamine. I'm talking about a culture-wide phenomenon that is snatching people up and carrying them along, convincing them that doing "more, better, and faster" is the path to happiness. Some people see it as the result of our increasingly wired society when children are texting their siblings sitting at the same breakfast table, and frequent fliers feel so deprived of their various devices by the end of a plane flight that touching down on the runway has become the universal signal that your suffering can end. Phones appear and the sound of finger tapping, beep dialing, and relieved voices reminds you that the "bar" is open.

I believe technology is only part of the story, however. Technology provides the tools for instant gratification in the same way a hypodermic needle provides an efficient delivery mechanism for heroin. That gratification comes from two places—the illusion of rapid connection to other people, and immediate access to information we feel we need, be it a Google Map, an investment insight, or the answer to a trivia question. If we look at the direction in which the tools are evolving, what we are seeing is a manifestation of this need for speed. We don't want to waste time speaking on our cell phones, so increasingly we send text messages. Email takes too long, so now we use Twitter. Typing a search query is too time consuming, so now an app allows people to speak into their phone, "Green's Restaurant, San Francisco," and up pops the phone number, a map, and an opportunity to make an online reservation. Although we claim we crave the connection to others, we don't want to "deal with" the ambiguities of face-to-face contact, the messy emotions, the meaningful commitment of unstructured time. Every outreach demands a choice: What is the fastest way for me to get exactly what I want?

What I am seeing in my practice as an addiction specialist is that, especially in urban areas, this speed trap is outstripping people's ability to manage, to fulfill all of their responsibilities, and even to cope. The idea that we literally have at our fingertips the tools to do so much more than we actually have the human capacity to do well has created an impossible bind that leads to chronic stress and a sense of failure. You do not have the ability to be on 24/7 like a computer, but you believe you should be able to keep going, and that you will be able to do so if you only try harder. And so you push yourself incessantly, creating an addictive spiral. You can't stop. And, you know deeply, if you never stop, you won't have to face and feel your limits, which sadly also means your failure. The cultural belief so rooted in our heritage that there are no limits to what we can achieve, and the tools of technology that do indeed seem limitless, have created a condition of chronic stress for us as individuals and for the culture in which we live. The American mantra that you can have it all is false, but we can't face that truth. Nobody can work 24/7 and nobody can do it all. But recognizing the reality of our human limits still means failure in our culture of win-at-all-costs success.

Society is captured in this out-of-control state of expectation and behavior. We do it to ourselves and others reinforce it. People reach out to us to demand what they want, twenty-four hours a day, seven days a week. We can no longer have a lovely dinner alone with our partner or our children, or even go on vacation, without constant interruption. We often wish we could freeze time and turn off the access, but we don't; we fret we will be perceived as unable or unwilling to keep pace.

We are suffering from this chronic stress. It causes health problems, it causes relationships to fall apart, it leads to emptiness and despair. We value the technology marketed as a tool to solve dilemmas and make our lives easier, and at the same time we feel trapped by the demands it makes on us. Multitasking, the buzz-word for "achievement" over the last fifteen years, has become the source of multi-problems.

As a psychologist, I have watched many people get caught in this conundrum and have seen how terribly it has hurt them. In the decade of the roaring nineties—the 1990s that is—I began to see a few people in my addiction psychotherapy treatment practice who weren't having trouble with either their own or a loved one's drinking or use of other drugs. They were feeling overwhelmed by their lives, by a feeling of pressure to succeed, and by their actual achievements. They were feeling and living out of control. On a fast track, they were enjoying the highs of work and financial rewards, yet they were also living in fear that they couldn't keep it up. By the time they got through my door, the fear was omnipresent and more intense than the pleasures of success.

As I puzzled about how to help my clients slow down and reclaim their lives, I realized that America's frenzied lifestyle—this thing I refer to as speed—has itself become an addiction. People are out of control in their push to do more, to always be on and available, and to never say no. Addiction means you cannot stop doing something—drinking, taking pills and more pills, shooting up, gambling, spending, overeating, staying on the computer till dawn—and you need to stop. The physical and emotional pain of stopping is too great, so you are pulled back to do it again. You tell yourself you can stop, and you really believe you will stop when you've had enough, finished your project, or met your goals. But this false belief simply keeps you trying to work harder to do more. With addiction there is no such thing as enough, no finish to anything, just more new goals to trump the old ones that are out-of-date before you get there.

But there's good news: Recognizing that this drive for speed is an addiction gives people a way out, a way to recover and return to a healthy and balanced life. As with other addictions, this is not a realization that comes easily. Before they begin the process of recovery, virtually all addicts reject the idea of limits. Addicts indulge in a fantasy of omnipotence, that if they are clever and determined, they can both feed an addiction and maintain a functional life and normal relationships. In reality, however, the addicted individual is in a downward spiral that may be hidden for some period of time, but that ultimately leads to a crash or multiple crashes—of health, of soul, of marriage, of career, or even a physical accident.

A patient recently arrived late to my office, tossed his cell phone on the sofa, and pleaded: "Can you help me control my phone? It's ruining my life." Dave laughed, but he meant it. In his view, his phone, supposedly a tool, was actually controlling him, and he was feeling burned out and frightened. As it happened, he felt reactive to his phone, needing to constantly monitor it, afraid of the onslaught of calls he believed he had to answer.

He was also caught in an emotional conflict. The phone, with its instant access to others, had opened for him a world of business success. Now he needed to hear its ring to reassure him that he mattered, that he was still in the game, so he felt a jolt of relief when the sound of Metallica signaled a call. At the same time it frightened him when this welcome sound interrupted his attention to his three-year-old son. "Daddy, don't answer! Watch me!" pleaded his child, who was building a tower of blocks. Dad knew he was in trouble when he was irritated and couldn't turn his phone off to focus on his child. He believed his phone gave him vital connections and he could control his use. Instead of recognizing his limits, he was furious that he couldn't do it all and he snapped at his son. This is the paradox of addiction. What seemed so good, so positive, so helpful, and so harmless in the beginning, ended up hurting him, and he was hooked.

This book is my story of what I've seen and heard in the last twenty years in my office, on the lecture trail, when teaching therapists, and in my own personal world. It's my view of what it is like in a society living with a rejection of limits and an addictive loss of control, and only beginning to wake up to it.

I speak from my own experience. This is my story of what I see and what I know—personally and professionally—about the culture I'm part of. I'm a reporter here, informed by my own experiences as a recovering alcoholic who came face-to-face with my own limits, as a child of alcoholic parents, and as a theorist and therapist for more than thirty-five years, working with people who were once out of control and are now engaged in a developmental process of change and growth in recovery. All of these experiences have shaped the way I see things.

But that's not all. In the twentieth century, a dominant view in my profession of psychology was a belief in the power of human will, the power of individuals to be in control—to be tough, to take charge of any problem or any situation. In this prevailing view of American psychology, there were no limits to what human will could achieve. If you don't like something, get a grip and change it. That same belief in human power was a cornerstone in the founding of America and it continues to be central to the country's values and character. If you're not in control, you're failing..

As a recovering alcoholic training to be a psychologist in the early 1970s I experienced firsthand a conflict in belief between traditional mental health theories and practices—based on a belief in human power, treatment of any kind should help people restore control—and the emerging field of addiction treatment, shaped by knowledge of the Alcoholics Anonymous (AA) program. In my view, these worlds collided around core beliefs about control and the limits of human power. While psychology believed in the human power to restore lost control, AA was based on a deep acceptance of the loss of control over one's drinking and the inability to ever reclaim control. AA was founded on a fundamental acceptance of human limits.

In working with recovering people who are members of AA, I have often heard comments about "normies"—normal people who can drink without problems. These are people who are not struggling for control. One joke goes: "Wow, if I could drink like you, I'd do it all the time." This is humorous because the alcoholic can't stop. He or she has lost control and eventually must stop completely. The alcoholic was never the normie.

Until now. As I've observed our culture over the last twenty years, I see that society has lost control. Society as a whole, and the people who make up society, now look and sound like addicts. People are out of control in their drive for speed. They are out of control in their behaviors, thinking, emotions, and the addicted lifestyle they create. Ambitious people and people who are simply caught up in a cultural wave believe they should have no limits, they can do everything if they only work harder and smarter, and success and a time-out lie at the end of an imaginary finish line. Yet they cannot stop their push to get in one more call, check off one more task, or play one more poker hand, behaviors that become robotic, automatic, mindless.

This is addiction: You can't stop. Your behavior becomes automatic. A voice inside warns that you really should slow down, but you don't have a brake that works anymore. You are driven by strong emotions of need and fear that become a compulsion to keep going. As you race into my office, finishing up a last call, you sink into the chair with a sigh as you apologize for being late. You are living the American dream. There is not much left in our culture that values or models restraint or limits, and you know an apology will do the trick.

I live and work in Silicon Valley, the heart of technology innovation and revolution over the last thirty years. I have felt the pace of my world increase dramatically in the last fifteen years, with pressures all around me to do more, go faster, and think smarter in every aspect of my life. I've felt it in my work, as more people call in crisis, out of control with alcohol or other drugs, hooked on prescription meds to wake up and go to sleep so they can maintain their fast pace, or frantic about an adolescent child who has shut down emotionally, turned to marijuana and all-night marathons of video games to cope with the constant pressure to keep up, to achieve, to push the limits.

I've felt it in my neighborhood with massive construction and denser traffic, with drivers gunning their engines on this residential street as if to show themselves and others that they are already behind and working hard to catch up. I've felt it in the local middle school, where for the past twenty-one years I've given an annual lecture to eighth graders. Early on I had a quiet hour to teach these kids about addiction, to engage with them in thinking about what addiction is and how widespread and rampant it is. I would ask them, "What is a craving?" Hands went up and voices shouted: "You've gotta have it; you need it." Does craving hurt? Is it painful? "Yeees!" What do you need? "Chocolate! Cheetos! Video games!" What is addiction? "You can't stop! You do it, you take it, and you have to have more." These kids already knew addiction. Today they holler out, "Music! Texting! Facebook!" and a new generation of video games. Chocolate is still on the list.

A few years ago my time was shortened to fifty minutes, which last year became forty minutes. There was no time to engage the kids. No time to go back and forth to hear them talk about craving, about an uncle who is an alcoholic, an older brother who found Oxycontin in the high school parking lot, and their parents who don't have time to sit down for a family dinner anymore. At the end of a rushed forty minutes, I felt my own failure. What did we just do together? We went through the motions. I started grasping for words when I realized halfway through that I couldn't cover it all and that many of these kids were waiting for the bell to ring so they could check their phones.

I said what I could about the fast pace of technology and Internet addiction in that short time window. Afterward, Keeshawn, a young man of thirteen, approached to tell me he was out of control. "I am that kid you described, the one who is up all night on the computer. My parents are screaming at me to stop, but I can't. My mind tells me to turn it off, but I can't. I *have* to play another round. People tell me I'm choosing to do this, but I'm not choosing. I don't have a choice. I can't get up for school, can't concentrate at all, and I can't wait to get back online. Please help me." Unfortunately Keeshawn's problem is not unique; I have heard this often. I told him that I understood and offered school names and community resources where he could find some assistance. I wished I'd had time to talk with him longer and to facilitate a link back to his school adviser. But it was rush, rush, out the door as we were told to vacate the room. My time was over. Yet another failure as a result of our constant rush.

I have encountered this pulsing sense of urgency—the craving and the need to be in action—in patients who talk about how hard it is to be in recovery from a chemical addiction and feel the un-yielding pressures of the workplace. As recovering alcoholics and addicts, they know they have limits. But they live in a world that denies this same truth. The normie of today denies the need for limits. Just like Maria, Dave, and Keeshawn, we all do have limits.

Living in Silicon Valley, I was in the bubble of the tech world at the beginning. Everything in the nineties and the first part of 2000 was going up. Everything was growing, expanding, and moving faster. There were no limits. But this was not a problem! This was success! Anything and everything was now possible. This was the start of something *big*, and you didn't want to be left behind. The sound of a ringing cell phone in a quiet restaurant was jarring and new, but it was also a sure sign of status: you were on to a major deal and you needed to take this call. That mentality soon became normal. Your need became everyone else's need to wait for you. The sound of a ring became a buzz in your pocket, but you had to answer then and now. There was electricity in the air, a contagious pressure to go, go, go. Anya described it: "I only have one speed. It's go. I am always on. Even in my quietest times and most intimate moments with others, my mind is racing ahead to what I'll say and what I'll do when I can check my screen. I can't listen. Listening feels like failure."

Because I lived at the starting gate, I was ahead of the rest of the country in experiencing this boom and no doubt had an earlier view of the culture's loss of control. Being an addiction specialist, I recognized the signs of a problem, and this made me a killjoy in many circles. Why would I want to burst this wild high? Why would I question the wisdom of such a pressured pace and lifestyle?

I worried about my daughter growing up in such an intense atmosphere, where "stressed out" was becoming part of normal teenage jargon. I began to think that the culture was addicted, that people were out of control in their drive to succeed.

One day while picking up the newspaper in my driveway I caught a moment with my high-tech neighbor, who usually left home before dawn and returned after dark. He said he loved the high of chasing invention and stock options and he loved his daily dose of adrenaline (sounds just like the heroin addict who feels the needle and then the sigh of relief). "It's a never-ending race," he said and then sighed. "But I'm running out of steam. I can't keep it up."

One day not long after, this thoughtful man left his job to figure out what he could do that wouldn't keep him in such an out-of-control frenzy and potentially ruin his life. At first he felt like a loser who would never be on the cutting-edge again, never welcome in the high-stakes locker room. Then he saw that he had almost lost everything—his marriage, his kids, his time for sports and reading fiction instead of just business books. He had lost his sense of downtime. Like Anya, Michael had just one speed. He had almost lost it all, because he believed he had no choice. He had to keep going even when this pace was robbing him of all that he loved. He has since rejoined the tech world but with a deep understanding of his human limits and the importance of slowing down.

Michael made the tough decision to set his own limits, even if it would cost him professionally. He sets his alarm for 5:30 a.m.

instead of 4:00 a.m. He set another alarm to leave the office at 6:00 p.m. for a sit-down family dinner with all phones turned off. At first he experienced physical withdrawal and a sense of loss. But he accepted his limits, got off the treadmill, and weathered months of fear. It was during that time that he deeply understood his need for limits. "When I am slow and reflective, thinking about myself, who I am and where I am, I see that I need more than one speed. It's a whole different way of thinking about success. I need *slow* in order to think, in order to protect my judgment. I lost the capacity to think and as a result totally lost my judgment. I made reckless decisions and did stupid things on impulse." Today he looks back, just like an alcoholic in recovery who hasn't had a drink for years looks back, to marvel at how he could have lost his way, believing he had no choice and that speeding through life was the high he really wanted.

Is Michael happy? "Well, yes and no," he said with a chuckle. "I know where I'd be if I hadn't slowed down and stopped being such a crazed person on a mission to attain higher status and wild success. I am happy and grateful that I have my family, that we are happy and loving together, and that I took the risk to slow down. But I have to say I sometimes feel a twinge of pain, of regret at what I'm missing, even though I know I don't want it and it's not even fun when you're so out of control and going so fast. Maybe it's nostalgia for the high of believing you never have to stop, just like an addict with the excitement and relief of a binge ahead. I'm happy now in a quieter and slower way. Would I go back? No. It was going to take me out."

This world of out-of-control, high-speed living is not only about technology, though that's what started the race. The advent of technology gave people the ability to go faster and to be always on, fueled by the belief that going faster was the path to success. The behaviors of constant, impulsive action, the belief that this is progress, and the feelings of intense pressure and frenzy have spilled over into all aspects of life. People are out of control in their drinking, their use of prescription medicines, their eating, their spending, and their use of all forms of technology. They are out of control internally with the constant buzz of one speed—on—as they "power" their way through life, unable to listen to others or emotionally connect, while they revel in the number of people they are "connected to" on their social media sites. The loss of control to speed has become a way of life.

Lest you think I'm proclaiming technology and the rapid advancement of technological capabilities evil forces to be slain and buried, let me assure you it's not so. It is not technology itself, but rather the loss of perspective about speed that is the problem. It's the absence of limits to anything that has become the problem.

Technology has many plusses. It is a leveler that may be the biggest equalizer and assimilator yet known in American culture. You have a cell phone—possibly even an iPhone—no matter how much you make, where you live, or what language you speak. But on the flip side, addiction has always been equal opportunity. An addiction to speed isn't limited to the middle and upper classes. It's now a philosophy of success in anything, for any class, any gender, or any ethnic identity. Young or old, rich or poor, black or white, gay or straight, you have to go fast and you have to keep going.

Despite my assurances that I am not against technology, you may be skeptical. I am accenting the problem of speed as a direct consequence of technology and the pace of rapid invention and competitive drive in a society with a long, proud history of rejecting limits.

The problem is not technology itself. I use these wondrous machines. I am not out on the stump preaching against the evils of Facebook and Twitter like Carry Nation and the prohibitionists railed against the evils of drink many years ago. I'm a happy oldie who grudgingly put down my yellow pad and pencil to write on my computer, and I have never looked back. I will go along with technology and I'm very grateful for all the lives now saved thanks to medical advances. If I'm ill, I want the latest and the best. So my struggle is not all or none. I don't want to do away with anything and I don't want to take away anybody's gadgets. I don't want to stop people from pursuing their investments and their opportunities as I pursue mine. But I do want to ask if we can slow things down without giving up progress.

I want to recognize that American society is now dominated by a deep conflict of interest: our culture demands speed from its members, and it results in loss of control. The drive for success through greater and greater speed becomes a chronic failure. I want to identify how so many of us have become addicted to speed, how this is encouraged and reinforced by our culture, and how seeing speed through the lens of addiction can help people reclaim their lives.

TWENTY QUESTIONS

How do you know if you're hooked? Many years ago, in the 1930s, Dr. Robert Seliger developed a simple questionnaire to help people determine if they were drinking too much. Known forever since as the Twenty Questions, these descriptions were long attributed to Johns Hopkins University and, inaccurately, to Alcoholics Anonymous. Then and now, individuals have been asking themselves these questions and finding the answer to the question: am I an alcoholic?

I have adapted the idea to the issue of speed as a cultural loss of control. Just like countless hundreds of thousands of people worldwide have looked at their use of alcohol, you can now ask: am I hooked on fast? As you read the list of behaviors, feelings, and ways of thinking that constitute the warning signs of an addiction to a speeded-up pace of life, see if anything fits for you. As I read this list in a lecture or even describe these signs in a social conversation, people often laugh with immediate recognition. Once you name it there it is. I do that! I think that! Oh yes, that's my feeling. Doesn't everybody? You mean it's not necessary? Not good for me? OMG! say Maria, Dave, and Michael.

Some of these questions may seem unclear or unrealistic. Some will be difficult to grasp at first. "Sure," you say, as you check numbers one, two, three, four, and on and on, "of course I have limits, but that's not how we live and operate in the world today. You have to get on board or you can't compete." But stop for a moment and really think about these questions. See if you can say yes to some of them, recognize that speed is a problem, and then begin to make small changes. As you read through the book, return to this list and see what else fits. Though it may be scary to really see that you don't have all the power you think you do, it will be a great relief over time. And as the world catches up to the recognition that everything is out of control, you will have faced that reality and taken steps to slow down.

So try it on. If just a few of these questions fit for you, read more. You will learn how society has fostered a wild, fast, speedy life as normal, and you will see if and how you are caught in this frenzied world of behavior, feelings, and beliefs.

Keep reading and you'll learn what is necessary to slow down and get unhooked from speed, and you'll learn how to do it.

Twenty Questions: Are You Hooked on Fast?

YOUR BEHAVIOR:

1. Do you want to slow down, but you cannot? Have you lost control?

2. Do you keep adding activities without taking any away?

3. Do you work longer and longer hours, but don't ever finish?

4. Do you treat other problems: sleep, anxiety, depression?

5. Do you act first and think later?

6. Do you check your email and reach for your phone first thing and last?

YOUR FEELINGS:

7. Do you feel internal pressure to live fast and act fast, which becomes a craving to "connect" more rapidly?

8. Do you feel empty if you are not in constant action?

9. Do you feel nervous without your tech gear in hand or pocket?

10. Do you feel the beep of your phone as a comfort that gives you a shot of adrenaline?

11. Do you feel you belong when you are rushing, stressed, and in action?

YOUR BELIEFS:

12. Do you believe you have no limits and you are entitled to live without limits?

13. Do you believe you should think, feel, react, and behave instantly?

14. Do you believe you will fall behind if you slow down?

15. Do you believe success equals fast and faster, and slowing down is failing?

16. Do you believe you should only feel good, only feel high; other feelings are a sign of failure?

17. Do you believe stress is the price of success and chaos is normal?

18. Do you believe that the "new intimacy" is through technology; less time for off-line relationships is the price of success?

19. Do you believe instant action is a virtue and you can overcome anything with enough willpower?

20. Do you believe all change must be big to count?

1

A Chance Encounter

In the spring of 2004 I was returning to my home in California. The plane touched down, and a fellow passenger and I began to talk. He was an engineer in the technology business, traveling at least 60 percent of the time. I had been in Minneapolis to promote a new book and teach.

"About what?" he asked, hitting the next right note in a ritual limited-space-of-time exchange.

"Addiction is my field."

"I've just stopped smoking—two weeks without," he said instantly.

"Good for you," I said. "That's a difficult withdrawal."

"What do you do with addiction?" he asked.

"I work with all addictions, every aspect of loss of control," I told him. Knowing he was in tech, I added that as an observer of the culture of Silicon Valley over the last decade, I witnessed a growing loss of control in his industry as well.

He smiled, an immediate signal of recognition. "That's it. That's me! Out of control. I run around, one call after another, one trip to the next. I can't stop. And I never get the feeling that I've completed a job, even if I've made a sale. It's always on to the next one. It's a feeling of racing against the tide with the undertow ready to swallow me up. I have to keep going, but it gets harder and harder."

He kept on talking, his speech getting faster. "It *is* like an addiction! Look at smoking. I got so I couldn't put one cigarette out without lighting up another. I'd be jumpy and shaking from all the nicotine, but I couldn't sit still; couldn't keep myself from reaching for the pack, holding that next cigarette even while I knew it wouldn't do the trick. Nothing does the trick. I'm just a racing engine. I always feel like I need to go faster, but I can't go faster. I've reached my limits in everything I do."

As often happens on an airplane, this man spilled the beans in an instant. He had been jittery during the flight and seemed ripe to tell someone how much he was hurting. I felt such compassion for him and smiled in understanding.

"I knew one day a few weeks ago that I couldn't keep smoking," he continued. "I've been coughing more and having trouble breathing. What am I doing? I asked myself. So one morning I didn't light up." He took a deep breath. "It's been fifteen days and I'm doing . . . okay. It was time." I nodded a sign of rueful agreement. If we're lucky, we get to the point when we know it's time.

The pilot advised us that we had set a new record for speed, arriving a half hour early at the airport. Ironically, that achievement left us sitting on the tarmac waiting for a gate. I told my new friend more about me and what I'd observed in the last few years.

*   *   *

Silicon Valley grew from a collection of former orchards on the San Francisco Peninsula and is now the nerve center of the high-tech world. It is the place where chips are made, software code is developed, and money is raised and distributed to thousands of energetic, smart people who believe they have world-changing ideas. It is an exciting place to live, but also, in my view, a perilous one.

In the course of the last fifteen years I watched an entire region lose itself in a world of speed. Both individuals and entire companies became obsessed with capturing and controlling cyberspace, the "new frontier of unlimited possibility." It was the unlimited aspect of the tech world that offered the lure to the explorer, the risk-taking entrepreneur and the gambler alike. For those wrapped up in the pursuit of these frontiers, Silicon Valley produced a new kind of high. People got hooked on speed!

A new business culture was born that paired investors with inventors, who together gambled on an eventual IPO that would bring them millions. The lore of a couple of geeks tinkering in a small garage became the blueprint for the path to success, a fantasy come true that anyone could emulate. This idea, and the thousands of small start-ups that followed this path, spread like a prairie fire, changing an entire county and much of the San Francisco Bay area into Silicon Valley.

Speed is the race, the drive to get there first. Speed is tied to the magic of instant success. Speed is instant discovery that promises billions in stock options and propels you to a Nobel Prize. It was, and is, all about fast—the fastest search engine, the fastest connection, the fastest way to get and spread information—and the high this race produced.

Twenty years ago this high led to a full-blown experience of addiction for many involved. The addiction was the unstoppable pursuit of fast and faster and the behaviors, beliefs, and emotions that fueled it and reinforced it.

This high-on-speed addiction spread through and beyond companies, crept over city boundaries, filled up the business and cultural space of an entire county, became a regional virus. Ours became a society captivated by its belief in the absence of limits, by grandiosity about the human potential to control what can't be controlled. The pursuit of technological discovery became a drive to conquer the new, unknown, uncharted territory of cyberspace. The lure of progress, success, money, and fame created a wave of contagion. You needed to get on board: don't wait, don't stop. Just like the alcoholic. Just like the "addictive mind."

The culture of the late nineties was a gold rush mentality of greedy frenzy. People were certain they risked failure if they took time to eat dinner with their families, go for a leisurely Saturday bike ride, or read a book just for fun. They were utterly focused on constant progress. People in the nineties worshipped the god of speed—anything worth doing was worth doing fast.

My seatmate stared at me, nodding in recognition as I described the tech culture of the 1990s. The upshot of what began as an exciting, profitable, even fun ride crept up on this community, just as an addiction can creep up on an alcoholic family. No one anticipated that this crazy push for speed—speed of the technology itself, and speed to discovery—would also be the root of personal disasters, of uncontrollable compulsivity, of endless pursuit culminating in an ultimate depression and despair.

From 1998 until about 2001, the "high" was so pervasive, so gravity defying, it was blasphemy to suggest we were due for a correction. Tiny companies with no revenue or profit would go public, and their stocks would instantly double or triple or go even higher. Venture capitalists were prowling the hallways of Stanford and other engineering schools, trying to lure young students to drop out and start their own companies by waving millions of dollars in start-up money at them. Doctors and lawyers who saw themselves as successful, well-off people were horrified to see twenty-something computer programmers snapping up perfectly lovely homes and scraping them to the ground to build bigger, better mansions with theaters and gyms and other money-is-no-object amenities.

When the correction came, it was overwhelming. Tech stocks collapsed, thousands of companies shut down, millionaires became penniless. I watched with sadness and silent recognition. I knew this had to happen because I'd seen it so often with people who believed they could drink all they wanted and never have to stop. I hoped the crash would give people insight, just like alcoholics who finally see that they have lost control. I hoped people would recognize what happened, how an entire culture became out-of-control. But shortly on the heels of the March 2000 crash, Google came along, and with its success came a whole new wave of minting money. Soon houses were selling for over their asking price, people were becoming overnight millionaires again, and a cultural wave of competitive bidding was set in motion.

In my therapy practice, people kept saying to me: "I can't keep up, and I can't stop. I can't work any longer, run any faster, or multitask one more thing, but I can't stop trying to do more. I feel like I'm failing all the time. I'm out of control. I know I need to slow down, but I'm frightened I'll lose everything."

Sometimes I was able to help these people see that the only road to relief from this addiction was to acknowledge their loss of control. When they recognized that they couldn't go any faster but they also couldn't stop trying to go faster, many could miraculously begin to slow down. Then and only then could they begin to change. But, I told my airplane friend, they have to *really* see it, like you did when you decided not to pick up your next cigarette.

We'd been stopped on the runway for a while, but now a gate was open. People sat still—they had to sit still—though many fidgeted with cell phones, ready to leap up when the Fasten Seatbelt light went off. And now, as we taxied to the gate, my new friend looked sad.

"That's me," he said quietly. He told me that he'd lost his wife and two children because he couldn't stop. He was gone all the time, and could focus on nothing but his tech world. He lost it all, or *all that was most important to him.*

Nice to chat, we both agreed as the engines quieted and people rose from their seats to stand . . . and wait. The plane unloaded in its own time, each person retrieving luggage, proceeding row by row out the door. The line doesn't move any faster than the next person. As I stood up and moved into the aisle, my seatmate and I exchanged sad smiles.

Who was this man, my airplane friend? Why is his story so touching, so sad, and so important to all of us living in American culture today? Here was a man who lost control of his life; he had a loving family, a wife, and two kids, a good job in high tech, and a good salary. Yet his life was falling apart. He couldn't limit his work hours, so his time at the office grew from nine hours a day to thirteen, then fourteen, and then he stayed the night. He lived in airports and socialized on airplanes, sharing his story with a seatmate like me. By the time he told me that he'd just stopped smoking and lost his wife and kids, he had fifteen years of out-of-control living behind him—trying to be successful, to have it all and to keep going. He lost it all, except his job, and that was no longer fulfilling or even exciting. Here was a sad man, a lonely man, wondering what had happened to his American dream. He had succumbed to speed.

This man went down on the wheel of the rat's cage, trying to pedal as fast as he could until he couldn't pedal anymore. His story is not unusual. He's a man who believed that constant stress—feeling chronically burdened and chronically unable to catch up—was normal. He believed that he had no choice, that he should be in control, so feeling the stress was his failure. He had to keep trying, even though his losses told him something was terribly wrong.

This is addiction: you need more and more of the same substance or activity even though you never feel full or finished, but you cannot stop. Addiction is a process with a slow or sudden start and then a growth curve that becomes self-perpetuating. Once established, addiction takes on a life of its own. But even then, you may not know it.

WHAT IS ADDICTION?

As I've marveled over the years at how much American culture believes in the power of the individual and the power of self-control, even while becoming more and more out of control, I've also noted an expansion in the definitions of what constitutes addiction. Food addicts, sex addicts, shopping addicts. Now I'm suggesting that we look at the fast pace of life from this same perspective. So let's ask: What is addiction? Why would my airplane friend so instantly realize that he was addicted to his jet-setting lifestyle and his compulsive pursuit of sales in the same way he needed his nicotine?

We used to think that addiction was only about alcohol—a compulsion to drink and an inability to stop. Over the years we came to understand that addiction can include more than alcohol. It covers all those other drugs—the illegal ones like pot, cocaine, meth, heroin—and legal drugs like painkillers. Addiction is the growing need for more and more alcohol or drugs to produce the same effect. The need for a drink turns into dependence and eventually into compulsion with an inability to stop. You have to keep drinking or using drugs, even when you don't want to. You have lost the choice not to. Addiction also covers behaviors like compulsive gambling, compulsive eating, and compulsive unhealthy sexual activity. You have lost the choice not to engage in those behaviors even when they are hurting you.

Addiction is ultimately a deep, self-destructive conflict of interest. It's a war within the self, which becomes a war within the family, and now a war within the culture. Addiction is a struggle by one part of yourself for control of another part of yourself, so you can't help but lose. It's you against you, and then it's you against all of those who would stop you.

Addiction Is a Behavioral, Emotional, and Thinking Disorder

The Twenty Questions at the beginning of this book focus on behavior, emotion, and thinking, the three prongs of any addiction. How does this work? When you're losing control of your behavior, your thinking becomes distorted so you don't have to see that you've lost control. Addiction involves such self-delusion and self-deception that it results in a massive perceptual and thinking disorder. You are committed to believing you are in control of yourself or others, so you simply deny that you've lost control. Along with muddled thinking come muddled emotions. Whether positive or negative, your feelings become a threat to you. They sit inside you, in your chest, in your stomach, and they seem dangerous, uncontrollable. They might challenge you and your denial, so you suppress them.

As an addict, you think you're managing your behavior, but you're actually distorting your perception and thinking, and working very hard to stop all of your feelings so you don't have to notice how out of control your behavior is. Addiction becomes a massive avoidance of an open, honest relationship with yourself and with others. Addiction shuts you down.

Addiction almost always starts as a solution to a problem. You may be trying to avoid anxiety or fear; you may be trying to have fun or relax. You may be trying to comfort yourself after a breakup with a girlfriend or boyfriend. You may be trying to fill a feeling of emptiness. You may be in nonstop pursuit of things that you want. You find the answer in a drink, a smoke, a pill, a pastry, a poker hand, the next big sale, or the next new app. You can become addicted when you feel like you need to change your mood, your thoughts, or your physical senses. This is called self-medication, even when the medicine is a behavior instead of a drug. It's something that promises to let you manage your behavior, your mood, and your thinking. Addiction starts out as a solution and then it becomes the problem.

Most people today accept that alcohol and drug use can become an addiction. Many also accept that behaviors such as compulsive eating and gambling are addictions. Adding to the list of addictions a compulsive need for a frenzied, pressured lifestyle may be harder to come to terms with. But after witnessing the increasingly frantic press of life in Silicon Valley, and after spending years working with the casualties of this pressure, it has become clear to me that speed is an addiction and that understanding this can be a key to recovering our health and balance.

2

The Evolution of the Idea of Speed

Through the decade of the nineties, I was busy watching people in my personal world and my professional practice struggle with a pace of life that was moving way too fast. They were out of control, and since I knew about addiction as a loss of control, it seemed like I was seeing the world as a 3-D caricature of the same thing. But I knew that raising the idea of a culture hooked on speed would be a difficult proposition at that point in time. This was a high on its way up, a huge new wave for anyone to catch. Nobody wanted to hear that there were tides and an undertow that could sweep you away. Just like the anticipation of a drug high, the rush of an IPO lit up our endorphins before we knew what these were. I had raised cultural alarms in the past and learned how hard it is to break a wall of family and societal resistance to recognizing problems.

In 1983 I was part of a group of professionals who came together to name and describe a new idea. This first meeting of fifteen men and women spurred the wildfire development of a national social movement of new awareness and legitimacy for children of alcoholics (COAs) and adult children of alcoholics (ACOAs). While the idea survived and flourished to help millions of children and adults over the last thirty years, there was also loud and angry resistance.

"Isn't everybody the child of an alcoholic?" an older gentleman asked me in a tone of exasperated impatience as he pondered funding a service for teens. "What are we supposed to do with all these children? And shouldn't the adults just get over it?"

This experience stayed with me for years as I plugged along with my research and writing about living with addiction. At that time I no doubt reminded myself that normies didn't want to be bothered with alcoholism as a health problem and they certainly wouldn't want to acknowledge the often terrible consequences of growing up with parents who are out of control. I also had known for years that many so-called normies had addictions of their own that they did not want to recognize. And perhaps this man had grown up with an alcoholic father or mother himself and carefully denied this reality all his life. Many people didn't want our band of ACOA-liberators to be so vocal. They didn't want us tampering with their life stories, which included denial of family addictions.

THIS IS SPEED

We see this same kind of denial today in our culture of speed. Speed is the loss of control. Speed is addiction. People have to go fast and then faster. Many people don't want to see it, don't want to name it, and don't want to change. Like the man above who thinks people should get a grip and get over it, many will say,

"What's the big deal? Everybody's going fast so that's how it is. You have to move quickly to keep up, to make progress, and to be a success." This kind of thinking is the core of addiction. You can't stop, you believe you shouldn't have to stop, and you don't dare try.

But, you might say, "Aren't you overreacting? Hasn't the pace of life always been a concern?" Yes. Worry about the fast pace of life is not new. Historians describe acceleration as a central feature of modern society at least since the eighteenth century. The issue of "progress," which has become synonymous with increasing speed and man's ability to be in control of it, has been a philosophical issue since the beginnings of recorded time. Socrates worried about the impact of the invention of writing on people's ability to think, fearing they "would cease to exercise their memory and become forgetful."

While worry about speed is not a new idea, the current impact of speed on our culture is unprecedented and unforeseen. It is now causing serious damage to us as individuals and as a culture. The highest power economically, socially, and within the family (as parents and schools push for kids to do more and more in order to "succeed") is now speed—moving constantly and moving fast. Fast means progress and success. Slow means failure. In the all-or-nothing American culture, fast means you win and slow means you lose. It's as if we have moved from driving a highway at fifty-five miles per hour to sixty-five miles per hour to one hundred miles per hour; we can't slow down for the curves, and we are crashing.

The pace and the compulsion to make progress are damaging us to such a degree that our very lives as individuals and as a country are threatened. Peter Whybrow, author of *American Mania*, suggests that we are in a "manic moment in the history of the planet when our biology is at war with our culture. As *Homo*

sapiens, we are not programmed to eat junk food 24/7, to be sur-
feited by video games, BlackBerrys, cell phones, and artificial
light, and to fly through time zones in a fraction of the time it used
to take us to sail by boat. It is no wonder that our minds and bodies are suffering."

And we are suffering. Many people suffer from stress so intense that it impairs their immune systems, contributes to heart
attacks, strokes, infertility, and speeds up the aging process. Stress
destroys marriages and tears families apart. Long-term stress can
even rewire the brain, leaving us more vulnerable to anxiety and
depression.

The quickest possible progress at all costs affects our institutions and our environment as well. Our air and water are polluted,
plastics and oil are invading the ocean, and our leftover carbon
dioxide is melting glaciers. We are facing economic and health-
care crises. Americans are working around the clock to make more
money and buy more things. We have gotten so used to feeling
driven, so used to constant motion or attention to our gadgets, that
we are out of control and it feels normal. We don't control our
technology; rather our technology controls us. We are addicted to
speed.

American culture is at a crossroads. Just like that small group
of us who raised the banner for children of alcoholics more than
thirty years ago, we must now ask: What is the impact of this fast
pace on child and adult development? What are the problems and
the costs of a cultural addiction to speed? How do we maintain the
best of technological advances *and* recognize and *accept* the problems created by these advances, which are now a serious threat to
the health and well-being of all adults, children, and families? Finally, how do we *change* from a culture addicted to speed to a culture that accepts limits and finds a healthy middle ground of pace

while not giving up progress and not sacrificing the best of American ideals?

Understanding that speed is an addiction will allow us to make the critical changes to heal ourselves and our world. This compulsive frenzy is an addiction every bit as much as compulsive use of drugs, alcohol, sex, or eating are addictions. And the path to recovery is the same. Applying the AA frame, the path to recovery begins with accepting our powerlessness, accepting the limits to our power and control. This first step is transformative. It continues with turning our lives over to a higher power, which means, at the cultural level, we search for something to believe in that is higher than ourselves and our own egos; something that is higher than the frantic chase for personal success. It means forming healthy attachments and cultivating sound, mutual relationships, while making community a priority. AA demonstrates through its steps for the individual and through its traditions for the group how to integrate the individual with others, how to focus on the self in the context of the community. This model can help Americans find a healthy middle ground of pace while not giving up progress.

MY TIPPING POINT

I first experienced the resistance in our culture to the idea that we cannot restore lost control more than forty years ago. I felt it when I took my first graduate class in psychology, a discipline strongly based, then and now, on the premise that humans have the power to regain lost control. As a recovering alcoholic, I knew how important it was to accept deeply the loss of control and the inability to ever reclaim control, but I was in a graduate program whose faculty and other students could not accept that perspective. In their view loss of control was a human failure you had to reject and overcome, not something you accepted. And so I experienced the same tension of rocking the boat with a radical notion as I did later when I joined with others to name "children of alcoholics" in the 1980s. A new idea that challenges favorite beliefs—for individuals, families, and societies—will almost certainly meet with huge resistance until denial won't work anymore. The new idea finally reveals problems that have become too big to ignore. Thus it was probably natural that I would begin to ponder the loss of control I was seeing in the culture of the 1990s. It was an alarmingly familiar experience for me, but an unwelcome reality to most of society.

The idea of speed as an addiction brewed in me through the decade of the nineties. I had my aha moment in June 2000 when I spotted Malcolm Gladwell's *The Tipping Point* in an airport bookstore, hot off the presses. As I read Gladwell's discussion of a "tipping point"—that moment when a new idea suddenly takes hold—it struck me that it is the same as the "turning point" for the alcoholic or the family that "hits bottom."

I started and finished that book on the long trip to Regina, Saskatchewan, where I was headed to teach about the alcoholic/addicted family and the process of recovery. The addicted family, both as individual members and as a system, becomes out of control right along with the addicted person. The addict becomes out of control in pursuit of a substance or behavior, and the family members become out of control in their efforts to stop the addict. The family that reaches recovery hits a turning point, a moment or series of moments that shifts their awareness, when they recognize that they've lost control and cannot get it back. These families must accept the reality that they cannot heal without a major shift in their behavior and thinking. So begins a process of radical change and new development for the family. This is what I believe is necessary in the culture.

A new idea becomes a trend, a new way of thinking and seeing the world—a paradigm shift—and it can create dramatic, transformational change, just like the path of recovery for the addict who sees "I have lost control." We need a tipping point in American culture, an aha experience, a recognition that society has indeed lost control and that our efforts to get back in control—to get a grip—are not working. If this happens, if people recognize speed as an addiction and if they can take advantage of the potential for change that this awareness offers, perhaps American culture can transform.

In the last five to ten years there have been many articles about the fast pace of life and its problematic consequences. I have incorporated much of that knowledge in these pages and provided an extensive bibliography at the end of the book. Speed as a cultural problem may be a new idea, but it hasn't been for lack of awareness. Many people are worried; some joke about their racing and their "ADD moments," while others are frantic and scared. But there hasn't been a tipping point, that moment when the whole culture recognizes there is a problem that requires serious attention. Why not?

ADDICTION AT THE CORE OF AMERICAN CULTURE

Most people can't see or accept the reality that the pace of life in our culture is out of control because the reality goes against the core of American character. There is a deep link between addiction and our national identity: the beliefs, values, and ideals that have long constituted the best of who Americans are also constitute the heart of their addictive thinking.

Addiction is behavioral loss of control, but it is more than that and it starts long before we've reached the point where we can't stop drinking, smoking, eating, shopping, gambling, or staying on the Internet until dawn. Addiction grows out of the way we think, believe, and feel about ourselves. The widespread addiction to speed began long before people couldn't stop texting, emailing, tweeting, and multitasking around the clock and around the calendar. This addiction has grown out of the beliefs that fostered the birth of American society. The concept of Manifest Destiny, a creed of entitlement that began with the Pilgrims' arrival, reflected the belief that Americans had unlimited power and could go anywhere and do anything. It is a core principal of national identity that has led directly to our national addiction to speed.

The widely respected writer Wendell Berry says that we live with a "disease of limitlessness." We worship our capacities to defy limits and cultivate a gambling mentality, going for the quick win in everything we do. Grandiosity and entitlement, key elements of addictive thinking, are seen as strengths of "American character." You are entitled to whatever you want, and the rules don't apply to you. It is this grandiosity and the false belief in human power that have to change, the false belief that the world is limitless. It is this false belief that is the core of a severe conflict of interest in American values and character that is leading us down a dangerous path.

Manifest Destiny validated the idea that it was the settler's right to own the continent, that there were no limits to progress, that the individuals constituting this country were so powerful they could conquer any problem. A favorite word of the time was *boundlessness*, the promise of endless opportunity. Yet the basic beliefs—unlimited growth, unlimited individual power—are the same delusions that constitute addictive thinking in relation to substances and other behaviors.

The values of Manifest Destiny crystallized into three basic rights:

1. You can have whatever you want and all you want.

2. You should be in charge and in control.

3. Your power to accomplish these feats centers in you.

Solidified in American character, these beliefs make it extremely difficult to recognize limits and to value slowing down. You are entitled to pursue what you want and to take what you believe you need because you've worked for it. That's the American heritage. Work hard, maintain a high moral code, and you can have what you want and be anything you want.

But there is more that makes these beliefs so problematic and leads to chronic loss of behavioral control. Americans have long favored an either-or mentality called dichotomous thinking—a way of thinking that is part and parcel of all addictions. You're either right or you're wrong. You're either good or you're bad. You've got all the power or you've got none. There are no shades of gray. This all-or-none way of viewing the world reinforces extremes in everything.

Either-or thinking is deeply embedded in American culture. Americans typically see their country as the best, the most favored nation. America is the most powerful country in the world, the richest, the most innovative, the most creative, and has the best democracy. Anything short of the top is a failure. This feeds our frenzy. We can say we want balance, bemoan our fast pace, and vow to slow down, but the American ideal is not a middle ground.

No one wants to be average; average is the graveyard for losers. So we rev up our engines to continue full speed ahead.

This type of thinking is also part of addiction. It's going after the *all* instead of settling for *none*. Addiction is the extreme of loss of control. The addict needs more and more of the substance to simply keep pace. There is no getting control in the race to have more. The race itself fuels a bottomless need. You always need more after the first sip of martini, hit of cocaine, puff on your joint, or rise to the top. These "successes" may spark exhilaration, but soon that feeling turns to fear and emptiness, with a hole inside that pushes you for more. The addict loses control of his behavior in the same way people in the culture lose control of their drive to go faster.

There has always been anxiety about change and an erosion of values in pursuit of Manifest Destiny and the progress it promised. Grandiosity, an inflated, false optimism fueled by beliefs in entitlement and no limits causes more anxiety and apprehension. These layers of anxiety and foreboding exist for growing numbers in the culture today. Some see that the notion of "no limits" now rules society and threatens to take it down. Many people feel a chronic underlying fear as they recognize we are, or we will be, hitting a wall of endless progress and confronting real limits. Chaos and dissolution lie ahead if society cannot slow down and begin to self-reflect.

The speed addict, like any other addict, doesn't dare stop to reflect and ask, "What am I doing?" Yet the absence of self-reflection is a key to what's wrong. Loss of control and polarized thinking wipe out the ability to slow down, to stop and think, and to question. Like my airplane friend, our culture needs to pause and ask, "What are we doing? Are we hooked on fast? How do our behaviors, our emotions, and our hallowed beliefs feed and reinforce our cultural loss of control?"

The cultural belief system grounded in Manifest Destiny has mixed with the reality (for now) of an unlimited cyberspace and unlimited speed of technology to make a toxic brew. Our cultural values and beliefs require people to live at high speed in order to progress, to achieve and not fail. People's lives become out of control. They become addicted to a fast pace just like the individual addicted to alcohol or gambling.

The drive for success and the deep beliefs of entitlement that still pervade the American character now require people to keep up an unsustainable pace. Yet people feel compelled to sustain it. The culture requires people to go full speed ahead, values maximum achievement and maximum consumption, and recognizes no limits. This cultural pursuit of endless progress becomes an exercise in massive denial as big as the notorious denial of the addict. People want to believe we are not losing ground as a culture, we are not limited, we won't age, and we won't die. These are all beliefs that are traceable to the grandiosity proclaimed by Manifest Destiny—that America was the land of futurity, that no one or no thing could stop the expansion, a God-given right. "Go west, young man, go west" was the cultural mantra that fed unlimited expansion in our early years as a nation. Today, it's "go west—to Silicon Valley—for fame and fortune. Don't look back, don't stop, and don't give it a second thought." Our Manifest Destiny today is speed—fast and faster at any cost.

SPEED.COM: NAMING REALITY

In the summer of 2000 I was preparing for a conference called Speed.com to be held in July at Santa Clara University, located in the heart of Silicon Valley. The purpose was to officially name and describe the fast, out-of-control pace that was now the norm in Bay Area life and spreading quickly across the country. Speakers would raise questions about this norm and its impact on individuals, families, and communities. By this time there were early signs of recognition across the culture, and people were raising questions about the wisdom of always being on the move, always going so fast. *New Yorker* cartoons from fall 1999 through summer 2000 portrayed the ludicrous and comical "insanity" of this Mr. Toad's Wild Ride. Articles appeared in the same magazine and other periodicals, describing the out-of-control lifestyle and the negative costs of our devotion to speed. Over-scheduling and double-booking were signs of progress and belonging. Money was falling off of trees for those in the know who could grab the right branch.

Few knew the stock market and the high-stakes culture had peaked about March 2000. But by summer people had a sense something was amiss. The high was now tempered by fear. At the conference, people had already experienced the consequences of decline. Yet many businesspeople said they could not speak openly about the out-of-control pace of their lives. They had to speak in secret about burnout. Working long hours and maintaining a fast pace were corporate requirements. The business culture would not allow acknowledgment of human limits or any kind of slowdown. The weakness in the stock market and the beginning of corporate crashes had to be temporary. People hung on fiercely to the belief this would be just a blip on the road of progress.

It wasn't a blip. It was a major, jerking halt that hurt many people. Yet others, and most corporate cultures, did not see, and don't yet see, that the frantic pace and rush of speed are a root cause of a severe cultural loss of control that is now causing great damage.

In fact, the taboos on naming the realities of speed are even greater today. Many tech companies expect their employees to put job ahead of family and help them do so by providing "perks" and "benefits" for them and their families that make it easier to devote longer hours to work. It is a new kind of indentured slavery as the company intrudes into personal and family life, demanding more time and loyalty with the promise of "success." People become afraid to say no. They see setting limits as an "opportunity cost," rather than recognizing the reality of the growing costs of their long hours and addiction to speed.

USA Today covered the Speed.com conference back in July 2000. This was news! The reporter captured the feeling of pride many people felt about their long work hours. Instead of complaining, some people wore their ninety-hour workweek as a badge. Who could work the hardest and the longest? One man jokingly called himself a speed freak, noting matter-of-factly that he works sixteen hours a day. "Time is our scarcest resource," he believes, so he is careful not to waste it.

And what would that look like? Well, like others who work in high-speed Silicon Valley, he owns a Corvette and a sailboat, but doesn't waste valuable business time enjoying them. He might relax at the computer for a few hours, but then it's back to fast.

Like countless others I have seen in my practice, I suspect the man knew, underneath his bravado, that he doesn't have a life, that he is driven by the need to stay in action, that he feels empty and frightened without the constant stimulus and distraction of nonstop work and moving fast. Many people function with a numbed sense of themselves and their worlds—on autopilot—a deadness they now consider normal. It is the feeling of being empty and dead that drives the addictive need for more action. People adjust to living like robots and constantly fuel the pump. The robot is likely to feel depressed and terrified underneath the action. He says he likes to go fast, but I'll bet he also knows he has to. The addict, the person who drinks "because I like it and it's relaxing," also hears the whisper inside: "You're really in trouble. You drink because you have to." Now the voice inside warns: "You've got to slow down, take a break. You can't keep this up." And then you soldier on.

Many people at the conference nodded in agreement as speakers described the cartoonish pace of life. Others said they had to sneak into Speed.com because they weren't allowed to openly talk about the fast pace as part of their job. Several people spoke from the floor of the large auditorium, looking left and right and over their shoulders, as they described the pressures to produce nonstop and not complain.

This conference provided a moment that could have been a tipping point for the culture. The name Speed.com labeled the reality, and the setting offered participants the opportunity to speak out loud about the pressures they felt in their work and family worlds and to acknowledge the loss of control they were living. The "new idea" was then presented in the popular press. But there was no tipping point. The power of the drive to go faster and longer in the race to progress and success was simply too great and too much on the upswing for people to see the danger signs and the realities of negative consequences yet. And if they saw them, their fears of stopping kept them in the race. Just like people fear withdrawal from alcohol, sleeping meds, overeating, or gambling, people feared failure if they wanted out of this trap.

Over the next decade I pondered the reality as I watched the norm of loss of control spread beyond Silicon Valley, across the country, and now the world. I listened to the denial at all levels of the culture, reinforced by the anguish of a nation that feared it was falling behind.

Yet there was also a sense of growing nostalgia for a slower time. The quieting that used to come as part of normal life—Sundays for rest and reflection, hobbies for broader interests, time for relationships with children and families, altruism and the sense of something greater than the self—has been lost in the race for more and faster.

The person who has lost control to addictive behavior must also believe in a false sense of limitless self-power. In a vicious circle, you continue to be out of control as you tell yourself you're just fine. Pretty soon you look speeded-up to those around you, but you can't see it. You can feel it though. Underneath the speed, you're terrified.

Today's addicted person, and the addicted culture, believes in the absence of limits. Both are out of control in pursuit of their own new Manifest Destiny: going faster and faster, conquering cyberspace, harnessing the unlimited, and reaffirming the denial of all human limits.

The permission of Manifest Destiny, so long rooted in the culture, has turned the American virtues of hard work and endurance into nonstop action and chaos. Manifest Destiny is a denial of limits. Manifest Destiny has become a belief in your right to have whatever you want, when you want it, as fast as you can get it. Manifest Destiny is a belief in the ultimate power of the individual. Today that manifesto forms the root of a vast cultural addiction to speed. Our era of loss of control, like the proverbial wind that moved the country west, is now sweeping all before it who cannot slow down or stop themselves.

3

Addiction to Speed

As I've worked away on this book, sitting at my computer, searching for a quick fact, moving text from chapter six to chapter three, and then moving it again to the end of chapter seven, I've thought many times how grateful I am for technology. If I can keep my patience and my own sense that this book will come in its own time, I'm okay. Sometimes, though, I'm all itch, like a drug addict tapping his fingers to try to keep from shooting up. I'm all itch because I want to finish this thing now, and not one minute longer. I need to finish it, so I must keep moving. I need the Twenty Questions, right now, no doubt about it! As the process of writing has gone from one to two to five years, friends say, "Can't you speed it up?" I ask myself the same question. The answer is no. I can't go any faster than the book that's emerging from deep within me. But I can and do make use of technology to help me simplify the writing process. No question, I do love my laptop and all the tools at my disposal.

There are many benefits to the cyberspace revolution: we can answer the simplest and the most complex questions in a heart-beat; we can access a wide range of information about any subject in an instant; and we can reach people anywhere on the planet in moments. The technology revolution has no doubt supported a transformation in our methods of knowledge acquisition and our ways of thinking, what Thomas Kuhn famously called a "shift in paradigm." It has also changed our way of life.

While we celebrate the benefits, the focus in this book is on the problems caused not by technology itself, but by the way it is used, the beliefs that underlie its use, and the unsustainable pace of life it has produced. The focus is on the fast pace of life as an addiction—the behaviors, emotions, distorted thinking, and per-ceptions that keep us out of control. What are the costs of this incredible "progress"? What happens when you go too fast? What are the consequences of becoming addicted to speed?

Gina is a perfect illustration of the costs of too much speed. She grew up in New York in the heart of high finance and high fashion and always loved the rush of her life. Graduating from col-lege, she happily got on the business bandwagon as fast as she could, working first as an assistant to a fashion designer and then as a buyer for a major high-end retailer. Gina loved the world of fashion with its short cycles of new style coupled with intense, condensed advertising and promotion. She was dealing with fall fashions in February and March. Pre-fall "early look" advertising started in June. As soon as the first merchandise hit the markets, the current season was old.

At age thirty-two, Gina left her high-speed job and moved west with her husband, a finance guy who was starting a branch office in California. By that time Gina had two children and needed a new career that would give her more time flexibility. She determined that the San Francisco Peninsula was the perfect place to start a new business as a personal assistant and organizer. People were chaotic, frantic, running around, and there was such a high pitch to everything. Her friends were on the rise, making millions, and buying two or three houses, and she constantly heard how fast they were moving and how pressured they felt. She offered to help a friend organize her closets and she was off and running. From fashion executive to personal organizer. After a few years she got as disorganized and out of control as the people she was helping. She felt guilty when she was not with her children and guilty when she was not working. There was a standard of success she felt she needed to achieve, and she couldn't live up to it without working so many hours that she was on the edge of exhaustion all the time.

Gina's experience wasn't unusual. There is awe and admiration for the "winner" who works an eighty-hour week, wakes up in the gym, passes his family in the driveway, says hello over cocktails, and goes to bed with Ambien. Gina's frenzied lifestyle finally made its toll evident when she suffered from clinical depression. However, although after treatment she recovered from the depression, the addiction to speed was not treated and a couple of years later she watched herself abuse alcohol and was diagnosed with chronic fatigue syndrome.

Gina had always enjoyed drinking and sometimes "partied" too much, as she called her wild binges, but she believed she was simply "taking the pressure off." As she recovered from her depression, she returned to the same work, the same pace, and the same guilt that got her into trouble in the first place, except now she was drinking more. She kept looking for medical diagnoses to explain her agitation and the loss of control of her life. She could not see that she had a role in her problems and that she would have to have a role in their treatment. No pill would "fix" her so that she could keep racing at full speed. She would have to begin to say no and set limits on herself and on what she could do for others and her work.

Because our culture values speed—in fact, demands speed—recognizing it as an addiction is nearly impossible. Instead, the difficulties of distraction, inattention, and changes in thinking this frenzy and pressure cause are often diagnosed as emotional problems and even psychiatric disorders.

The media recognized the cultural push for speed early on. More than ten years ago journalists were describing their own personal experiences with the tidal wave of speed and its addictive qualities of greed, grandiosity, and omnipotence. Their stark and often frightening stories offered the first warning signs to a culture that was hell-bent on pursuing speed at any cost. Gathered together now, we can see that these early commentaries sounded a compelling alarm that we are only now beginning to grapple with. Just like the addict in recovery looks back to tell the story of her descent into loss of control, these stories offer the same retrospective lens into our cultural spiral into speed addiction.

In describing his stock market addiction in the *New Yorker*, David Denby defined a new kind of personality "produced by rapid shifts in capital . . . a person who is morally promiscuous, whose character has the liquid properties of cash."[1]

A 2007 *New York Times* editorial talks about the addictive quality of BlackBerry messaging, how the devices are referred to as "CrackBerrys," and how it was harder to quit than smoking.[2]

And in April 2009 author Judith Warner published a telling letter to the editor in the *New York Times* in which she wrote about taking Ritalin in order to meet some impossible deadlines. The medication served its purpose, albeit with some uncomfortable temporary side effects, but Warner ends her article with the acknowledgment "that memory indicates to me, very strongly and very simply, that there are limits to what we are supposed to do."[3]

DEBILITATING STRESS

What are the negative consequences of our cultural and individual addictions to speed? First is the physical and emotional state of stress. There is an alarming increase in stress-related disorders of all kinds for all ages, beginning for many young, elementary school-age children who are struggling with obesity, depression, anxiety, attention disorders, and all kinds of learning disabilities. The exhausting fast pace of life promotes over-scheduling and overstimulation, which become chronic stressors. These lead to behavioral, mood, and attention disorders.

Recently a new illness of speed has been named. Adrenal fatigue syndrome, described as "chronic fatigue lite," is directly related to stress. Dr. Marsha Seltzer reported: "This depletion syndrome linked to adrenal functioning is real—and treatable . . . We must learn to simmer down, unwind, let go—or at least quit obsessing about our 401(k)s."[4]

Efforts to solve these problems remain within a fix-it mode and, in that sense, keep the out-of-control, compulsive cycles going: how to get a grip on the problem without changing anything. But people are trying to fix the wrong problem. They think there is something wrong with them, a failing, or an illness, because they can't do more. They look for books and articles to improve their time-management, consultants like Gina to help them organize, or drugs to treat the reality of their human limits and the "disorders" they now have as a result of stress. Sadly, these physical and emotional disorders become "the problem" and are treated

directly without a link to the underlying stress that causes or contributes to them. There is thus no change in the disconnected
relationships, the fast-paced environments, or the excessive demands that children and adults are trying to meet.

A research project at the Stanford Graduate School of Education called S.O.S., for Stressed-Out Students, has identified serious problems for high school students who are literally stressed to
the breaking point by too many hours with too many demands and
too much activity each day. This study concluded that going so fast
is not good for kids. Sleep disorders and emotional problems including anxiety, depression, and all kinds of behavioral disorders
and addictions have become the stuff of normal teenage life.[5]

This research spurred a different kind of fix-it. A free period,
a shocking throwback to an earlier, quieter time, was reinstituted
at a local private school, seemingly based on the understanding
that kids could not slow themselves down without a change in the
structure of their day and changes in expectations of what is
normal.

This change is important for several reasons. First it was a response to the right problem and a direct challenge to conventional
wisdom and school policies that emphasized the importance of
adding work to keep kids competitive. In the last two years there
has been more conflict between parents and local schools about
what is best for children: accenting the need for kids to do more or
realizing the importance of time-outs from the pressures of constant action. While it may seem obvious that everyone needs
downtime, my patient Reynaldo, a ninety-hour-a-weeker and parent of a son in high school, illustrates the opposite, prevailing
view: "A free period is an opportunity cost and an opportunity lost
from what you could be producing."

The reinstatement of a free period was also important because it illustrates the need for top-down policy interventions to alter expectations and norms. Without the support of the administration and school board, a free period can easily be condemned as evidence of laziness. Reynaldo would call his son a slacker for letting up on his drive to produce.

Awareness about the dangers for children of too much stress, stimulation, and confusion is not new. Working for *Sesame Street* in the 1960s, Ed Palmer designed an observational study of preschool kids watching TV to learn what works in program design to engage and hold the attention and retention of preschool children. Palmer's findings surprised him and many others who thought that creating excitement and stimulation was the best way to get kids' attention and keep it. Wrong. Just the opposite. They found that children turned their heads away from too much visual and verbal stimulation. Instead of excitement, the kids became confused by multiple images and multiple voices talking at the same time.

So what do these studies tell us? Teens need a free period. They need time to be quiet, to reflect. We all do. And young kids don't want to be overstimulated and confused at all—never mind constantly, in the misguided belief that quiet time and old-fashioned play will reduce their competitive edge.

From an increasingly younger age, people are treating their stress disorders by turning to other addictions. They are attracted to alcohol, other drugs, compulsive overeating and under-eating, gaming and gambling online, and spending in an effort to give them a feeling of internal control. When that doesn't happen and they instead feel more anxious and out of control, they may move to prescription drugs. It is easy to get a diagnosis of ADD, chronic fatigue, sleep disorders, anxiety, and mood disturbances when you're a young person today. With the diagnosis comes a prescription for Ritalin or medical marijuana. If a teen has trouble getting a prescription, just walk the halls at the local high school or check online for the nearest supplier. Kids can instantly buy every kind of drug today: stimulants like Ritalin or Adderall, painkillers like Oxycontin, and sleep meds like Ambien.

A few years ago a parent told me she had helped her teenager get a prescription from the pediatrician for medical marijuana. She and other parents were convinced that it was better to make the smoking legal as a medicine than risk jail or a police record for the illegal purchase and use of this substance. These parents did not see the problems their kids were trying to treat. They did not see that the pressures from them and their adult world were causing the stress.

In the last five years phone calls to me from frantic, frightened parents have increased dramatically. Their teenagers and young adults are dropping out of their lives. Holed up in dark, locked bedrooms, hooked to the computer, smoking dope and taking uppers and downers to regulate their attention and mood, these young people cannot "log off." Many of these kids will get to addiction treatment on the route to slowing down and recognizing their limits.

One parent recently said to me: "Our college-age daughter will not slow down, will not get off the computer, or get off the pills she takes to stay awake. She says she's got to get to Wall Street as fast as possible. But she's getting sick instead."

Instead of recognizing the cause of the problem—too much pressure, too much speed—people are adding alcohol, all kinds of other drugs, and prescription medicines to treat the consequences of our loss-of-control lifestyle. Instead of recognizing the fallibility of the belief that people can do as much and go as fast as they wish with no limits, they turn to other methods of control.

They ask their physician for a pill to help them work faster and sharper. It is a medication-managed world we are passing on to our children and reinforcing for adults.

This has created multiple layers of loss of control and addictions for boys and girls and men and women of all ages. People are addicted to their work, to the computer, to going fast, and they maintain this loss of control through their addictions to drugs of all kinds. By the time these people get help, it is a long road back.

CHANGES IN ATTENTION AND THINKING

From the beginning, technology prophets saw problems, but widespread recognition was muted in the drive for innovation and the pursuit of wild profits now associated with high risk and speed of development. The emphasis on speed and constant action reduces or wipes out reflection time, and a quiet mind is where creative and deep thoughts are born. Try pausing right now. Look up from this page and close your eyes. What do you feel and hear? Sit quietly for a few minutes. Then open your eyes and look around. What do you see? How easy is it to focus on your surroundings? And to focus on your senses—your smell, your sight, the sounds, and what you can touch that will not blink, ping, or buzz you back? Are you rolling your eyes at me? What's this hokey-pokey stuff? You have too much to do to spend time becoming aware of your inner and outer worlds. You need to get to action. But ironically, the more you push yourself to act, without any quiet time at all, the harder it is to be creative and the less you actually produce.

Vannevar Bush, an early pioneer of the idea of the harmful effects of speed in technology, saw these ironies. He discovered that the speed of incoming information was eroding creative thinking rather than automating the routine aspects of thinking as he had hoped. According to Bush, scholars were lost in "managing the record," leaving them less time to think, absorb, create, or interpret the data.[6]

Decades later author Susan Cain wrote in the *New York Times* that people are more creative when they enjoy privacy and freedom from interruption, old-fashioned qualities of life that are now out of style and devalued.

Think about it: Do you have your phone turned on and nearby all day and all night? Do you answer that ring wherever you are, whatever you're doing? Do you think this is normal? What everyone does? Or maybe you don't even think about it? Now it's part of you. Holding up his phone ten minutes into his session, my patient Reynaldo joked: "Don't leave home without it." He glanced down to see who was calling and answered. Then he quickly cut a deal, sighing as he pressed the "End" button and looked back at me. Ah, how easy it is and how important it is to be available instantly. Reynaldo couldn't see yet that he had traded a connection with himself and me to make some money. He had a hard time getting back to the much more painful topic he was opening with me.

David Levy, professor at the Information School at University of Washington, concerned about the impact of technology on scholars, educators, and students, wrote that we were "losing the time 'to look and to think' at the very moment we have produced extraordinary tools for investigating the world and ourselves and for sharing our findings." Levy wondered, "How has it come to pass that technologies developed to make more time to think have seemingly had the opposite effect?"[7] What kind of irony is this? The great discoveries, the new solutions, soon become the problem? The new technologies are "self-propelling," which is exactly what happens with addiction. The desire for a drink, a pill, a roll of the dice, or a ring of the phone becomes a craving and then a driving compulsion to follow through. Addiction takes on a life of its own.

Multitasking, an outgrowth of the demand for increased speed and, until recently, a valued solution for dealing with masses of information, also stimulates internal chaos and inattention— serious problems for anybody at any age. But for years now we've simply chalked up this chronic confusion and new memory loss to unavoidable costs we pay in order to go so fast to get so much. But how is increased confusion a good thing? In fact, now we're learning that multitasking is nothing but trouble. Multitasking may interrupt and diminish learning, productivity, and even friendships. Young people may still believe that multitasking boosts efficiency, while in fact, it actually takes longer to get things done. Talk about bursting the bubble! Switching your attention reduces your efficiency and skill. You cannot concentrate on either task. In fact, you're trying to focus on everything. You hear it all, even what you used to be able to block out.

Is this true for you? What else are you doing right now? Do you have your eye on your in-box as you read along? Do you have your phone close by to happily interrupt you? That ring is a much more welcome information byte than the challenges on these pages. Do you really want to read more about how you're fooling yourself? Are you really not more efficient when you're juggling?

Miranda, a high-tech executive, often said with pride that her greatest skill was juggling her "eight plates of focus" from the moment she wakes up until the moment she crashes eighteen hours later. "There is only multitasking for me. I don't see that I have any choice. So I have to believe I'm doing a great job with everything, even though I know deep down it's not true. My staff follows behind me to pick up the pieces, and my kids have stopped asking me to pay attention. What am I doing? There's something wrong with being so important that I have no time to really focus on anybody or anything."

There is now concern that technology is even changing the way people think. The culture of technology values efficiency and immediacy, which also leads to a dumbing down of information intake. According to *Atlantic* contributing writer Nicholas Carr, people become "decoders" of information, skimming to pull bytes rather than piecing together a deeper understanding.[8]

What are we doing? We're all headed toward the goal, and we miss the journey in between. We don't see it anymore and we don't register the experience. This is the result of striving for shortcuts and efficiency. We stay on the surface of everything and no longer value depth. Taking the time to read a long article or to engage in a long conversation that goes back and forth with deepening complexities will cost us too much in lost outcome. There is nothing to savor anymore except the anticipation of the next win.

And never mind that we don't value deep reading anymore. Looks like pretty soon we won't have the mental abilities or the patience to slog through anything. We find that our concentration drifts quickly and repeatedly no matter how hard we try to pull ourselves back to the page. Then we feel impatient and frustrated, feelings we don't like and want to change. So you stop reading and turn to your screen. Soon you've moved from an inner state of quiet calm to a hyped state of pushing buttons and scanning your favorite sites. Feels much better, you think. The anxiety of the quiet state has become too much to bear.

Reynaldo first came to talk with me because, although he was a very successful corporate executive, he did not have close or meaningful relationships with his wife, kids, friends, or colleagues.

People had been upset with him for years, which he knew, but he never knew why until the reasons poured out at a family intervention for his young son who was hooked on opiates and alcohol.

Reynaldo believed his kid just didn't have enough motivation or strength of character to tough it out for success. His son said he could never be good enough or work hard enough to please his father. There was no end, just more pressure and failure in his father's eyes.

Week by week, as Reynaldo came to therapy and came to value the quiet space and inward focus, he began to question everything he'd ever believed in, especially the chase for greater and greater success. Reynaldo learned to slow down, though his old values still haunted him. At the end of a quiet, slow meeting with me, he contemplated: "What's my takeaway here? I just can't see what I've learned from this. I started out at point A and ended up back at point A. What's different? Nothing I can see. Taking this time is one big opportunity cost."

I suggested that he view it as an opportunity. We had the journey in between points A and A. And in that journey was the difference. We'd seen the sights, talked back and forth, felt awe and sorrow, and shared a deepening of relationship that is only possible in a quiet, open, vulnerable state of feeling and mind. We both had to stop *doing*.

Reynaldo wasn't sure, but he stayed open to finding something he never knew he was missing and was never going to find with the way he was living his life.

Yes, technology may be changing the way people think, and whether they think, and racking up serious personal costs. Listen to Bryan, a proud techie in his early twenties: "I *love* my gadgets. I love technology. I love the excitement of pushing a button and making things happen. It's a great high. But I really did have a bad feeling one time in class when the teacher asked me to trace the path of my answer. All I could tell her was which buttons I pushed. I couldn't think about how I got to the answer, because I didn't get there myself. My BlackBerry did the work. I felt very inadequate in that moment."

Have you been there? Think about the last time you felt confused, couldn't remember what you'd said, or where you were supposed to be. "It's all in my iPhone, not in my head." Think about the time you went blank at the party. You didn't know how to carry the conversation so you looked down to check your messages. Or you looked for something to add to the discussion from the gadget in your hand.

Why does it matter that we know how we got the answer? Storing information internally, building a cumulative internal depth of knowledge, and knowing what it means are baseline essentials for healthy child and adult development. We need a sense of mastery that comes from learning deeply. And it is mastery from within that leads to self-esteem.

Josie said she always thought she'd be smarter with her iPhone in hand, but instead she felt stupid. "Everything is faster and there is no end to the information out there. But it's out there, not in here, inside of me, rumbling around as I digest and ruminate," she said. "Instead of thinking more, I'm thinking less."

Along with outsourcing their knowledge and know-how, people with divided attention may not deeply integrate new information and may have trouble applying it later as a result. It's as if they've lost muscle. With one eye on the iPhone and one on the teacher, they slip into a trance of rote learning, a numb mental and emotional state that doesn't permit digestion. You can't get to a deep understanding, so you tell yourself you don't need to. The answers will be there if you need them. But then it's harder to learn and you start to look like a kid or a grown-up with attention deficit disorder. You can't focus and you're easily distracted."

We've cultivated the psychiatric illness called attention deficit disorder (ADD) as a cultural phenomenon because it works to excuse our failures to keep up. ADD is a euphemistic way of saying, "I have limits." Unfortunately, many people with speed-induced attention problems are now being treated for this illness with medication, along with every other conceivable disorder of stress, so they can keep up.

The distraction that is part of speed can have devastating consequences. Talking on cell phones while driving (now against the law in many states) increases your risk of being in an accident fourfold. Text messaging also increases inattention and raises sixfold your chances for an accident while driving. The negative consequences of not paying attention are claiming lives.

While technology has succeeded in speeding up or taking over the routine, repetitive logical processes of thought—you simply program the address into your GPS and Siri takes over—the chaotic, out-of-control experience of information overload was not anticipated. I hear it all the time. Listen to Frank: "I'm on overload. I can't take in any more data on this project, but I have to. I'm making list after list and pushing out my deadlines, my meetings, everything. I used to be able to schedule a social dinner a week or two ahead, but now I start looking for time a month or two out. I'm big into time-debting. You just keep saying you'll get to it, and then you push it off. Nothing happens on the first shot anymore.

"Information overload also means I can't make sense of things. There are too many choices and I can't sort through the plusses or the minuses. Look at buying a new car, a new refrigerator, or planning the details of our vacation. I finally hired a personal assistant to get me out of the information mud.

"Here's the worst part: I make so many more mistakes than I ever did because I'm going too fast, not reading closely, not listening closely. I cannot take time to read the small print. But then look what it costs me. I often feel behind and out of the loop. How come I'm so often saying, 'Why didn't anyone tell me?' and I get looks of dismay. Oh, I didn't read far enough in the email."

The trouble for society today is not the remarkable advances of technology, but the unforeseen drawbacks, especially the loss of time, rather than the gain in time that was expected. You lose time as soon as you decide to log on to Facebook and then follow an advertising link to find out how to lose ten pounds of tummy fat without leaving your chair. Next you click for the day's headline and click back again to check the stock market. Ooh, you were up two hours ago and so was your mood, but now the ticker has taken a dive and so has your mood. You are in the throes of a repetitive cycle of checking and checking again, a victim to the ticker tape and its arrows of gain or loss.

There's a trap here with time. You no longer think you can afford to take time to do anything. So you just sit there. As long as you don't start, you won't feel overwhelmed by the enormity of the task in front of you and the panic that you don't have time.

Instead of being freed up, people have become enslaved to the addictive experience of trying to get control of themselves and the vast amounts of information they cannot absorb or harness. You're like the rat on the wheel: pedaling faster and faster but going nowhere. Yet you convince yourself that you will get there— you'll start the project or you'll finish the project once you read this last citation; you'll lose the weight once you've evaluated all the diet plans; you'll make the call once you've done your background work; and you'll get married, have children, and live a real life once you've made your millions. In a word, you'll stop your addiction once you get control. It's backward and it's an illusion.

Most people still believe the answer is simple: go faster, try harder. You pump yourself up with slogans—"get a grip," "just do it"—to try to get a different outcome. You race for a while, trying new shortcuts, writing more lists, to accomplish more in less time. You really believe there's something wrong with you that you can't get control, but it's not going to happen. The constant focus on trying to get control is the core experience of addicts who don't want to recognize the reality of their loss of control.

DISTURBED RELATIONSHIPS

Once again when we look at the impact on human relationships, we find irony in the progress we think we've made. Is it really progress? As the computer facilitated communication through email, we began to use it as a shortcut to avoid direct person-to-person contact, which takes too much time. Then came social media with its promise of creating communities that would expand our contacts exponentially. But wait, we wouldn't have to meet anymore, because that takes too much time. We wouldn't have to learn how to talk to people face-to-face, how to develop an initial attraction into a deeper friendship or intimate relationship. Not necessary anymore, and it all takes too much time. Everything is now. Everything is impulse. You just go for it. Count your friends and that equals relationship. No wonder people feel so empty and so unsatisfied.

But could we see that we were replacing our human relationships with a new attachment to our technology and the pursuit of speed? That we had stopped talking on the phone, sitting down with our children and partners for dinner and conversation, sitting on the sofa later when the kids are in bed or doing their homework to check in on the day and listen to our spouses. No, we sit across from each other and text, read and write our blogs, and look on Facebook for what's new with you. We catch up with our nearest and dearest in 140 characters. So many of our relationships are like the grocery list. Tap it out and cross it off.

At night, as we fall into bed, we mentally check off our lists: Did I pack the lunches for the kids? Did I send that email to the boss? Did I kiss the kids good night? Did we schedule sex for Thursday? No, we didn't talk together in real time today. But we'll catch up with that. I'll put it on my list for tomorrow.

For many people, their relationship to technology and speed has become more important than, or even replaced, human relationship. This is the nature of an addicted relationship. People now have an intense emotional investment in time, money, and a fast pace. That's what counts, just like getting to the first drink at 5:00 p.m., the first hit of meth to wake you up, the first bite of the pastry that soothes, the first bet at the online poker table. Your relationship to your wife or husband, your business partner, or your close friend takes second place or no place once you've got to be online, once you're on the make for success. People addicted to fast and faster are missing, or they have lost, healthy human relationships that would mediate and help them contain this new relationship to technology and speed.

The human brain is wired to be dependent. Infants need to develop a strong attachment to a caregiver because it is through dependence on the other that infants learn the basics for their ongoing healthy development. A loving interaction with a caregiver teaches an infant how to think and how to manage his or her emotions—what is called today self-regulation: to get excited, to get energized, to calm down, to soothe him- or herself when experiencing discomfort. It is in this human interactive process that the ability to control impulse is born and developed.

Healthy human attachment facilitates restraint of impulse and an ability to slow down through the emotional bond and the reciprocal communication that begins before birth and before words, and evolves throughout our lives through language and emotional connection. Instead of acting on impulse for instant gratification, we learn as two-year-olds to "use our words" instead of biting, hitting, or pinching our playmates. At any age the less we share emotionally with another and the less we feel able to talk back and forth, the more isolated we become. This kind of isolation can lead to depression or to addictions of all kinds as people attempt to fill the internal hole. Impulse comes to rule.

But even finding and maintaining friendships is often a form of multitasking these days. People post again and again on social media sites like Facebook, seeking the rush of accumulating "friends" and "likes." People count these hits as connections or even friends, but these are not relationships. You pressed "Accept" and you may or may not develop any more knowledge of each other or ever engage in a direct exchange. Yet you tell yourself you are connected, but an expansive Internet world of close friends is an illusion.

Deep human relationships are built on face-to-face interactions that involve emotional engagement back and forth. We evolved as human beings to be in emotional connection, with deepening bonds nurtured by listening and empathy. When you evaluate your worth by your number of social media friends and shift the method of building friendships to quick, short hits on the "Accept" or "Like" buttons, you change the nature of friendship. Without emotional engagement, you are left with a virtual list of contacts, not friends. Instead of a few long-term close friends and even your most intimate partner, you gather superficial, short encounters.

No wonder so many people feel lonely and deeply unfulfilled in their relationships. Many say they don't know how to establish an intimate bond or they don't have time anymore. Young people often have no idea of what an intimate, open, vulnerable, and trusting relationship is. They think human relationship is a commodity. You shop for friends and you market yourself. We have radically shifted our deepest understanding of what constitutes closeness, commitment, and connection. We are paying a huge price already and it will get worse. We are eliminating our value of being real in the drive for image enhancement in the pursuit of success.

Recently a college professor spoke of a class exercise that became "out of control" in the best way. Following a writing exercise in autobiography, students shared excerpts accenting their emotions. Twenty-year-old Romy spoke of the "connections" she had always valued in elementary school and how she felt she'd lost them when she became so hyperactive in high school. Now in college, she didn't know what it was all for. "What's the purpose of working all day and all night? I'm one of the privileged kids, part of this wonderful experience at this great school, and I feel empty." One by one each student in this seminar related a sense of chronic stress, emptiness, and loneliness. As they let it all out, they also began to cry. Every one of them. Ironically, they said they hadn't felt this connected for years. They were telling the truth to one another, listening, and feeling.

Luckily, Romy had solid experiences building close friendships as a child, so she knew what she had lost in the rush and chronic frenzied pace of college. She and the other students in the class felt overwhelmed by the power of their emotions and the truths that poured out about the loneliness they all felt. Their class experience of overwhelming emotion was positive, they all agreed. But several felt awkward at the next class. Did they need to be emotional again? Would they feel demands from others to stay this connected? Some were scared of the burden of such intimacy. Where are the rules? Where are the boundaries?

When you've settled into a world of instant contact, impulsive action, and quick cutoffs, you don't know how to build a relationship over time or to value a longer process. A grad student told me about describing his efforts to find a girlfriend he could marry: "Taking all this time to get to know each other is inefficient."

Many parents, high on speed for so long, are becoming aware of the serious emotional costs of technology immersion and the fast pace of life it demands. "You think you are so engaged with your kids and family, and it's all an illusion. Your kids have to tell you to put your phone down and pay attention, to look up instead of down."

"Dad, we're talking about our summer camping trip. Don't you want to be part of this?" ten-year-old Sean asked his father at the dinner table. Dad often missed dinner, and when he was present, he was preoccupied. "Earth to Dad, Earth to Dad, come back," pleaded his son.

For a while, this dad bragged that he ate dinner with his kids at least three nights a week. But when he reminded Sean that he was home more than other fathers, his son handed him a list of the nights he'd been at the dinner table in the last month. Dad held his impulse to yell and looked at the numbers. It wasn't true. It couldn't be that he'd only been at the dinner table four times in the last month. Sean knew. Dad thought he was involved, but his illusion of engagement was self-absorption.

Dad cried as he told me he'd lost his father to alcohol. Never, ever did he think his son would lose him to his addiction to speed and his drive for success, his multitasking, his obsession with his iPhone, and his inability to really listen.

What about couple love? Intimacy? Raina had been a successful computer programmer for more than ten years, in demand by the most prestigious tech companies in the Silicon Valley. She lived and breathed computers and believed she had a good life.

Raina and her husband, Omar, had been married for five years, but they'd drifted apart. After a fast hookup through a computer dating site, they found compatibility in their mutual devotion to the tech world and the fast pace of advancement. But they quickly found they had no time for each other. Both were driven to work harder and longer to make more money and be more successful. They saw spending time together—a date night—as an obstacle on the road to success and agreed they didn't need it.

So they had no time to really develop intimacy. They lived parallel lives, side by side at their computers. They could talk tech, but they couldn't talk feelings. They hadn't learned about emotions growing up because emotions weren't valued. They were taught that feelings should be hidden, kept to yourself. Plus, feelings complicate life. If you're going to talk about what you feel and how you feel, forget speed and efficiency. Forget success. You'll be adding valuable time to every interaction and dragging each other down. Relationships should be transactional. Do the deal. As soon as you start to talk about feelings, you're done. Now you're sucked in and trapped. What's the most efficient way to be in relationship? Agree to leave emotions out of it.

So Raina and Omar didn't have feelings. They suppressed every hint of emotion until all of life was about getting things done. But ironically, there was something they couldn't achieve. They had no idea how to get to know each other and be in a relationship that went deeper than tech talk.

This couple didn't get as far as seeking help. They just didn't have a marriage anymore. Agreeing amicably to separate, they waited a long time because they were too busy. Raina, who started individual therapy three years later because she was having anxiety attacks, said she had no idea she and her husband had problems. They thought this was what a relationship was. You both work ninety hours a week and pass each other early in the morning and at night.

In therapy when asked to describe her relationship style, Raina said: "It's like parallel play. I don't listen. When the other person is talking, I'm thinking ahead to what I'll say. Or I tune out. I just don't grab hold of a thread and pick it up myself. Too much trouble. Relationships with people take work. I feel alive if I'm racing inside, so I stay primed to the buzz of my iPhone, my closest relationship. That sound gives me an instant jolt of relief and rescue."

Another couple, married for thirty years, had always maintained their close, loving bond by checking in every night—staying current—about all things emotional as well as practical. They also tried to hold on to a long walk together at least once a week. But as they both became more successful, they became too busy to keep talking together. It didn't take long at all for the distance to set in between them. Luckily, Janelle felt the change quickly.

She told her husband she needed him to be present emotionally for her, even if he didn't think he needed it for himself.

Janelle and her husband caught themselves in the throes of speed and all its costs. They weren't about to settle for a robotic, get-it-done relationship that was void of feeling. But it took focus and effort to slow down and start talking deeply again.

Think about your closest relationships. Are you in a committed relationship now? What does this mean? What kind of connection do you and your partner have? Is it all action, all getting things done? Do you feel close because you share your lists and check things off every day? Is parallel work and play your operative mode? When was the last time you looked each other in the eye and talked? Shared deep emotional truths without feeling criticized or defensive? When was the last time you cried together?

Do you see the absence of interaction as part of relational life today? Is this absence the cost you pay for keeping up, the price of success? Now look at your Twenty Questions again. Is your list of yeses growing? Are you beginning to see that you've actually narrowed your world, even though you'd swear it was just the opposite?

STRESSED CHILDREN

What is this addiction to fast doing to our children? Are we modeling unhealthy behavior and sowing the seeds of a future generation that is socially crippled? Are we neglecting our children emotionally? Are we less available to give them engaged time and attention? Is time with our kids another burden we avoid?

Many children raised in unhealthy, addicted, or otherwise traumatic families grow up afraid of others, reluctant to trust anyone besides themselves, and vulnerable to addiction. They learned a hard lesson: the very people you must depend on are the same ones who abuse you and create the frightening, dangerous conditions that constitute the everyday environment of your life. Out-of-control parents wreak havoc on the basic safety and security of emotional attachment with their children. Children living with the trauma of any loss of control may grow up to be wary of others and to believe they can depend only on themselves. This damage has been widely accepted for children of alcoholics or drug addicts. Can we accept that this is true for children of speed addicts as well?

May, who ruefully calls herself a nineties wunderkind, recalls: "My parents were never home. They were always working, always after success, which was supposed to be good for all of us. We were going to have opportunities!" When they were home, they were racy, antsy, impatient, yelling. Basically, they just shouted orders. Life was nothing but getting things done. You had to be productive. You had to be working on something, chop-chop. Talk about over-scheduled!

"We had no time for thinking, no time to talk. I remember running from one activity to the next and wishing so much for quiet time. I used to get that in school and I loved it. Then everybody got worried about getting into college and there went quiet time.

"I don't think there was ever any *now* to contemplate and enjoy. There was this edginess that filled our lives. That's what we felt. It was an intense out-of-control pace that never, ever slowed down. I grew up believing that I had to be successful, but I had no idea how to do that. I felt I had to take care of myself, but I had no idea what that meant or how to do it, except to keep running. I really grew up afraid to stop."

Carlo described the erosion of his family until the whole thing collapsed. "We all lived with a rush, rush, rush sense from morning till night. We could never go fast enough. My dad was running to work and couldn't stop to listen, my mom was rushing us off to school and couldn't listen, and we just grew quieter and more resigned. No one could see or talk about the bad place we were all in because of this push for success. Then one day they told us they were getting a divorce. No kidding. Nobody had any connection anymore. We had the big house, the gadgets, and nothing going on between us. It was pretty sad."

What does this new world of speed mean for our children? It affects them in every way and much of it is not good. While many kids love their technology as much as their parents do, they are also showing the same signs of stress and distress, illnesses of all kinds, and psychological problems caused by chronic internal pressure to go faster and produce more and better.

Kids need close, loving bonds with their parents and an environment of parental attention, reasonable limits, and guidance. Kids need time in relationship with their parents, but it is time that has slipped away. Many parents are too busy to provide much of anything and abdicate involvement in their children's lives. They are preoccupied with their own addiction to fast and busy, having traded human relationship for tech support.

Kids are developing behavioral, thinking, and emotional problems due directly to neglect, overstimulation, over-scheduling, and too many pressures. They have impulse disorders, too, as their parents, friends, and school all push them to more action. They are not given limits nor are structures and boundaries valued. Action and impulse are the currencies for success and the core of behavioral addiction.

Kids' thinking is skewed as well by the effects of pressure on their attention and the rush to outcome. Get the answer as fast as you can. Breadth of topical facts achieved by a "horizontal" sweep on the computer is valued more than depth achieved by delving deeply into one subject. These values reinforce the need for greater speed.

Plus, experiences and definitions of success and healthy relationship are skewed by the drive for speed. Many kids haven't experienced slow time at the dinner table with everybody present, so sitting together over dinner to share the day's news and emotions is seen as an energy drain. Many kids consider this kind of attention to relationship a major *cause* of stress. Panic rises in a child who feels compelled to get back online, back in the game, and back on Twitter, checking in with friends. For many, social media has become the social world.

THE NEED FOR HUMAN RELATIONSHIP

Everybody needs human contact and deep human connection. Everybody needs human relationship. We don't grow up healthy and we don't survive without it. Yet this bottom-line fact of human dependence is also something many people scorn, fear, and avoid. This denial and aversion to human need for others is a key part of all addictions, including our unhealthy hooked-on-speed dependence. We happily believe that we are self-sufficient.

People who have lost control to addictive behavior have a false sense of limitless self-power. They don't believe they need anybody else, and in fact, consistent with a dominant American value, they feel they *should not* need anyone else. American culture has always viewed dependence as weakness. Ironically, the weakness lies in not realizing and refusing to realize how dependent human beings actually are. When people are not allowed to develop healthy dependence, it increases unhealthy dependence—the kind of dependence that defines addiction. Addiction is a relational problem. Addiction is a dependence on "other" that's gone awry. It's a need that's become out of control.

Being addicted interrupts normal development, no matter how old you are, and it even sends you into a backward spiral. You begin to feel, think, and behave like a child—a needy, greedy child. We could call this immaturity, and it is, but it's much more. It's a regression to a primitive level of development: your whole sense of self becomes dominated by impulse and a loss of control of thinking and emotion. This immaturity is inherent to all kinds of addictions, which are now characterized by a feeling of intense need, entitlement, and the drive to have it all now.

It's a fact: humans need other humans. Yet people recoil at the whole business of human need. They turn inward instead, relying on an illusion of self-power and a denial of need, especially emotional hunger. We need to accept this need as healthy and learn what healthy dependence is. This leads us directly to spirituality.

A SPIRITUAL AILMENT

Spirituality is a big concept in our culture with as many personal meanings as there are people. We would all agree that spirituality is something we value and maybe need as human beings, something that promotes our health and well-being. We might also find some agreement that spirituality involves an experience or state of awe, wonder, and connection, defined as an experience or state that we feel and know as bigger than ourselves. Ironically, we might see connection as exactly what people addicted to speed believe they have or are seeking to find. Yet for speed addicts, this pursuit is a terrible trap: They are looking for connection through the elevation of self-power. They look for connection through the exercise of human will to overcome and conquer all limits.

In the context of addiction, I see spirituality in relation to human dependence. We do not exist alone. And we are not the ultimate power. We exist only in relation to other human beings and, for many people, to something greater than ourselves.

A concept of spirituality has always been a part of the Alcoholics Anonymous program, though what that spirituality means is open to interpretation by every autonomous member of this fellowship. In my view, it involves an acceptance of human limits and human need, with a reliance on "a power greater than ourselves."

As we'll see later on, spirituality also involves a focus on service, on something higher than personal gain, a reaching out away from self-absorption.

We are caught in a fundamental spiritual ailment—a belief in self-power gained through the push of a button, a belief in speed and action for their own sakes, and a belief in the power of endless input, stimulation, and information. We believe in a god of speed. We are lost in our strivings for self-power and terribly afraid we're really powerless. Technology can lead to a loss of self-esteem. We no longer feel competent without buttons to push or a gizmo to hold. We fear that we're not really smart, and that we're empty inside. This fear is the truth for many who can't function without their props.

What about you? Have you known this anxiety? Do you watch it sitting on your shoulder or rumbling inside, waiting to fill you with dread when you pause for breath? Do you pat your pocket to calm your nerves while you wait for the next opportunity to pull out your phone and check for messages? Do you know that you don't have the power you believe you should have? Or that you could have if you weren't failing all the time?

We are alone, though we relish our "connections." We have a pseudo intimacy, achieved via the mediator of technology. We've lost our ability for self-reflection and to be together, focused on the other and each other. Moments culled away from tech devices or pursuits outside of ourselves cause anxiety and panic. Yet we still think this is good. We think we like this state of frenzy.

And sadly, racing full-throttle becomes for many the heart of spiritual pursuit. Spirituality—the reality of our human dependence and the need for something greater, as I define it—becomes the chase itself and the illusion of reward. Many people drive themselves nonstop toward a goal. When they reach it they look for another goal and another drive because the fantasized reward is empty. The end of pursuit is futility, fear, and another round of "start your engines."

Our business-model culture places production and profit as the highest goals, the something greater that lies just beyond. If you sold one hundred widgets today, just imagine what you can do tomorrow. The market is limitless. The stock market has no ceiling.

Spirituality has become the chase for more, the entitlement for endless progress and unlimited profit. Shareholders are the bottom line. There is nothing greater to look toward, nothing greater to aspire to. There is nothing greater than the power of self to drive toward success.

Is speed an addiction? The next chapters will discuss in detail how people who live in a compulsively frenzied state show the hallmarks of addiction, with all its disordered behavior, feeling, and thinking, with all its devastating effects on their lives.

4

Behaving Like an Addict

The Twenty Questions you encountered in the prologue invited you to think about yourself and your relationship to the pursuit of fast and faster—speed—as a central feature of your life today. You found these questions in the early chapters as descriptions of loss of control and addiction. Now we highlight the Twenty Questions directly to help us explore the triple components of any addiction: your behavior, your feelings, and your thinking. The next chapters will show you why "just do it" often isn't enough when you want to slow down but can't. You will also see what it takes to change and you will learn how to face yourself, your family, and a culture that now pushes you to never slow down, never accept limits or make tough choices.

Twenty Questions

YOUR BEHAVIOR:

1. Do you want to slow down, but you cannot? Have you lost control?

2. Do you keep adding activities without taking any away?

3. Do you work longer and longer hours, but don't ever finish?

4. Do you treat other problems: sleep, anxiety, depression?

5. Do you act first and think later?

6. Do you check your email and reach for your phone first thing and last?

As an addiction specialist, I have treated people for all kinds of addictions over the years. When I first began this work, most people accepted the existence of alcohol and drug addiction. However, there was a lot of resistance initially to recognizing addictions as other unhealthy behaviors. It wasn't easy for people to accept that eating could become an addiction, that gambling could become an addiction, or that profligate spending could become an addiction. But it made perfect sense to me. They had in common the utter powerlessness over the substance or behavior along with the thinking distortions, the defenses, the emotional pain, the endless downward spiral. As I watched the movers and shakers in my hometown area of Silicon Valley wind up and implode, it became obvious that an addiction to speed has the same things in common. If we look at the story of Jack, we can see how the dynamics of addiction are present in his devotion to speed.

Jack was a small-town guy with a big appetite for more of everything. He loved his life and believed there was only opportunity for him if he worked for it. He grew up in Arizona one of three children. Somewhere in early adolescence he went through a transformation from scrawny little kid to a muscular six foot two inches. His blond hair turned dark, but he kept his striking blue eyes. He became aware that people paid attention when he entered a room. When he was a high school freshman the football coach encouraged him to join the team, and by his junior year he was captain. In the winter he played basketball and in the spring he ran track and played baseball.

His folks were adamant that sports not get in the way of his studies, and he maintained a 3.9 GPA despite his busy schedule. He wanted to go to an Ivy League college, so he paid a lot of attention to his résumé. Debate team, student council, class president, Big Brothers volunteer, Habitat for Humanity volunteer. His mother would look at him and smile. "You're amazing." His grandmother would shake her head. "I don't know how you fit it all in," she'd say over and over again. "No problem," thought Jack. "I can handle anything." Not that he didn't feel overwhelmed sometimes, but he'd forget the tension when he heard a cheer go up from the bleachers.

Jack was surprised when he started Yale University that the demands on his time and effort multiplied like stars in the midnight sky. But those stars promised sparkling rewards, too. Jack found he had to study much, much harder than he did in high school, and he frequently found himself at his desk at 2:00 a.m. He awoke bleary-eyed to his alarm in the morning, bolted from bed, splashed water on his face, and charged across campus to his advanced calculus class. Despite the pressures, he found time to write for the school's newspaper and play intramural sports. After all, he knew he wanted to go to grad school.

He met Maureen, a tall, lanky redhead with a withering wit, when he was a junior. He'd never forget his first view of her. He was standing by his dorm when Maureen and a friend ran by in track shorts. He whistled at her and she shouted back, "Put your money where your mouth is, honey." She, like Jack, was bright and achievement oriented. They were married his first year in graduate school.

After Jack got his MBA, the couple moved to San Jose, California, where he got a job at an Internet start-up. Maureen joined an established tech company as a finance vice president within a month of their arrival. They didn't have to bother with much ladder climbing. They had been groomed to start close to the top and that's exactly what they did.

Life went well for them that first year as they settled into the exciting life of Silicon Valley. Maureen had the cachet of her company's name and the aura of the big time. She wore a corporate photo badge along with 20,000 other employees worldwide. She carried benefits for both of them and could be the stable earner.

Meanwhile, Jack had options. He played the high-risk gambling stakes of the start-up. As part of an unknown one-room gang of eight guys, Jack had the thrill of constant risk and the push to get the product to market and the company to an IPO.

Neither Jack nor Maureen had ever brought in so much money before, and it was a heady experience. They bought designer clothes and high-end cars. They became thoroughly early adopters, buying every new tech gadget as it hit the market. When Jack's parents came to visit, he casually opened a $250 bottle of scotch, the kind his father had purchased for special guests. His dad motioned a tip of his hat to Jack. "You got it made, son," he said with a grin. Jack couldn't have agreed more. He shook his right hand and blew on it as he rolled his virtual dice.

Before the year was out Jack and Maureen were beginning to experience some of the downsides of their high-end lifestyle. Both of them were working sixteen-hour days. They didn't see much of each other, and when they did, they were too tired to talk. They were often grouchy and irritable with each other. Maureen could ease back and shorten her days occasionally to ten hours, but Jack didn't dare. Plus, he didn't want to. He loved his work and the excitement of creating something new that would make him millions. Jack quickly adopted the mantra of finding "the next big thing." After all, isn't it true that everything important must be big, and there are no limits to how big, how much, or how fast?

Jack had the gambling buzz. If someone would have asked him if he exhibited any of the behaviors outlined in the Twenty Questions of speed addiction, he would have proudly acknowledged behaviors number two—he kept adding tasks without taking any away—and number three—yes, he worked longer and longer hours and never finished. But that's the way life is now. You just keep pushing things off. Everybody works that way. Jack smiled as he nodded yes to number five—of course you act first and think later! That is the *only* way to win. And Jack added another "of course, that's obvious" yes to number six—"I reach for my iPhone constantly, first thing and last." Jack didn't think number one fit him—he didn't want to slow down, yet—and he certainly didn't think he had lost control. What about number four? No, Jack maintained. He wasn't treating any sleep, anxiety, or depression problems, even though he regularly took a sleeping pill to help quiet him after midnight so he could get a few hours sleep. But Jack didn't think he had a problem with sleep. Anybody would need some help to quiet down if you worked as hard and as intensely as he did. So the medications were a support to enable him to keep going. Taking sleeping pills simply helped him work smarter, faster, and longer. Jack was proud he could answer yes to the four questions he did. He believed these "action first" ways of living were the keys to success.

Although he and Maureen made good money, they still had to stretch to buy the house they wanted. They didn't worry about it though; they anticipated that they'd soon be making much more. They wanted to stay in line with the rest of the Valley, and Jack got a Porsche. Maureen continued to drive the luxury Mercedes they got when they first moved. It was easy to rack up debt in Silicon Valley because it never showed. People just keep piling it on, knowing they would have more than enough to pay off debts in the future.

It took several years for Jack and Maureen to recognize that there was any problem. They both wished for more time together and wanted to start a family. Still, they reasoned that working these long days and maintaining the fast pace would pay off. They could retire young and wealthy. But Maureen wasn't getting pregnant. They were often too tired for sex and it didn't work anyway. She was dropping weight unintentionally and her period became very erratic. Her obstetrician suggested that she was too stressed and frantic all the time. Maybe she could try slowing down and giving more time to their relationship. They agreed but couldn't change anything. They were afraid if they slowed down they'd fall behind.

Next came sleep problems, which Jack had maintained he didn't have. They just couldn't quiet down enough to relax into natural sleep. As time passed relaxing enough to get to sleep naturally became more difficult, especially for Jack, so sometimes he took an extra sleeping pill. One pill didn't do it anymore. But then he would awake so groggy it was hard to think. He started getting horrible headaches, and the doctor told him he simply had to give himself a break. He decided to take a couple days off to rest, sleep late, putter about the house, but he felt anxious and out of sorts. He couldn't make himself pull out the spade to plant the lavender Maureen had bought. His legs seemed to have a mind of their own. It was almost as if they walked of their own accord to his desk where he switched on his computer. All he could think about were Carl and Ahmed solving that problem they were working on without him. He checked his email every few minutes to see if they'd contacted him. He texted them to see what they were working on. The text came back immediately: "Think we got something here, man." His craving to be in the office was so strong it almost felt physical. Headache or not, he was heading back in.

Jack and Maureen had slipped into speed addiction. They both shared the high of the adrenaline rush to invent and launch and then to outpace the start-up down the block to get to the IPO. What a high! Jack couldn't come down and he didn't want to. But he couldn't keep it up. He was racing compulsively to work harder and longer and he was spending compulsively to reap the rewards. Jack was out of control. Maureen was, too, but she didn't show it as much. She looked blankly at the Twenty Questions at first, not able to see herself at all. She realized that Jack had a problem, but if he would just slow down, they'd both be okay. Just like many partners of alcoholics, who drink right along with their more visibly drunken mates, she didn't recognize that she was a speed addict, too. Jack could be the "identified problem" and she could hide from view. After all, she told herself, she came home some days by 7:30 and even fixed dinner.

Just like an alcoholic, a prescription drug addict, or a gambler who cannot resist the urge to bet it all, Jack and Maureen were out of control and couldn't stop. And just like other addicts, they had no idea what was wrong. What do Jack and Maureen have in common with alcoholics or drug addicts, with compulsive spenders, or compulsive gamblers?

HOW AN ADDICTION TO SPEED WORKS

Just like an old-fashioned addiction to alcohol, an addiction to speed has multiple levels. It is a behavioral, thinking, and emotional disorder. *Behavioral*: You cannot help but act on your impulses. *Emotional*: You feel anxious—you've got a knot in your stomach and a little voice inside that tells you something might be wrong. Instantly, the impulse to fix the anxious feeling with a drink, a drug, food, sex, or even technology kicks in. Quick action will give you a temporary feeling of control. It's a vicious cycle. *Thinking*: You have to believe this isn't the case; you have to believe that you are in control. This is called denial. You lie to yourself so convincingly that you think you are telling yourself the truth. Addiction—the combination of out-of-control, impulsive behavior, uncomfortable, even scary feelings, and distorted thinking—begins to feel like the air we breathe. But it's noxious air. Ultimately the search and cycle produces a wasteland of emptiness.

For alcoholics this is the inability to say no to a drink, even when it threatens their jobs or families. They pretend to themselves that they can control the drinking. They feel lousy when they can't, but they rationalize the drinking. They tell themselves they need a little boost to get going or to quiet down. Another glass of wine won't hurt. Didn't the doctor say it was fine? After all, look how hard they've worked. It's important to celebrate and to take care of

yourself. And look at the headlines about the heart-healthy benefits of red wine. No problem here. I'm just taking care of my heart!
Many of these people will run with these permissions and ease into
compulsive roles, routines, and rituals, repeating them without
question. The trouble is the glass of wine before dinner becomes
two, then three, with more rationalizations. Soon the nightcap is
actually glass number four or five, but who's counting? Then they
begin to lose parts of their lives that are precious to them—they
can't think clearly after dinner and they start to nod off while reading to their kids—ultimately losing everything most meaningful.
It works the same way with drugs, gambling, spending, all addictions. People lose a connection with themselves and those they love
as they slip into the terrible compulsions of addiction and the denial and rationalizations it takes to keep from seeing it.

This is also how it works with speed. Jack had miserable headaches, couldn't sleep, couldn't find time for his wife, and yet he
wasn't able to stay away from his office for even one day. He tried
to garden, but found himself in front of his computer instead. He
was checking his email constantly and reaching for his smartphone
to text his colleagues. He was losing his relationship with his wife,
his chance to have a family, and his health, but he couldn't stop his
compulsive and constant focus on the office.

Our culture encourages—even demands—that we do more,
produce more, never stop. We forget how quiet time and a calm
atmosphere feel.

Or we never knew it. A proud computer geek since he was
fourteen, Perry caught the wave of high-tech frenzy when he recognized that he lived smack-dab in the heart of all the innovation
and he could get right on board. In high school Perry had several
summer internships at local tech companies and knew he could
easily start his first job after graduation at $100,000. And this was

before he went to college! Imagine what kind of starting salary he'd earn once he graduated with an engineering major. Perry could hardly hold still to finish his education. He'd remind his parents, "Bill Gates didn't graduate and look at him!"

Perry wanted to get going in the tech world and he didn't want to be stopped. "I felt like school was an undertow, operating at a slow pace that held me back. Fast was it, all there was. You move fast, think fast, and you don't stop. I loved the high and I hated every reminder that life is more than the computer. Not for me. I didn't want limits.

"My parents worried that I was addicted to the computer and to being so speeded up. I am and I love it! Fast is my life. Fast is what I want."

Carrie, sixteen, had the same sense of internal drive, but for her it was a need to constantly "connect," to be in touch with friends and to get feedback on Facebook and Twitter so that she was indeed part of the in group, a player. Carrie told her parents she had to answer her texts instantly, even if she was in class, at the dinner table, or doing homework. The sound of the ping says, "Get back to me *now* or I won't be your friend."

Following a recent lecture I gave about speed a therapist who works in a college health service noted that the school had to set strict limits on cell phone use during class. When a professor asked a female student to put her cell phone away, the student said no, began to cry, and explained through sobs that her friend said she had to answer instantly to prove she was her best friend and more important than anything else. When your friend needs you, you have to be there! This sense of urgency and desperation to respond is just like the craving for the next drink or bite of chocolate or the urge to get to work like Perry experienced.

ADDICTION IS BEHAVIORAL

Addiction is a loss of control of behavior: you can't stop doing something once you start. The actions are driven by instinct and impulse. You take one more puff and one more until you're hooked on smoking. You take one drink and you have to finish the bottle. You chisel that corner off the cake to even it up and soon you've eaten the whole thing. You log on to Yahoo! and you can't get off. You intended to just be a minute, but somehow you lost track of time. You've got a compulsion to keep at it and you do, even if the consequences of not stopping are horrible. Ironically, and sadly, the behavior probably started out with good intention. But when you can't stop, that drink, pill, or roll of the dice puts you in deep trouble.

We often look at people whose behavior is inappropriate or annoyingly repetitive and intrusive and think, "Why don't they stop this?" We are skeptical and intolerant of the notion that they can't stop. But that's what addiction is. You're doing something you can't stop even when you want to.

As we have seen by the examples of Carrie and Maureen, speed addiction is not just a man's problem. And it's not confined to the tech world. Today women of all ages, economic status, and ethnicity know they can be and do anything they want. They've seen and heard that opportunity waits for them to step up. But how can they manage? How can they do it all? Society says you can achieve more, have more, but society doesn't tell you how to get it, and definitely doesn't tell you what to give up to get it. If you are not supposed to have limits, why do you have to give anything up?

This has been a huge cultural conflict for women since the early days of Betty Friedan, feminism, and women's liberation. Times have definitely changed, but the conflict remains. Now, many teenage girls know they are supposed to do it all, but they don't know how to do it all, except to push harder and longer. You accept stress as a given. You know you won't sleep much, and somehow you'll figure it out. Above all, it's taboo to say you can't do it all. So you keep at it and then you can't stop. You become a speed addict, and then you add food, nibbling as you power through your homework or your twelve-hour workday, watching the numbers on your cell phone light up with an interruption that is both welcome and threatening. You need to get that call and you can't afford the time to take it. You can't get out of this nonstop push. At least you've got the Adderall to get you going and the Ambien to slow you down when you can't slow down for yourself.

Ironically, because of the progress females have made in every domain over the last forty years, men now have the same conflicts. They, too, are supposed to do it all and to have no limits. Saying yes to question two, men keep adding more without taking anything away. Men now must juggle the needs of their spouse and children, along with the impossible demands of work.

Men and women both try to keep going, operating robotically on impulse, without ever questioning, "What are we doing?"

ADDICTION IS AN IMPULSE DISORDER

Addiction is impulse without restraint, impulse unimpeded by reflection. You've got the urge, the craving, the nasty feeling of intense need that fuels the drive to do it again. The primitive feeling of urge turns into action that begins to drive everything else. The individual is dominated by feelings of intense discomfort and need followed by an impulse to act instantly to soothe these feelings, only to start it all over again.

Sherrie was a woman on the move. No one and nothing could stop her. Starting as a TV reporter in the field, she took the early-morning stories and waited for the anchor desk to open a seat for her. Sherrie had an angry streak that went with her ambition. She developed a reputation for pushing her way through, walking over anybody in her way. Colleagues called her "the Bulldozer" behind her back, noting that Sherrie was determined to plow, scratch, and manipulate her way to the top. She was destined to be a star at the anchor desk and she didn't look left or right or backward at the damage she was leaving in her wake.

Sherrie could only act. She only had impulse, the intensity of need. She was enslaved by her own internal drive to succeed and out of control with her impulses to make that happen. Nobody could reach Sherrie. If you tried to talk with her, to worry about her, to confront her, she talked over you and said you were jealous. Sherrie was on her own, heading for the top with a wild impulse disorder fueling her reckless drive.

Impulse is primitive, before words. It originates in the brain, and you feel it in the body, the tight shoulders, the quick inhale or the coughing jag, the jittery stomach. It often doesn't become a recognizable feeling because an action follows so instantly. It was impulse that drove Sherrie and impulse that Jack was responding to when his legs carried him unbidden to his desk and his computer.

Impulse is not bad, not unhealthy, not even immature. Impulse is perfectly normal. It's in all of us as infants and as adults. As we mature, we learn to recognize our impulses and to give them names—a pang in the stomach becomes "I'm hungry," which immediately becomes an impulse to eat or, if we pause, we can choose to eat or to delay. A tightness in your chest or abdomen becomes "I'm afraid," which becomes an impulse and perhaps an action to flee or hide or go to sleep. Or we learn to pause, even with a feeling of panic, and ask ourselves, "What is this feeling about?" A feeling of arousal becomes "I'm turned on," which becomes an impulse to engage in sexual activity. We can either act on the impulse immediately, or pause and imagine a time ahead when we can be physically or sexually engaged.

With maturity the individual can stop to think, reflect on an impulse, and choose how and whether to respond. Sometimes impulse wins out and sometimes it doesn't. The person waits for the physical sensation of feeling to move to a level of language and thought. Recognizing and articulating the feeling can soften the intensity and the need for an instant response. Words help contain impulse. Words become mediators, allowing an individual to become conscious of a feeling or an impulse to act and taking time to decide what to do. Words allow delay and time to choose. This is what an angry child who is throwing a toy is learning when her parents say, "Use your words."

Use your words is exactly what you can say to yourself when the urge to go faster, to answer the phone, to write one more email at midnight threatens to once again take over. You watch yourself do it again, but you don't stop. That's what it's like to be out of control. The trouble is you don't have a parent to step in and tell you to use your words. But nevertheless you need to be interrupted. You need to stop or be stopped. It can be you and your words.

Later in the book I'll provide tools to help you interrupt yourself. You'll learn new words and actions to help you begin to watch your impulses float by as you no longer automatically act on them. It's not easy, despite your wish that it could be as simple as "just stop it," but it can be done.

Addiction is young, even infantile, because it is so automatic, so linked to nerves and impulses. The addict in a state of need or arousal is just like a baby. Babies are a bundle of nerve endings, gurgling and crying out for comfort, nurture, or movement. They are dominated by impulses and feelings that require attention. If gratified, infants usually settle down, calm and secure.

If they do not receive adequate response, babies will cry harder, deeper, longer until they get a response or they give up. So infants learn to signal, to reach out for food and comfort and to be in motion, all normal tasks for healthy development. These are the same kinds of behaviors that later can become the repetitive actions of addiction, the compulsions that seem to come from nowhere and are unstoppable. Both Jack and Maureen were metaphorically crying harder, deeper, longer when they repeatedly turned to their frenzied, endless workdays to soothe their anxiety. They believed that working more would save them from falling behind, yet pushing harder, deeper, and longer always increased their anxiety. It was an unfixable trap. They started with anxieties about being able to keep up, to always win and be a success, and they piled on more anxieties from trying so hard to keep going. Then there was the anxiety about the costs of this vicious cycle. Could it be that Maureen and Jack couldn't get pregnant because of the stress? Were they causing their health problems? These are tough truths to see, so people seek something else—action, escape, relief, soothing, more, more, more—to get a feeling of control, to be able to change an internal discomfort. An impulsive, automatic action will become so routine that the individual can't link it to a thought or feeling.

Sherrie woke up with drive to get moving, to charge ahead; it just felt physical to her. "Just do it," she reminded herself all day long. She felt lucky she had the drive! Imagine if she couldn't get moving like some of her colleagues. She pushed and shoved, but couldn't stop to reflect and didn't want to. To her, acting on impulse was equal to success. You don't ask why or "What am I doing?"

In the culture we hear the infantile conflicts of addiction when grown people say that they're going too fast in their lives and they have to get a grip, slow it down, but they don't change. They think if they treat their depression and insomnia, they'll be fine. So sliding into number four of the Twenty Questions, they seek medication for these ills, rather than slowing down and quieting. They are baffled when they remain dominated by impulse and repeatedly lose control of their behavior, staying up all night surfing the Internet, staying at the office even when a husband or wife is waiting with dinner for them, or texting when they are reading a bedtime story to a child. They are treating the wrong problem.

Developmental theory helps us understand this dilemma. It is scary to realize that impulse, a primitive level of development, actually rules. That's where we are as a culture. We're becoming a playground of impulse dominance that often requires one public apology after another.

Is this you? Do you tell yourself that you can always apologize if you overstep, insult someone, forget an important meeting, or miss your deadline? Do you know that you can apologize for being angry, drunk, abusive to a coworker who isn't fast enough? You apologize for saying too much or showing too much online. And then there's that moment when you finally spew out your hatred like you always wanted to. But, oops, then you realize it was too much. Just say you're sorry, and it's all forgotten.

Is this you? Can you now think about the words *pause, reflect, stop to think about it*? Can you imagine introducing the notion of an adult time-out? These will be the key words that can help you interrupt your mantra to act on impulse and the automatic behaviors that seem to have a life of their own. We'll see more how these words can help up ahead. Now let's turn to the feelings of addiction.

5

The Feelings of an Addict

In the last chapter we addressed the first six of the Twenty Questions, which focus on behavior. You answered them and thought about whether they apply to you. Are you out of control in your drive to go fast and faster in your life? Do you recognize yourself as a speed addict from your behaviors, and if so, are you getting yourself ready to slow down?

Most people think that addiction means loss of control, and it does. But people often think that behavioral loss of control is all there is. If you just slow it down, stop robotically touching, patting, and reaching for your iPhone 24/7, change from working eighteen-hour days to fourteen-hour days, you'll have it licked. Well, here comes news that really won't be news to you. Addiction is more than behaviors that you can't stop. In this chapter, we'll look at the emotions of addiction, the feelings that push you to keep going and the feelings you'll encounter when you slow down.

Twenty Questions

YOUR FEELINGS:

7. Do you feel internal pressure to live fast and act fast, which becomes a craving to "connect" more rapidly?

8. Do you feel empty if you are not in constant action?

9. Do you feel nervous without your tech gear in hand or pocket?

10. Do you feel the beep of your phone as a comfort that gives you a shot of adrenaline?

11. Do you feel you belong when you are rushing, stressed, and in action?

At the Speed.com conference at Santa Clara University people mingled in the hallway outside the auditorium during breaks, sharing stories of the corporate pressures they were experiencing to go faster and faster. Some were revved up and pacing the halls, anxious for the next speaker to give them answers. They identified already with the loss of control and wanted a fix. Some expressed annoyance that we couldn't tell them how to "get control." Others felt discouraged and powerless to have any impact on the intensity of their work environments or their lives.

I heard people saying things like this: "I can't stand the pressure inside. I hate the feeling of being so hypercharged all the time. But I can't live without this feeling, either. As soon as I slow down the feeling of anxiety wells up inside and I look for something to take it away. I dread going to work and I dread not going to work. I feel trapped in my own skin and in my life." This is what it feels like to be out of control, to be an addict.

I was hearing the same kinds of things from these people that I heard from all types of addicts in my practice: they felt tremendous anxiety when they did not have their drug, and they felt trapped by their craving and their inability to stop. For a speed addict, the fast pace of life and the emphasis on action cover or distort emotional awareness or experience. Feelings of all kinds are redirected into doing something; then you don't have to experience the feeling. Yes, you're worried about falling behind, a fear that seems to cover everything else. But under that big fear, you've got a lineup of other major worries you want to avoid recognizing. Maybe you sense your marriage is falling apart, or your teenager is smoking pot and playing World of Warcraft in his closet all weekend. Are you over forty and still don't know if you'll ever really feel fulfilled as a working mother? All of these feelings can be frightening to face and even scarier to do something about. So speed—trying harder and going faster—steps in to take the pressure off of knowing what you're feeling, just like alcohol and any other substance or process addiction (food, gambling, sex) puts the lid on your real emotions. All your worries can be conveniently stored underneath the pressure to move fast and the urgency we call stress. The emotional dynamics of a speed addict are the same as those of an alcoholic or any other addict.

THE EMOTIONS OF SPEED

Emotion can play a couple of roles in the beginning of an addiction. It might be that an individual is drawn to a particular substance or behavior because it makes him or her feel excited. Moving at breakneck speed can release adrenaline and other chemicals in our brains that feel thrilling. Combine that with a "win" and the reinforcement is ferocious. Why would you slow down? The high of fast feels so good.

Children often love the feeling of spinning wildly, screaming in real or feigned terror on the roller coaster, or holding their breath to see what happens. Many young kids thrive on the terror of a horror movie. They are old enough to separate fantasy from reality and thus to enjoy a foray into loss of control of emotion that will end when the movie is over. Adolescents can feel a normal turbulence of hormone-stimulated emotion that is exciting and often threatening. Adults often seek the excitement and pleasure of out-of-control sexual feelings.

On the other hand, addictions can also begin in the need to escape feelings. Sometimes thrill-seeking becomes the driving force, giving people a sense of excitement while warding off emptiness and depression that loom underneath. People often take a drink, smoke a joint, turn to sex, or get really busy to avoid experiencing unpleasant feelings or any feeling at all. Emotion is normal to human experience, but many people are not comfortable with feeling. They fear or avoid feelings of any kind, positive or negative. Feelings don't seem neutral or safe. Many people fear that their feelings will end up hurting them. They'll feel too much—sorrow, grief, anger, lust, to name a few—and they won't be able to stop feeling. Many people ward off tears because they fear that once they begin to cry, they'll never stop. Ironically, people are most afraid they'll become out of control if they really open up to feeling. Emotion carries a threat of tremendous danger.

The three aspects of addiction—emotion, impulsive behaviors, and distorted thinking—are mutually reinforcing and are like three strands of a necklace that get tangled; the more you try to unravel the necklace, the tighter the knot becomes. Eventually the strands become chains that choke you. As people avoid them, the feelings get tangled with thoughts and behaviors. For example, anxiety pushes for taking action (behavior). Take a drink, push the buttons on the keypad, gulp the smoothie. This in turn pushes for an explanation (thought). "I got overwhelmed so I took a drink to relax." "I thought I'd miss some important calls if I took a break so I checked my messages constantly." Or "I was scared about the test so I quieted myself with a cool, quiet puff of weed."

Anita had been moving up the corporate ladder quickly. When her and Felipe's first child was born, Anita had changed jobs, received a big promotion, and worked eighty or ninety hours a week. How was she going to make this work with a new baby? She took a few weeks off and hired a full-time nanny. But she still had to figure out how to pump her milk and shorten her work hours by more than half. Anita was certain her colleagues and bosses now considered her a part-timer and would no longer relate to her as a high-level peer. That's what happens when you start a family. That's how she had seen it happen for others—women and men— who wanted to shorten their workdays but still be in the top tiers.

Felipe, who was a high-power driver just like Anita, agreed to make it home earlier in the evenings so he could help with the baby and so he and his wife could spend some time together, but he carried his BlackBerry with him. He never disconnected, and even when he'd awaken at 3:00 a.m., consumed with some problem at work, he'd jot notes on his phone.

But despite his drive, Felipe convinced Anita to take a week off and go to the beach in South Carolina when their son was almost a year old. Anita was ambivalent about the vacation; even though she was so wired and anxious all the time, she was reluctant to take time off because it would just make it harder at work when she returned. There is always more to do, so how can you relax? But Anita was tired, stressed, and craved more time with her family, so she eventually gave in. When they got there, she felt anxious. She kept pulling her phone out of her pocket to check her email. She'd play with her son for about five minutes and feel utterly impatient. All she wanted was to get back to her BlackBerry to look at the latest publishing news. Her industry had been in a state of wild change for the last few years, so she was sure her timing to start a family put her job even more at risk. She was driven to fill up every minute of her day with tasks to keep her anxiety at bay.

Although she couldn't admit it to Felipe, on some level she knew that if she stopped to think about how driven she was, she'd get scared. Who would support their family's lifestyle and who would pay the bills? They couldn't keep up on one income; plus, her job had always been more dependable than his. Worse than these worries was the pit she felt in her stomach when there was too much extra time. She would start to get sweaty and anxious until she could do something. Action made the feelings go away. At the same time the actions she took also left her empty.

Anita was sure she had a mood disorder. She had been depressed before the baby was born and afterward, as she lived with a terrible fear that she couldn't do it all. The worst feeling, and the one she tried hardest to push away, was her worry that she wasn't giving her son enough attention, enough love and care as she juggled so many balls every day. Would she regret her choices later on? "Well," she told herself, "don't look now. You can't do anything about this. Speed it up and work smarter. That must be the way out."

What is the feeling of speed? Speed is an internal sense of intensity, of urgency. You may feel it as a drive to be in motion and not stop, which can produce a feeling of being high. This drive can also be anxiety, masquerading as a feeling of excitement, a high that pushes for more action. Or this drive can be your effort to control anxiety. You actually feel shaky and scared, uncontrollable feelings that you can push away by jumping into motion. You feel the vibrating pulse of the smartphone in your pocket, and it pulls you out of the feeling of emptiness that was beginning to surface. You have become so used to focusing on gadgets that quiet time now brings anxiety. Or you watch yourself rush your kids constantly, rush your husband to get off the sofa. Rush, rush, rush. That's your normal feeling, so any letup tells you there's something wrong.

Recently I was talking to a twenty-something, high-tech couple about speed. Carmela makes education videos for elementary and junior high students, while Wilson is a creative guy in the audio world. Both identified with the issues of pace and high intensity, which they love. Carmela noted that her videos must be entertaining, especially funny, or kids won't maintain their attention. "They don't want to be bored and they don't think they should be bored. The video has to emotionally engage the student, provide a fun experience, or the child will not pay attention or stay with it. Today's expectation is that everything is fast. If you've got a forty-five-minute video about *A Tale of Two Cities*, you'd better find the humor."

As we talked over a leisurely, intellectually stimulating dinner together (we were visiting old family friends), our conversation became more animated. Carmela, Wilson, and his sister Abby, all gave examples of speed in their own lives and some understanding of what's gone awry.

Abby said she and Wilson had grown up eating dinner with the family every night, a ritual that taught them about relationship and gave it importance. It also gave value to slow time. Carmela nodded, noting that she, too, had family dinners to teach her about relationship and the value of conversation and listening. When Carmela and her friends go out to dinner, they put their iPhones in the middle of the table. Whoever picks up the phone to answer it during dinner pays the whole tab. *Yay!* we all cheered. But why leave the phones on? And why not put them out of sight? Leave them in the car? Is it possible to contemplate being engaged with others, feeling connected directly through conversation that builds and deepens as you slow down and let in other feelings besides the rush of speed? I wonder if Carmela, Wilson, and Abby all had their phones on and at the ready in their pocket or purse the whole time we were eating.

In a world of speed you also pick up tension from others. There is a contagion of intensity: feeling, pace, and constant motion are all around you and you absorb it. It's like an alcoholic going into a bar. The sight of the bar can trigger a craving for the feeling of relief or experience of camaraderie that came with the first sip. When there's a buzz all around, you start to feel it, too.

Speed is also a feeling of pressure, a different feeling than the high of intensity. When you feel pressure it interacts with your behavior and your thinking. You feel pushed, feel you need to go faster in order to stay ahead, or even just to stay afloat. Many people believe they are always behind and are therefore always trying to catch up. There is no pause and no feeling of success. Instead, you live with a belief, perhaps not even conscious, that you are never quite making it and you must keep trying. If you stop, you really will fail.

You may feel the pressure as a craving. Maybe it keeps you going or maybe you don't like it. With addiction, you get both. The pressure may become the drive of impulse. You are suddenly moving, thinking that your actions will quiet the pressure. You're drawn to keep drinking even though you don't like it anymore. Now you're drawn to stay "connected" through your gadgets, even when you long for a break, a quiet time you nostalgically remember before you were loaded down with technology and had to respond. You want to keep it going and you have to keep it going. You don't want to stop and you believe you don't dare stop. This is addiction.

You can see this dynamic playing out in Judy. A highly successful medical researcher, Judy had a knack for designing creative, groundbreaking studies that would bring in the big grants. Trouble is, she then had to do the research. The need to keep the money flowing interfered with the slow time she needed to be in her lab. It was a catch-22 for her. Judy knew how to work hard and she knew how to work smarter. Judy could make a small grant grow. When she first scanned the Twenty Questions, Judy laughed. "I do see myself in this list, but it's all good! Why do you think I'm such a success?"

Judy lived by the philosophy of if you've got a problem, fix it and fix it fast. For months Judy had pressed her partner, Maya, to do something about her use of opiate pain medication. Maya was glassy-eyed and nodding off during their quick dinners and out-of-sight for most of the evening. At first Judy thought the Oxycontin was just for the pain from Maya's hip surgery six months ago and before that the chronic back pain that had plagued her for years. But then Judy was worried and angry. Why couldn't Maya get it together and get off this stuff?

Maya couldn't get it together. She couldn't get off. After a dangerous fall Judy took her to the emergency room, where she was admitted. After several days Maya was transferred to a ninety-day residential addiction treatment program. Judy was relieved that Maya was in treatment, and she was furious that she had to participate in the family program. She could not see that she had any role in Maya becoming addicted. Judy worked hard, provided for the family, and now this.

Judy agreed to individual therapy instead of having to go to "those meetings" where she would have to listen to all the poor folks who had become out of control. She knew she was in control. She could manage her life and the lives of most of the people around her. It really was a slap in the face that her partner had gotten out of control and she hadn't realized it.

After Judy had reluctantly come to her therapy sessions for about six months, she began to wonder about herself. Having maintained at first that she didn't feel anything but good and strong, Judy now entertained the idea that she didn't really know what she felt. The pressure of working hard was all she knew.

Then one day Judy realized that she does have a regular, major feeling: stress. That's what she knows. It's with her all the time. "I think maybe there are other feelings underneath, but stress— that sense of constant pressure—covers everything," she told her therapist.

Judy said she could never keep up. She lives with a backlog of "things to do" on her BlackBerry. She thinks about what she can check off today and most of these to-dos don't get done. Not today. Not tomorrow. "I've got work projects, scheduling soccer, gymnastics and dance for the kids, getting the heater fixed and the carpets cleaned. But it's weird," she said. "I hate the pressure I feel to complete these tasks, but it's oddly comforting to see that list every morning. So I can tell you I feel like I'm failing all the time, that I'll never catch up, and I don't want to tackle any of these tasks. I don't want to finish them. Somehow I need that pressure."

It took Judy another six months to see that she, like her partner and all those "poor folks" attending support group meetings, lived in a state of being out of control. Underneath her feeling of pressured stress, she found sorrow and a sense of loss. What was all this for, really? What was she striving for that would make all this pressure worth it? All the fighting with Maya and the kids? All the strong foundations of their lives that now seemed to be crumbling? It's the loss of the dream of having it all. The loss of the illusion that she could do it all, but especially that she had the power to change anything and anybody.

How could she cope with the realities she was recognizing? She had been out of control for years in her drive for success and, therefore, unavailable emotionally to all who were close to her. Her partner is the one who'd become addicted, she believed. Yet her family members were upset with *her*.

Judy learned to recognize her emotions, to name them, and to tolerate feeling them. She marveled at how she could have lived her whole life without any awareness at all that she had feelings. Judy was a thinker. That's it. And she was an action gal, too. That was strong. You get in there and take action. She had no idea she'd become out of control and no idea that she'd been running away from her own deep feelings for all of her life. Nobody ever asked Judy about her feelings. Judy knew what pressure was, but that was all.

After about a year of therapy, Judy pulled out those "silly" questions she'd laughed at and started reading them again. "Oh, my God," she sighed. "This is really me, one question after another, and it's not good."

Judy grew up frightened of her emotions. She could hear the voice of her hardworking, single mother urging her to push ahead: "Don't let the teasing get to you. Brush it off, and don't cry. Be tough. You'll never get ahead if you give in to your feelings." Judy was sure feelings must be bad, at least to the degree she couldn't control them. How do we, like Judy, come to understand all emotion as normal and positive, even if feeling is sometimes painful?

Experiencing emotion and stopping to reflect on it before acting is known as "self-regulation," a key to healthy emotional, cognitive, and behavioral development. Self-regulation is an internal thermometer and a brake we all need. You get to a certain point of feeling and then you stop and give yourself time to calm down.

People learn how to self-regulate when they are infants and children through the attachment bond. The infant responds to the most primitive physical feelings with rooting and sucking motions and cries of distress or coos of comfort. When a close caretaker regularly responds appropriately, the infant develops a sense of safety, or a "secure base," as the attachment researcher John Bowlby famously called it. The child comes to count on the fact that he or she will be quieted and calmed by the soothing physical and emotional presence of a parent. Feelings can be felt, known, and expressed. Parents communicate a value and acceptance of emotion within a tolerable range for themselves and their children, knowing that wide swings of emotional loss of control are frightening.

Over time the child internalizes the ability to self-regulate, and then the growing child, adolescent, and adult will be able to tolerate a wide range of emotion, channeling it to healthy behavior and thinking and to relationships outside the primary family.

THE EMOTIONS OF ADDICTION

Failures in self-regulation are central to the experience of loss of control—which includes all forms of addiction—and to a culture that is now dominated by pressure and speed. Failures in self-regulation are characterized by distractibility and impulsiveness, along with a preference for choosing short-term benefits over long-term gains, traits that are dominant and valued in today's culture. Addiction is full of wide swings of emotion, from the lowest low to the highest high. People stay in action to avoid feeling these wide swings and the loss of control they represent.

It is very difficult to teach someone self-regulation, at least until the student is aware that she needs it. As you've seen so far, the first step toward self-regulation is awareness that you don't have it, that you're out of control with speed and the emotions that drive it. Only then can you think about slowing down as something you might value rather than as evidence of your failures. Later on we'll see how you become aware and how you then can begin to change. This whole process is paradoxical. Self-regulation is much more a result than a fix. It's a result of slowing down and looking inward, exactly what scares you.

Judy was pretty even emotionally when she began her research career. But as she worked longer and longer hours, she felt wider extremes of feeling. Sometimes she felt so high she couldn't stop moving. Then she'd get to the point where she would collapse, exhausted, and drop out of life for a few days. She'd withdraw from her partner, sleep a lot, and get depressed. As she progressed in therapy, she tried to explain to Maya what she had been feeling. "I couldn't stop jumping around and staying wired. It felt like it was me—excited and going for the high—but then it wouldn't. Soon it would feel like it was happening *to* me, a tornado whipping me around. I wasn't in control of it at all. It wasn't even a high at that point. I wanted to stop, but I couldn't. I'd have to wait it out until I ran out of steam. And then there'd be nothing left in me. I couldn't move."

The emotions of addiction are infantile, just like the behaviors and thinking. A basic feeling of need can translate into hunger, excitement, stimulation, greed, longing, anger, boredom, or count-less others. The individual feels a need, a hunger for something, or an intense drive to act, and immediately works to either deny the feeling or gratify it. Many people fear emotion, so denial may be a first response, followed perhaps by displacement. Judy prided her-self on never feeling anger. When a surge of fury toward her boss arose in her, she'd reach for her cell phone to check her messages instead of recognizing her anger. No messages. She'd stay on the phone, reviewing her photos and then her schedule. She'd con-vince herself once again that she was not an angry gal. Later on she'd explode at the driver next to her, waiting for the light to change. Then it wasn't her anger that was the problem; it was the bozo next to her. This justification gave her permission to displace her emotional loss of control.

SHUTTING DOWN EMOTIONALLY

Addiction often results in the "closing off" of all emotion, expres-sion, and perception as the addict is traumatized by his or her loss of control. The addicted person feels and knows deeply that she is out of control and fears that any other feeling will blow the lid off. The addict often mistakenly believes that her loss of control doesn't show, so she holds herself tightly, lest her feelings of fear, panic, remorse, sorrow, grief, or even joy and happiness disrupt her tenu-ous, false sense of control.

Trauma is emotional disorganization and paralysis, a state of overwhelmed immobilization, withdrawal, and depersonalization. You exist with a foggy feeling of being separate and fundamentally different from others. You feel a threat of danger, an absence of emotional or physical safety, and a fear of feeling. Traumatized people fear that any feeling will be experienced as "flooding" and uncontrollable, leading to destruction or annihilation. This fear leads to constriction and progressive blocking of mental functions. Memory, imagination, association, and problem-solving abilities are all impaired.

Like victims of other traumas, including natural disasters or interpersonal abuse and neglect, people lost in the compulsive repetitions of speed addiction experience a state of helpless surrender. Instead of seeing, feeling, and believing that they are driving their march to success, they begin to feel that they are out of control, thrown around by the forces of speed and the fast pace of life. You roll with it, or you fall by the wayside. Your helplessness reminds you that you really don't have control. You go with the flow or it swallows you up.

This was Anita. She was tired, worn out even, but she kept pushing. You mustn't give up, even if all you can do anymore is just show up. Your heart isn't in it, but you don't dare stop.

Or people feel an acute sense of danger—they are not going to make it to the finish line, they are going to fail—characterized by a hyperalert and hyperactive emotional state. They can't turn off, can't sleep because they are caught in the intensity of a wired state.

Most addicts do not recognize that they are traumatized until they are near the end of the line in their active addiction or until they are actually in recovery. Until that state of panic, the danger that addicts feel is the danger of being unable to satisfy a craving. To quiet the danger and the craving, they take the drink, the snort, the pill, or the pie, and then deny that they have surrendered to the traumatic state of loss of control. Again, they will not likely recognize their loss of control until later because they can explain it away.

Anita maintained that she was on the way up, that she was

driving toward success. "This can't be out of control, and it certainly can't be a problem." Rationalization steps right in to make everything okay. You are just going to make one more call, do one more email at midnight, and stay at work past dinner so the boss will know you are committed. Everyone should understand. These are sacrifices you make in exchange for being seen, being known, and going up the ladder.

People exclude, redefine, or distort information or events that are overwhelming or overstimulating to ward off unmanageable anxiety. As we'll see in the next chapter, this emotional chain in the necklace gets tangled with the thinking chain. The individual "uses up" cognitive capacities by constant scanning. You keep checking your phone, your iPad, your email to be sure you haven't missed anything. You return to Facebook, even when you just left it, to be sure you've taken it all in. You stay in an agitated state of alert so you can always save your kids should they need saving. They never have been in that kind of need, but it could happen. You know this is your guilt keeping you on alert, but you can't let it go and relax.

Many people who are hooked on information-gathering experience mounting anxiety as they recognize that a particular field of available information is too vast, too wide, and too deep for them to ever fully grasp. And so they turn to scanning, hoping to pull out bytes, or kernels of information, that will give them a "good enough" sense of the point or meaning.

Too often, it doesn't work. As we'll see, they have traded depth for width and, as a result, may miss in-depth understanding, seeing the surface of an argument or description as equal to the whole.

It's like riding the top of a wave. You skim over the surface without sinking into the depths of the water. You see the top and you feel the exhilaration of riding the wave, but you don't know what's below the surface. Sometimes this doesn't matter, and it's not even the point, until you get caught in the kelp lying just below your vision.

There are countless emotions that we can recognize, feel, deny, or act out directly or in disguise. We can be mature and know our feelings and discuss them. We can also deny or hide our emotions because we feel afraid, but still remain mature. Or we can go a step further. We can be immature and infantile and act out our feelings inappropriately in ways that hurt ourselves or others. Many people who are now out of control in their race for speed started out as mature, able to know their feelings and to discuss them. But as they succumbed to the pressures of speed, they soon felt fear, which they needed to deny. Finally they begin to look, act, and feel immature in their behavior, thinking, and emotion. Driven by the pressures of speed, they are dominated by impulse, which lowers their capacities for higher-level thinking and an emotional inner calm. An out-of-control culture drives people to primitive experience and function so that "normal" begins to mimic the level of three-year olds.

This is a layering process. We can all remember times when we let loose, said too much, yelled too loudly, and didn't stop to think before racing through the red light. We've had times when we wished we'd counted to ten before speaking, and many people have a rule to wait thirty seconds before pressing the "Send" button on the email. These minor glitches used to describe the everyday ups and downs of emotional life.

Not today. Impulse drives the culture, backed up by a belief that if you don't act *now*, you'll miss the chance. What about you? Have you acted too quickly, before thinking and regretted it? How often? How much has speed, pushing the envelope to say more and tell more, or just daring yourself to be "out there," caused you embarrassment, shame, or a baffled sense that you don't know what happened. You felt the urge and went for it.

Look at the five questions about feelings. Do they fit?

Sadly, these five and all the other Twenty Questions are now a measure of what's normal in the culture.

6

Thinking Like an Addict

In the last two chapters we explored the behaviors and feelings that constitute two strands of the addiction necklace. You asked yourself the six questions about your behavior in relation to speed and you tried out the five questions about your feelings. Maybe you had a lot of yes answers in both domains and maybe you were convinced: this is you.

But perhaps you weren't so sure. Let's turn to the third and final strand of this interwoven necklace to see if your clarity sharpens. Let's look at your beliefs and how you think, parts of human nature and function called "cognition." This is how we understand ourselves and others, and how we make sense of things, which is important to us: As human beings, we want things to make sense. When we're out of control we want to explain to ourselves how this can be, or not be, and why being out of control is really a necessary, good thing. Or if it's bad, we need to explain to ourselves why it won't last long.

Our deepest beliefs guide us in every aspect of our lives. Our behaviors and feelings will either be in sync with what we believe and value or, if they're out of sync, we'll be working to explain why this is necessary for the moment. Let's look at the last nine questions to ask what we believe, and then look at the impact of these beliefs in every aspect of our lives.

Twenty Questions

YOUR BELIEFS:

12. Do you believe you have no limits and you are entitled to live without limits?

13. Do you believe you should think, feel, react, and behave instantly?

14. Do you believe you will fall behind if you slow down?

15. Do you believe that success equals fast and faster, and slowing down is failing?

16. Do you believe you should only feel good, only feel high; other feelings are a sign of failure?

17. Do you believe stress is the price of success and chaos is normal?

18. Do you believe the "new intimacy" is through technology; less time for off-line relationships is the price of success?

19. Do you believe instant action is a virtue and you can overcome anything with enough willpower?

20. Do you believe all change must be big to count?

When Judy went reluctantly to therapy at the urging of her partner's treatment professionals, she was utterly convinced that the only problem was her partner's addiction to opiate painkillers. She had no awareness that she, too, was an addict because, as an addict, her thinking was distorted. It made perfect sense to her that she wanted to, and should be able to, work eighteen-hour days, race home and sleep fitfully for a few hours, and start all over again. It made perfect sense because the third chain of the addiction necklace she wore was distorted thinking.

An addiction to speed is supported by absurd thinking distortions in society—for example, it's normal to awaken to a beep at 3:00 a.m. and check your email. It's normal to sit across the hall from people and email rather than discuss with them in person. It's normal for a meeting of fifteen people sitting around a conference table to all be focused on the screens of their open laptops, typing and reading to one another, but not listening. It's normal to work several days in a row without sleep.

David Denby, a film critic and writer for the *New Yorker*, was an early participant-victim and observer of the high-risk, high-speed chase for wild profits that was taking American culture by storm in the year 2000. In a personal essay he described the demand for unlimited motion in our culture today and the addictive, gambling mentality and behavior it was creating: "When we're talking Internet time, the ideal person would not sleep. The 'New Economy' offers the chance to get rich. So you need to ask yourself, is risk something I can afford to avoid?" This is the thinking of loss of control, of addiction. There's a prize to get, money to win, if you only take the risks and keep moving. Don't stop to think. Don't be weak and let the risks give you cold feet. Don't stop yet. Go ahead and roll those dice again. You do have to work harder and smarter, and you have to stay in motion, but the rewards will come in an avalanche at the IPO, just like the jackpot of silver dollars that pours out when you finally pull the lever at the right time in Vegas, after countless, robotic, empty efforts, manning five different slot machines, running from one to the other. Ah, exhale. The payoff came. Denby said this thinking drove him and millions of other investors to repeated cycles of euphoria, panic, and collapse, the feeling states of addiction.

Just like Denby, you can see and hear the money pouring out of the machine or, like the drinker, you can taste the martini at 4:00 p.m. as you sit in an endless meeting and quiet your irritation with an image of the green olive in the clear, icy gin that awaits you. Your anger turns to expectation and the high of the reward. That's euphoria as you ride the wave that will crest with your first sip that you know is coming soon.

Then comes the panic. There might be an end to the upswing. There was a drop in the stock market and a problem in housing. But no, you reassure yourself, the movement is up. It has to be up. Any downward ripple is just that, a ripple. And if you're the drinker, fantasizing about the martini you'll soon savor, you also can feel the panic beneath your pleasure. This is the start of not being able to stop. This first drink will become your loss of control. But you don't let yourself see and feel that part. You tell yourself the drink is your reward for working so hard and tolerating the stresses that are part of your successful life.

Then comes the collapse. The endless physical motion, the stresses of the high-risk gambling emotions and mentality—the three strands of the addiction necklace begin to choke you. One day it will all collapse.

But we are not there yet in the culture. Addictive thinking still comes to the rescue as much as it also fosters the loss of control.

This distorted thinking is promoted by a pervasive fear of falling behind. Anthony Lavia, president and CEO of Flexstar, wrote, "As we in the high-tech industry have come to know, competitive success is all about speed and a commitment to a concerted course of action. Like a proactive company, our society needs to 're-engineer' our system and our processes before we fall irrevocably behind."[1] He worries about a trend toward a "committee-style of decision-making," with all its inherent failure due to delays and inefficiencies.

This CEO spells out a central addictive belief: you can't stop, you don't dare stop. Don't accept or yield to limits, or you will fail. Write another text, check another email, stay online in case you need to act. You might miss the big one. Any pause, any delay, and you'll fall behind. There is only constant motion. And be careful of thinking too much and taking too much time to reach decisions, which can happen with committees. What used to be considered prudent and wise management now carries a sense of timidity and cowardice. Take that risk! Keep going! Pull the lever on the slot machine, roll the dice one more time, buy the house a round to close the bar and have another bite of chocolate. You deserve it.

"Who knew," said a lawyer friend of mine. "One of the key beliefs of addicts is embedded in corporate policy." She said the corporate world will never stop its pressure for speed, which she related to the drive for profit. "Companies don't care if people don't talk, or if they're popping pills, as long as they're producing. They will never agree to slow down for fear their shareholders will sue. The corporation exists to make a profit for the shareholder and that is the bottom line." You don't slow down because you'll fall behind and you will lose profits. This is the way they think.

This belief system has become so pervasive that it reaches even into expectations for elementary school students. The elementary school system in Tacoma, Washington, supported a ban on recess, based on the belief that "children should be trained early to slot themselves into the fast-moving information economy."

By the time I read this news I thought I was desensitized to shock. But no, I felt a chill of disbelief and even greater worry about our kids. Can you believe this? What are we doing? I automatically asked myself. Are we so blindly working to program robots driven to success? Robotic children, medicated for stress disorders?

After I mentioned this ban on recess in a professional lecture, a professor of child development approached me and shook his head. He told me he felt overwhelmed and helpless to fight the cultural and educational tide of what he sees is a bandwagon belief in what is really false progress. His studies about the importance of play for all aspects of healthy child development were now being rejected as folly and a waste of precious time. "What will be the costs to our children?" he lamented.

We skew and distort our perceptions and our thinking to support our value of "fast" and the belief that we are entitled to have what we want and to go after it. We are entitled to move quickly, to make progress, and to embark on forward movement. Advertising shouts that a product or experience is quick or brief to hook us into an instant purchase. When you search Google for movie times, up pops the "get-it-now" ad for your instant tummy tuck. That ad and that image call out to you to press now and sign up for this miracle weight-loss tool. "I deserve it" is today's mantra for "go ahead, act on impulse." And so you do.

And here comes another ad in the middle of the hockey final. Enhance your performance. Up your top-gun appeal. Get instant results with the newest app or the newest manly, tough-guy fragrance that promises results beyond your wildest dreams.

Anything that is fast has to be good. We disparage the opposite: *slow, endless, forever, infinite,* words that sound like an old-fashioned 78-rpm record dragging along at 33 rpms. "Dragging along" is not a good state. We have come to believe that slow is boring. We believe we should not have to wait for anything. Waiting is lost time, lost advantage, losing. Why wait in line, why wait to buy something, why wait for anything?

The intensity of the high, the pressure to move faster, and the beliefs and values attached to speed are causing corporations, as well as political, social, and cultural institutions such as schools to crash into a wall of limits. The biggest example is the scandal surrounding the crash of banking and other financial institutions in the spring and fall of 2008 when a wall of previously unknown limits stopped the tsunami of unlimited loans and financing. One of the biggest financial companies was not rescued. It was allowed to fail, which started an avalanche of fear in the corporate and monetary corridors of society. That fear instantly crossed all boundaries to touch the rest of society, as what has come to be called the Great Recession came on with a crash.

Companies dissolved and individuals lost their savings and their homes. Wild gains in profit and the pace of betting came to an abrupt end and the economy collapsed. Grandiose thinking—there are no limits and no end to this wild ride—had created an addiction like any other. It was a loss of control—behavioral, emotional, and cognitive. Society was forced to slow down, but not to accept the reality of limits. People licked their wounds and waited for the next big thing. You live now—fast—and pay later.

Before this reckoning management and the workforce in Silicon Valley and many other corporate worlds were already out of control, victims of their own unrealistic goals and expectations. But nobody saw any problems. Hiring was on fire in Silicon Valley, where there was a shortage of workers. Yet the cost of living was also on fire, rising so high that many workers and service providers were priced out of the housing market. Your children's teachers, nurses, and many service people were stuck in a two-hour commute each day for the privilege of working in such a wild and promising environment.

Companies expanded their facilities as well as their workforces, which created a building boom. The price of real estate skyrocketed like the stock market and crashed in the same way. Binge building, buying, and selling of properties became the rash, high-risk Monopoly game of the 1980s and 1990s. Bet it all. Beginning in the fall of 2008, empty commercial spaces and housing foreclosures became the hangover penalty for this out-of-control thinking, feeling, and behavior.

While many of these companies were stopped by the crash, very few questioned the beliefs, values, and thinking that caused their loss of control and the crash they experienced. The culture and individuals continue to believe in the false illusion that people can and should work more, give more, and that this speed is progress. Like Judy concluded in her first reading of the Twenty Questions, the belief in no limits is normal in the culture. It's what we strive to fulfill. We are ironically entitled to be hooked on fast.

It's like the irony of the drinker who says, "Don't tell me I can't have another drink. I can get drunk if I want to." And the eater who says, "I'm entitled to eat what I want, when I want, even if I'm full." It reminds me of the three-year-old who says with her hands planted on her hips: "You're not the boss of me." I'm entitled to be hooked on fast because I want to succeed, I want to have it all, and you're not going to tell me otherwise.

The corporate world, and our culture at all levels, has been hijacked by the promises of cyberspace. It is the unlimited world of possibility that now can function like a drug. You may be drawn to the addictive feelings of excitement—the high, the energy push to move fast, live fast and not stop for anything. You may be drawn to the risk that pumps your adrenaline. This new high-on-speed addiction is the best antidepressant you've ever found.

And you may be just as afraid of this lure—the craving, the rush, the promise of something good from the gaming table or the ad that pops up in the middle of the Super Bowl—and of what you know deeply: that you want to slow down, but you can't. There it is again, question number one. Do you want to slow down but you cannot? Have you lost control? This is the captive corner of addiction, a captive corner that now holds the highest beliefs and values in American society. You now believe so firmly in the need to keep going that you shun hobbies, quiet time with your spouse and vacations. The whole idea of time off scares you.

Time off now leads to emotional and physical agitation and a fear that failure lies just around the corner. Many people live with a constant dread, a feeling of impending doom. This fear, this dread is not an illusion. People are afraid they can't keep up, and it's true. They can't. Like rats in a cage, pedaling furiously until they drop, people are falling off the wheel. But as they distort their perceptions and thinking, they see work-fanaticism—the elevation of work as the highest calling, a belief that work demands and deserves your nonstop time and attention—as the solution instead of the problem. People convince themselves that if they only work harder and smarter and keep trying to do more, they will be successful—whatever that means. But they never make it. As one of my patients said a few years ago, "You only think of the end; and you definitely don't think twice about the means. Anything goes in the pursuit of your success. Cheating, yes. Lying, yes. It's a marketing strategy. My mother taught me how to scam the system, which I've been doing since third grade. There was no room for failure in my family. Just gold stars."

HEALTHY AND UNHEALTHY THINKING

Like the capacity to have healthy attachments and the ability to regulate emotion, the ability to think in a normal healthy way begins in infancy. As infants and toddlers, healthy interaction with our parents and other caregivers lets us grow into active thinking, reflection, and language, the great mediators of human relationship. We've got primitive instincts in us all, but language, cognition, and speech make us more than our reflexes or our impulses. When a child's attachment to parents is fundamentally healthy, thinking and language promote self-regulation and the safety of mindfulness. Thinking and language give the child, and later the adult, the possibility of control over impulses and actions.

Parents and children will naturally encounter blocks in this process. When communication is open and honest and the needs of both are acceptable, the navigation can move well. But in the normal course of bumpy development, things can go off course. For example, a child with delayed language may develop anxiety she cannot communicate. She's too young to tell her parents what she's feeling, so everyone begins to worry too much and perhaps to intervene too soon, causing a downward spiral of unnecessary corrective efforts. Or parents freak out when a child brings home less than an A. The pressure for perfection then becomes the overriding atmosphere in the home, creating its own tension and anxiety. This is especially common in our speedy world driven by a belief in progress as the gold standard.

In the course of "normal" development, parents and children can both resort to cognitive distortion to hide or deny basic needs or wishes. This turn toward defense can be perfectly normal: An embarrassed child hides her developing sexuality, or a twelve-year-old boy stops talking because he's afraid his voice will crack; a parent, instead of doing anything, just waits for a child to grow out of her aversion to school, which then happens. Or it can become the overriding means of seeing and interpreting the world, as happens with addiction.

This is what we've been exploring: how people deny that they're out of control and explain just why being out of control is necessary at the same time. As Josh said heatedly, "I have not lost control, and I need to work this hard and this fast. I need to watch my iPhone constantly, and never slow down, or I will fail."

We use thinking and language to facilitate clear communication and understanding. We speak clearly and directly; we say what we mean, regardless of the anticipated response. We can also use thinking and language to hide the very same communication and understanding. We might speak vaguely or with circular logic. We say yes and no at the same time to avoid taking a stand. We don't quite get to the point or we shroud it with questions and uncertainties. For instance, you need to give your employee a poor evaluation, but you are worried she'll sue you for harassment because she is an angry, impulsive gal, so you focus on her strengths and minimize her obvious and problematic shortcomings.

Thinking and language can clarify or obscure. You say what you mean and engage in a reciprocal dialogue with maximum mutual understanding. Or you think and speak unclearly in a way that confuses your listener, which you may or may not realize. You may be feeling anxious and therefore much more concerned about your performance and image creation than your meaning. An extreme of this kind of confusion is called confabulation. You are all over the map. No one can follow what you mean. Sadly, many people approach this level of confusion today because they don't listen to others and thus cannot respond in a thoughtful manner that embraces complexity. People are often working to give an impression of clarity and understanding while they're not listening.

Virtually all human beings learn to use thinking and language to clarify and to obscure. Ideally, individuals will grow to be more open than closed in acknowledging reality, and more honest than dishonest in accepting human limits. It is a balance.

As people move toward addiction, their thinking becomes increasingly defensive and distorted, so much so that the defenses are no longer normal and healthy. When the individual becomes attached to alcohol or to a behavior such as eating or spending, the feeling of need intensifies and the need for pretense grows. The individual recognizes unconsciously that the need is growing and the behaviors are becoming problematic. A drive to hide this reality from herself and from others now overrules a desire to be open. She doesn't want to see how much she needs that extra pastry. He doesn't want to see the look of disappointment in his son's face when he says no to shooting hoops because he needs to keep working. The recognition of need and the growing loss of control bring feelings of shame and guilt. How can I be so needy? How can I turn away from my child?

The individual adds a thinking disorder to the beginnings of behavioral loss of control. Now the person uses distorted thinking and language to deny, explain, and reassure that indeed there is no problem with behavior.

Jack's wife, Maureen, whom we met in chapter four, was drinking cocktails at midnight to help her come down from her long, frenetic days. When Maureen got home before Jack and started dinner, she began drinking wine as she cooked. It wasn't long until she was addicted to alcohol as well as to her fast pace. It is common that people become addicted to alcohol or drugs as they try to control the symptoms of their addictions to speed. Maureen could not allow herself to know she was addicted to alcohol. To keep herself from doing so, her thinking grew more and more distorted. She frequently had a pit in her stomach as she poured her first glass of wine to keep her company as she cooked. On a subconscious level she was beginning to realize that the wish for a soothing glass of wine had become a driving need. To calm herself and to let herself continue to drink without guilt or worry, she would tell herself that she didn't need the wine. She was wound up tightly after her day at work, and she just wanted a touch to help her unwind. She would tell herself she would find it much easier to help Jack calm down when he got home if she were already calm herself. When she had fleeting doubts and fears again, she gave herself a pep talk: "I'm a strong person. But I need to unwind or I won't be able to sleep and if I can't sleep I can't work."

The pressure to distort comes in all guises. Benita tried to raise a difficult issue at her tech company's retreat. Tempers had been rising as people on her team felt the pressure to finish an impossible project ahead of schedule. Benita had yelled at her colleague that there was no such thing anymore as "on time." "I am always late, always running behind. Yes, I'm making more mistakes and, yes, I've gotten sloppy. What's to care about anymore? Let's just say we're done and move on to the next project, which is already late." Benita had learned it was important to deal with problems directly, so she calmly stated that she wished to talk about the tension on the team. She was met with looks of dismay and a stunned silence. "Oh no," she thought. "I've broken the rules and said too much." Whispering a quick "oops" to her colleagues, she moved on to the next topic. During a break, her boss cornered her and whispered intensely, "You can't talk about tension. Call it something else or go around it."

Is it really the word *tension* that can't be talked about? Or whatever is causing the tension? Often it's both. If you say the word *tension*, you'll have to open it up. You'll have to name it and the whole place could go up in flames—just because you said it.

Then you have to deal with whatever the underlying issue might be. Same danger. Naming a problem makes it real. This was one of the most important aspects of the children of alcoholics movement in the 1980s. You broke the rules. You said it. You named the reality. The labels "Children of Alcoholics" and "Adult Children of Alcoholics" broke cultural, familial, and medical denial: These names, and the detailed descriptions of the realities of parental alcoholism, called it like it is. You give it a name and you make it real. That may happen with speed as well. It is shocking to really see the underbelly of our loss of control in pursuit of fast. A friend who moved away from the Bay Area more than ten years ago came back for a visit and sadly noted: "I have a quiet, calm life. This fast pace and the materialism I find here are hard on the soul."

Addiction requires massive and often profound distortions in logic, which in turn drive thinking and cognitive operations to a primitive level. Addiction makes people sound stupid if you listen closely.

Rachel, the third-generation daughter of Czech immigrants, grew up in Chicago's inner city. She heard Czech spoken at big family gatherings and always felt proud of her heritage. Rachel had occasional housekeeping and babysitting jobs in high school to earn spending money and to help with the family's bills, but she always knew she was a child of opportunity, that she could grow up to be whatever she wanted.

From the time she could hold a pencil or tap on a laptop, Rachel loved to write. She composed stories, poems, songs, anything that popped into her head. In ninth grade she won her first local writing contest with a short story about a group of girls who lost a pal to an overdose. Her story was pure fiction, but Rachel's friends had begun to experiment with drugs, though she herself hadn't tried them yet.

However it wasn't long before she did. She started with pot. Just a hit from the joint going around the circle. Then she tried a few little pills. Uppers and downers, her friend called them. She felt buzzed and liked it. Soon she added alcohol, but that was kind of boring. Along came meth and she was home. Rachel grew into her twenties as a writer with a "little habit."

Rachel laughed as she recalled her crazy thinking when she was using drugs. "I really didn't make sense, but I didn't know that. I thought I was on top of things. I maintained that drugs helped me fulfill my potential, that I used them to enhance my creative juices and that I was never out of control. That's because I was never without something in my system. I was just a 'normal' writer, but 'normal' was always drugged."

Rachel illustrates the core pathology of addiction. She has to first deny her loss of control and then explain the loss of control that really exists in a way that will allow her to maintain the behavior. This is a recipe for primitive, even ridiculous distortion. You deny, then you explain what you've just denied in a way that lets you keep doing what you're doing.

One of the thinking distortions characteristic of addiction is dichotomous thinking, or black-and-white thinking. Dichotomous thinking functions as a defense against the anxiety of loss of control, the feeling of being overwhelmed. For example, Henri lived on the cusp of panic. Juggling more plates than he could ever really manage, he convinced himself that he enjoyed this pace and stress. Henri believed that there is only one direction and that's forward. You pause, you reflect, you go backward and that's failure. You are right or you are wrong. Make your decision, cross it off your list, and get onto the next matter. This kind of assured, take-charge thinking and action looks like competence. It lets people structure perception in a way that minimizes ambiguity, inconsistency, and uncertainty. Unfortunately, it narrows and distorts as well. It eliminates the need to deal with vague, uncertain, or unpredictable perceptions or feelings. It eliminates the need to integrate apparent opposites or complexities with many contradictory dimensions.

Life is not this simple. Life is not efficient nor are most things predictable, yet we often believe in this age of speed that making a fast, impulsive decision is more important than whatever it is you're deciding. Just do it. But this kind of thinking is actually disabling more people, more often. Dichotomous thinking reinforces the value of simplification, thus elevating the need for denial and obscurity. All-or-none thinking arrests cognitive development. People can't move to the highest levels of formal operations.

THINKING AS A DEFENSE AGAINST REALITY

The crazy logic that helps people remain blissfully out of control is what's called in psychological jargon a defense mechanism. We've all got psychological defenses. We can't live without them. I decide to stay longer enjoying the sunset, even though I've got an early meeting the next day. Seems like this is a wrong choice so I rationalize the decision as good for my mental health. Even though it probably *is* good for me, I need a way to make it okay since I am sure it is *not* the right choice. Up steps rationalization to give me permission. Or I use projection: I look at my daughter and suggest she might need a sweater when I am cold. These are everyday tricks of thinking that we can often recognize with a chuckle. But when you're addicted, your use of defenses becomes standard operating procedure that overrides your ability to recognize important realities.

Defenses are mental strategies—thinking distortions—that we keep out of awareness if possible. They are ways of perceiving and thinking, of knowing and judging—technically cognitive devices—that all of us use to cloud or alter reality in order to avoid discomfort or emotional pain. As we engage in self-deception, these distortions work directly as painkillers; they create blind spots in our perception and awareness. Any reality that is difficult, undesirable, threatening, or painful—the types of situations we all face daily—can be shunted aside with our defenses. They help us to sidestep it, minimize it, explain it as something else, or simply deny or reject it is happening.

I've been describing psychological defenses and distortions in thinking to therapists for years, highlighting the ways people use language to deny or explain something unpleasant, something they don't want to see or know. We don't have to go to textbooks or even a therapy session to hear such distortions. They are all around us. They are the stuff of sitcoms, the basis of comedy, the buildup to the joke. And they are the stuff of pain. Rachel confused cause and effect, which allowed her to rationalize her continued drug use. She convinced herself that her "little habit" fueled her creative juices, rather than the reverse. Her "little habit" was stifling her access to her inner world, which resulted in a stiff, frozen writing style. She was "off-kilter," but she thought she simply needed to add a touch more meth and better-quality weed and everything would be fine.

Henri also had defensive reasons for his chaos and stress. He believed his colleagues were jealous of him and would look for any weakness to challenge his competence. In fact, Henri wasn't at all convinced of his abilities and thus projected his own uncertainty onto others he was sure would want to take him down.

Defenses all involve distortion in perception and thinking, a take on things that helps people cope and often ensures they will not change. Defenses are probably universal to the human condition. We couldn't survive without them. Yet when we rely too much on defenses, when we need to block out reality or change reality, we're in trouble. Defenses should help us cope with reality, not distort it so we don't have to face it.

Yet we look at the Twenty Questions and see that defenses have helped us distort and avoid the realities of our behavior, feelings, and the kinds of beliefs and thinking that have gotten us hooked and kept us hooked. If you believe you have no limits and that you are entitled to live without limits, number twelve of the Twenty Questions, you're going to need a lot of denial and skewing of premises to keep from feeling like you're failing all the time, which you'll find in questions fourteen, fifteen, and sixteen. You simply ignore the realities that you have to sleep and eat and can't be turned on 24/7 like your computer.

And like Henri, if you believe you should think, feel, react, and behave instantly, number thirteen on the list of Twenty Questions, the spinning plates will give you a constant challenge. You deny that this pace and the reality of your limits is any problem at all.

On it goes through the rest of the questions. You need denial, rationalization, projection, and all the other defenses we'll soon explore to keep this house of cards—you—intact.

Cognitive defenses follow a developmental ladder, from the most primitive mechanisms (repression and denial, which are out of awareness) to more conscious mental constructions (rationalization and projection) to attentional mechanisms (like isolation, selective inattention, and automatism), defenses that are common to everyday life and now are also the result of speed addiction. The highest level of defenses—intellectualization and altruism—are often part of healthy coping. In fact, they will be part of your recovery from speed. You can feel your drive to answer your phone, your desire to act on your feelings and your behavior—yes, you tell yourself, go for it. You need to act instantly. Then a voice inside reminds you to take it easy. You tell yourself that you are more than impulsive actions, that human beings were given brains to think about things and to use reason. In fact, as we'll see ahead, this intellectualization will be an important step in interrupting your addictive behavior. But it can also work to shield people from emotions that, while threatening, they need to feel. Learning to know the difference can be a challenge for us all.

The same is true for altruism. You forego self-interest in the service of a higher principle or need. Just like intellectualization, you're going to strive to develop this character trait in recovery from speed addiction. So how can it be a defense? Well, it works as a defense when you can't pay attention to self-interest at all. You cannot see that your family needs you as much as your good works. You also may hide self-interest—greed, for example—in the cover of a higher purpose. You are raising money to feed the hungry knowing you will get the city award for service, which will build your image and your business. Is this defense? Is this manipulation? Is this smart marketing? It can be all three. Remember, we need our defenses. We're in trouble when that's all we have and they limit our ability to see and accept reality, which is what happens with addiction.

Addiction requires extreme, primitive defensive mechanisms, which push people to a lower level of behavioral, emotional, and cognitive function. What are these defenses and what do they look like?

REPRESSION

Repression has come to mean such total cognitive and emotional blocking that we don't know what we don't know. This defense is so primitive that we never know we're using it. We block out all kinds of feelings, perceptions, and cognitions that might cause us pain: unacceptable sexual wishes, aggressive urges, shameful fantasies, awful feelings, and upsetting memories. The thought or the memory is simply erased. Because people have forgotten that they've forgotten, they don't know what to remember or even that there is anything to remember.

People can also forget that they've lost control. With alcohol or other drugs, this might be a blackout. The mind erases conscious memory of everything, even though the person is awake and functioning. Big chunks of time disappear. The mind can also erase perception, cognitive awareness, and memory of unbearable and traumatic experiences or incidents people are told to forget.

It happens all the time with speed addiction. Henri came to therapy after a particularly bad experience of plate spinning. He set his alarm for 4:00 a.m. so he could get a head start on a day that had too many important demands: the company board meeting, the IPO, and his daughter's high school graduation. In between he was supposed to meet with his architect and see his banker to sign the loan. And he had to work out. Henri didn't make it all. With terrible remorse, he apologized to his business partners for racing into the meeting more than a half an hour late, and to his wife for completely missing the meeting to finalize the architect's design. When he rushed breathlessly onto the graduation field and realized his daughter had just received her diploma while scanning the bleachers in search of him, he gave up. "I've hit bottom," he said to the therapist. "I don't want to live like this anymore. Tell me what to do."

Henri apologized to everyone, yet within a few days he canceled his therapy and was back in the spin mode. What happened to the memory of his loss of control? "What loss of control? Oh, that didn't really happen. I'm in control and I can manage." Could Henri really block all of this out? Yes, he could. He had promised himself he would never miss an important event for his daughter and so, according to Henri, he didn't miss it. He simply decided he had been there and that was that.

DENIAL

Denial is a primitive defense, but it's not repression. Denial simply says it isn't so, when it is. It's the ability to simultaneously hold a version of reality that you *really* know, but don't *accept* and verbalize. You've got a deep knowledge of reality in your unconscious, but you do not consciously recognize that same reality.

You have to distort a lot to make denial work, but you don't recognize that's what you're doing. Denial says what you feel is not what you feel. Denial is a cornerstone of addiction, securing the secret of loss of control. Denial requires a lot of tinkering with reality. It takes a lot to simply blot out what is really happening.

But blotting out is exactly what we do. Denial is in high gear for our behavior, our feelings, and our thinking—what we believe are the keys to success. It's as if we consciously, even proudly, refuse to see that we are out of control.

People who are out of control with speed may tell themselves they'll "get a grip" when they finish this project or they'll turn off their phone tonight when they go to bed. But they never turn it off. Jack and Maureen both used denial when they told themselves they really weren't spending too many hours at the office. Anita used denial when she told herself that bringing the BlackBerry home from work was not disturbing her family life. Judy used denial when she told herself her partner had a big problem while she had no problem. Rachel used denial when she told herself that using meth made her a better writer. Thus it was a supplement and not a drug. When you are living with strong denial, it's hard to hold on to a different reality. It's hard to remind yourself that what you see really is what you see and there's a problem with those who need to deny it.

RATIONALIZATION

Rationalization is a more conscious and more proactive defense mechanism. Rationalization gives you reasons why you need to keep going, but you still have to distort a lot to make it work. Judy sat with her phone in her hand in a therapy session, debating whether to take the call. She sighed and said, "That's a six-million-dollar call right there. I can't wait until later. I have to take that call or I'll lose the grant. I won't take any calls during our next session."

Jose's family offers another example of rationalization. His father gambled and his mother got depressed and ate. They were both out of control all the time, but his father rationalized that he was letting off steam and his mother rationalized that she was taking care of herself. His father said he had a right to play since he worked so hard. His mother said eating made her feel better when she was lonely. Rationalization involves excuses and alibis, the deceptions we create and come to believe are true.

Many people also rationalize overstuffed schedules. They see them as a sign of belonging, of being part of the in crowd. Or they see them as being needed and important. Lorena came to my office complaining of stress and long work hours. She also said she loved her job, particularly her sense of being so important to so many people. She was seeking help because she was having trouble responding to a thousand emails a day, and this worried her. She was beginning to feel inadequate and was drinking more each night when she arrived home at 9:00 p.m., but she was sure she could easily stop drinking once she figured out how to answer all those emails. Instead of recognizing that she couldn't possibly answer this many messages, she wanted help with time management so she could "work smarter." She rationalized that drinking helped her cope, even though she was having trouble waking up on time and often had bad hangovers. We alter the way we think about things so we can excuse ourselves and not have to change anything.

Judy used to believe it was her partner's volunteer activities and not the opiates she took for pain that kept her overtired and irritable. This belief was pure rationalization. Judy's rationalization kept her nagging at her partner to cut back, an idea that triggered panic in Maya and sometimes sent her into an angry tirade. Judy was right that Maya was working too hard and going too fast, no doubt about it, but she was rationalizing when she paid attention only to Maya's speed and not to her other addiction, to opiates.

PROJECTION

Another way to deny the reality of out-of-control behavior is to project distorted thinking and feelings. We recognize the behavior, thought, or emotion, but believe and act as if it belongs to someone else. Our own feelings of anger become someone else's anger toward us. Projection lets us maintain behavior, thoughts, or feelings but not recognize them as our own. The person who is racing around out of control is quick to see his neighbor going even faster. She's got the problem, not me.

Projection was occurring when Judy was sure that everything wrong in her family's situation was her partner's opiate addiction, once she finally acknowledged this truth. What Judy didn't let herself see was that she'd come home after working a twelve- or fourteen-hour day and couldn't slow down or relax. So she'd explode. She'd suddenly scream at her partner for not having dinner ready, and then she'd head for her den to have a drink and get on the computer again. She'd end up eating by herself sitting at the screen. When Judy registered the meaning of the Twenty Questions, she became quiet. "Number twelve," she whispered. "I didn't think I had any limits so I was constantly furious with Maya because she so obviously had limits."

ISOLATION

Isolation used to be thought of as an emotional defense against engagement, a protection from insight and from the threat of intimacy. Isolation could work well for some people as a way of coping with life's demands, and it was a problem that brought others for help. Isolation blocks out feelings that go with an experience, but not the facts of the experience.

Now isolation has new meanings and works in new ways. For instance, isolation is present in the generation of speed addicts who are cut off from their own thoughts and feelings by the chronic push for action. This isolation from themselves, which they may feel as a panic of emptiness, may also translate to anxiety when they are out of tech touch and thus don't feel connected. Isolation is a defense against feeling and a consequence of not feeling. It serves double duty: you can protect yourself from the pain you feel at being so emotionally cut off from your kids, and you are cut off emotionally from your kids because you are too busy, too fast, and too out of control.

SELECTIVE INATTENTION

Selective inattention edits out the unpleasant or threatening parts of an experience. It is a true multitasking defense, offering emotional protection and a way to cope with speed addiction, and is a consequence of speed addiction that may cause new kinds of problems. Simply failing to notice is the most common, everyday defense. "Oops," a person might say. "Missed that one." Selective inattention is a prominent part of speed. Skimming along online like you're on a Jet Ski and going no deeper than the now-hallowed "power browse" creates inattention. Individuals can't focus; they feel a chronic sense of internal confusion and chaos. Difficulties with attention can be directly related to multitasking that's gone awry and to the screening out of others that accompanies a focus on gadgets.

Now nonstop action feels overwhelming and impossible to stop. Loss of control to constant motion numbs feeling, which keeps the fear at bay. When people can't race any faster, they begin to tune out. Selective inattention steps to the rescue. They ignore emails. They tell themselves they'll answer the calls later. Eventually they invoke the new mantra: "I forgot." These two words have become a way out.

Many people addicted to speed can't remember ten minutes ago. The blanking out of memory that is so common to people who are moving too fast may look like repression, and may even work like repression in the brain, but it is also connected directly to the refusal or inability to let information in to begin with. People describe their selective capacity to receive input as a "Teflon shield," a focus on internal rush and intensity with an inability to listen, concentrate, or absorb anything more than a sound byte from the external world.

Selective inattention protects you from so much of what you don't want to know or what you can't control. You learn to exclude, redefine, or distort information or events that herald danger. It made Judy crazy when Maya fell asleep at the dinner table, shutting her eyes and simply checking out, with a forkful of mashed potatoes poised to go down as soon as she came to. Judy wanted to shake her, an impulse she knew wasn't right, so she shut her out. "I just won't see this anymore," she recalled telling herself, and she didn't see it anymore. This is an example of how cognition interacts with emotion and behavior. You use an attentional defense to quiet emotion, which you hope will also quiet your intense need for action. If you can't screen this out and get some sense of control, you'll likely turn to a fast behavioral action. Do something quick, you tell yourself. You can make this feeling go away, you can alter the reality you don't want to see by getting into action.

AUTOMATISM

Automatism is another defense mechanism that has become part of normal behavior in the culture of loss of control. Automatism means we do what we do automatically, outside of awareness. We fail to notice what we're doing and we miss the sequences of our own behavior. This used to be called "spacing out" or "glazing over." The driver misses the exit and "wakes up" in the wrong town. Today automatism is a normal state of being for countless individuals who are caught up in speed and have checked out of awareness. They're not actively thinking. Much of their day-to-day operations are on autopilot. It is a way of protecting against too much input or input that is unpleasant. You don't deny it or explain it away. You miss it. Automatism, like selective inattention, is part of the mindless, numbing state of living in constant contact without connection. Automatism and selective inattention, which can be both useful and problematic psychological defenses, are now commonly used as part of an addiction to speed. You tell yourself— rationalizing—that your robotic behavior and your fragmented attention and memory are part of your focus, part of your ability to cope with speed and be great at it. You are someone who can play this game. You can live like this. These defenses keep you from seeing what you are sacrificing as they take you away from yourself and from others. They put you on automatic pilot for much of your daily life, ironically reinforcing the consequences of speed.

People who are addicted or who live with someone else's addiction tend to rely on primitive defenses. They might be thirty, forty, or fifty years old, but they look and sound like young children, at least when it comes to speed. The distortions in thinking reinforce out-of-control behavior and emotion. The out-of-control person in the culture today behaves with a sense of entitlement and grandiosity, throwing temper tantrums when the world doesn't go her way. We see people having to wait who are frustrated and full of rage at the imposition. The addict, operating at a primitive level of impulse and thinking, rebels from having to learn playground rules, from having to share, wait her turn, or live with parents who say no.

Fourteen-year-old Jesse went to his computer first thing in the morning, checked his cell phone and laptop all day long, and rushed home to get back online for five or six hours until bedtime.

His mother became concerned when he wouldn't accept her limits on his screen time, refused to come to the dinner table, and screamed at both his parents for their gall at setting limits. Jesse now had sleep problems and was constantly irritable. His teachers called for a meeting because he was sullen in the classroom and threatening on the playground. Jesse locked his door and screamed that nobody could tell him what to do. People who are out of control in their behavior are dominated by the thinking abilities of a young child. Jesse behaved and sounded like a three-year-old who tells his mother, "You're not the boss of me." Underneath his bravado, he was terrified of his compulsions. He really couldn't stop and he knew it deep down.

At fourteen, Jesse knew that question one was true. He had lost control; but he didn't want to stop. Jesse got to number twelve and paused: "I'm not supposed to have any limits. Nothing should get in my way. Nothing should stop me." He scanned numbers thirteen, fourteen, fifteen, and sixteen and put the page down. "These all fit. Yes, I should think, feel, react, and behave instantly. Yes, I'll fall behind if I slow down. Yes, success means *fast* and *faster*. You don't dare slow down. And yes, I'm supposed to feel only good, even high on this wild ride. I'm supposed to be grateful for all this privilege and not waste it. This is a lot to live up to! I'm fourteen years old!

"Just listen to my parents harp about getting ahead. They can't stop telling me about how hard it is in the world today, and then they yell at me when I won't get off the computer."

Jesse's parents want the best for him. They are frightened he won't be able to compete in a world that is going and growing so fast and demanding so much of its adults and children. Jesse's parents push themselves as much as they push Jesse.

Is this a family on the extreme end of speed problems in our culture today? Yes and no. They know they are in trouble and they feel out of control, an awareness that makes them out of any "normal" range at this point in time. Most parents and children have no idea there is any problem with their pace and their thinking about it. But Jesse and his parents are also a "normal" family, the new normies I described at the beginning. These are parents who believe the Twenty Questions and fiercely fight to teach their kids to push harder, faster, and smarter so they can succeed in the world. These are parents who have bought the societal mantra that more time on the computer, more time working on building your résumé, more time in action—doing—will be the path to success.

Remember my airplane friend? One day he paused and asked himself, "What am I doing?" And that moment started him on a new path. We need to ask that question now: what are we doing to ourselves, and what are we doing to our children?

7

Reaching the
End of the Line

The three-strand necklace of addiction—out-of-control behavior, volatile and frightening feelings, and distorted thinking—threatens to strangle our world.

The pressure to be constantly in gear to avoid failure causes extreme emotions, which in turn reinforce distorted thinking. There's the promise of the drug high, of the relief from pain, the euphoria of action without limits. Then there's the fear of not being able to stop, the fear of loss of control that looms. Finally, there's the collapse of the high and the fear of what's next. The end of the cycle brings despair, remorse, and disgust—core emotions of addiction. In pain, the person vows never do it again, which will sadly be an empty promise. There is only the illusion of self-control, not the reality. There is only speed.

From an increasingly younger age, people are treating their stress disorders by turning to other addictions. Instead of recognizing the cause of the problem—too much pressure, too much speed—people are adding alcohol, all kinds of other drugs, and prescription medicines to treat the consequences of this loss-of-control lifestyle. Instead of recognizing a false belief—that people can do as much and go as fast as they wish, with no limits—they turn to other methods of control. This has created multiple layers of loss of control and addictions. People are addicted to their work, to the computer, to going fast, and they maintain this loss of control through their addictions to drugs of all kinds. Dylan gives us a composite portrait of the speed addict today. His experience in losing control and in finding his recovery will move us into the process of change.

Dylan is twenty-three years old. He has had a steady job at Safeway in the Marina District of San Francisco for about two years, during which he moved up from stocking shelves on the night shift to assistant produce manager on the day shift. He is bright, motivated, and thinking about applying to college. He thinks he might want to get a business degree and start his own small company.

Sounds good, but until three years ago Dylan was out of control, high on just about everything, just about every day. He had almost flunked out of high school and didn't much care what happened to him. Sullen and angry at his parents for pushing him too hard, he had simply dropped out of his life, telling himself he'd be fine. He would make it with odd jobs. Nobody had to work as hard and feel as stressed as he had during eighth grade and the first part of his freshman year of high school.

"I was moving right along freshman year. I liked school and I could see a bright future ahead. But I started to have trouble keeping up with my classes. I never had to study and now I had to, though I didn't know how. You don't know how if you've never done it, if you always got it or coasted through. I didn't recognize it at the time, but I was feeling scared. There was constant pressure, stress. I was confused and lost, running from place to place, trying to finish schoolwork, go out for the team, build up my résumé with after-school activities. It was bam, bam, bam. Keep pushing. I was like a little machine, pumping out the work, speeded up and out of control. But I was also depressed, really down. I just couldn't keep this up. Then my friends got some pills—uppers. I tried them and it was the greatest feeling I'd ever had.

"Now I could do anything. Then I tried it all. Didn't take long. We had a 'store' on campus—our 'drugstore' we called it. You could get anything in this back bathroom near the gym.

"I never once thought I was in trouble or worried where I was headed. I took a big turn, but I never registered it and didn't look back. I really felt dumb in the regular world, trying to keep up. Everything was too fast and I constantly felt like I was slipping under, drowning. I liked this smaller world where I felt powerful. I became a dealer and soon ran the business during breaks. I was supplying my friends and a whole bunch of other kids I didn't know. I was big man on campus. Why would I question this? I told myself I'd stop when it came time to study or take the SATs. This life gave me a time-out from the pressures of competing all the time. I always thought I could get back in, but it didn't happen. I was hooked so badly, there was no stopping. I was out of control, but I thought I was completely in control. I thought I could manage my life because I was doing drugs. Everyone else was scared of life, but not me. I'd figured it out."

You can hear the behavioral loss of control and you can hear the thinking distortions. You can hear Dylan's emotional distress and fear before he found drugs. He was going under, drowning in the pressures of his teen world. Dylan on drugs wasn't worried. He wasn't feeling out of control. He'd found a route to deny it. "You just tell yourself you're in control and then, by God, you are."

Dylan sees that he lost about six years of his life. He's got another chance now and he feels lucky he got it while he is still young. He can pick up from where he stopped at fourteen and get back into his life. Dylan says he lost control. He sees the irony that he found drugs to help him get control of a teen world that was moving too fast for him. He simply found another addiction.

"I feel like I was addicted to working hard in school, to trying to be perfect. I kept pushing and trying harder to do more. It became out of control. I'd never stop. My parents would yell at me to turn off the light, to shut off the computer and get to bed. But they also pressured me to get good grades and were just as angry when I got a B or wasn't showing enough drive to succeed in school. There was no winning here. I just kept doing more. Pills helped me stop, but then I was off and running again, addicted to them. In the last two years I've slowed down, taking one step at a time. I stopped my drugs, got help and began to take responsibility. I worked at the sober-living house until a few months ago and have used the Safeway job to give me a daily routine. I've got regular hours and I don't go beyond forty. I pace myself and now I feel like a human being again. I have to be very careful not to get hooked on my computer, or to start feeling scared that I'll fall behind in this crazy society. I stay clean. Otherwise I'm out of control with drugs and I'm out of control with life."

People addicted to substances can lose years of their lives in the foggy state of addictive compulsion. They wake up and reach for a drink and go to sleep with a drink. The need and impulse to use control them, and they keep it going with distorted thinking. People addicted to speed have the same kinds of consequences.

They, too, may lose years of their lives caught up in the chaotic, confused inner state of compulsion to go faster and do more. They wake up and push the keypad on their smartphone and go to sleep with a last scan for messages. The need and the impulse to stay online control them. They constantly distract themselves from serious attention to anything else. They tell themselves: "You're a man on the move. You're making progress." They tell themselves: "You're a powerful woman, able to do it all," until you scream at your husband and kids and slam the door behind you.

People addicted to substances, food, gambling, sex, spending, the computer, the TV, and to going as fast as possible suffer ruined marriages, physical and emotional illness, impaired thinking, an inability to quiet or reflect, and a deadening of creativity. You become a robot, whether you're drinking, shooting up, snorting, eating, tossing the dice, clicking the "Purchase" button, or turning your computer on. You're on automatic pilot and you can't stop. There goes your higher self. There goes your motivation.

Who are we now? We no longer recognize that we have a choice about much of anything. We go with the flow, and the flow is out of control. We've acclimated to constant sound and action. Quiet moments signal that something is wrong. We call this constant movement progress. We brag about our workload and our skill at multitasking, while we also bemoan the stress we've come to accept as normal. We need to slow down, but we don't know how. We think there's a light at the end of the tunnel, a place where we can safely stop, but that light is now an illusion. Check off one task and three more are piling up.

Despite the extreme stress, the idea of setting a limit scares just about everyone. If we can't keep up, we'll be left behind. We'll be on the losing side. Yet this is the only way out. We are at a turning point. We must acknowledge that we've lost control. We can't keep going. We can't keep up. We must all, paradoxically, declare ourselves the losers.

We've followed the threads of society's addiction to speed and increasing loss of control. We've connected the dots of Manifest Destiny, with its core beliefs—in American entitlement, exceptionalism, and lack of limits—to a cultural belief in the rightness of territorial expansion that translated to the conquest of cyberspace. We've seen how the key parts of the individual—behavior, emotion, and cognition—have become wildly out of control, and the individual in relation to "other" full of flawed and troubled dependencies. Chasing the higher power of speed has become the center of twenty-first-century spirituality.

Is the culture in trouble? Yes. Are individuals and families in trouble? Yes. Can this be changed? Yes. We can be contributors, even leaders, in all the sectors of American life, from politics to business to labor to education, without being addicted to speed. We can participate fully and richly, using the full range of technologies at our disposal and still keep our balance and sanity, but this requires recognizing—and accepting—that we have limits and must live within those limits. This is a big *but*. It requires recognizing the conflicts of interest that exist in the culture that will pull us into the same wild, limitless thinking and actions. It is a shift in perspective; instead of looking totally outside yourself for motivation and energy, you learn how to use your own new, honest code of ethics and personal responsibility to guide you as you interact with external circumstances.

The American belief in Manifest Destiny defined progress as geographical expansion without limits. When most of the world's territory was claimed, outer space took over as a goal of exploration and expansion, and in the late twentieth century, cyberspace offered an even better, quicker potential for conquest. The promise of discovery and ownership of unlimited virtual space unfolded within the same thinking patterns that have always characterized American identity and its sociopolitical systems. There was no need to recognize limits or accept restraint. We can choose to stay on the path of the industrial revolution, repeating and reliving its values of maximum speed, maximum efficiency, and maximum output. Or we can choose to change.

America is the sum of its people, and a change in its culture will start with a change in its individuals. How can people who have been steeped in these cultural values since birth and who have become hooked on speed change? We'll see in the next chapters that we need to challenge core American beliefs in entitlement and limitlessness, as well as our definitions of success if we are to return to any kind of life within limits. We will have to accept failure, declaring ourselves the losers in our race to have everything with no limits. It is in this "failure" that we can set ourselves on a successful path, defined in terms that incorporate health and balance and the joy of real relationships—with others and with ourselves.

PART 2

Recovering from a
Lifestyle of Speed

8

Stepping Off the Rat's Wheel

"My name is Raj. I'm an alcoholic.
I lost control of my drinking."

"My name is Jack. I'm a speed addict.
I lost control of my life."

The first step in recovery from addiction is the hardest step: admitting we are failures. For an alcoholic this means admitting he can't control his drinking. For a compulsive eater this means admitting she can't control her eating. For a sex addict this means admitting he can't control his compulsive sexual behaviors.

Speed addicts have to admit failure, too. Held snugly as we are in the arms of America's values and definition of success, this is a daunting admission. While it's an admission that paradoxically will allow speed addicts to be successful at a sustainable pace of life, it may feel at first like jumping off a cliff and being in free fall. Addicts at the beginning of recovery don't know just where they'll land or what they'll feel like when they do.

Recovery comes in fits and starts. The speed addict may approach the cliff, pull back, and crawl slowly toward it again, and do this many times before he takes that leap of faith. Change is a halting process, one that circles back on itself, takes side trips, and even takes time off. You must expect that recovery will be bumpy, but there is a tried-and-true way to make this change. It's the twelve-step program of Alcoholics Anonymous. AA provides a model of recovery that has worked for many kinds of addictions and provides a model for healing from speed addiction as well.

Jack, the man who graduated from Yale, married Maureen, and took a job in San Jose with an Internet start-up, ultimately followed the principles of AA, as modeled by a friend named Raj. Jack had suffered many health setbacks, almost lost his marriage, and had several car accidents. He went through some convoluted pathways of change on his recovery journey, as he relied on the support and modeling of his friend. Here is the story he tells:

> *I'm slower now. I'm not supercharged all the time and I'm often quiet inside. I move more thoughtfully, I stop and think and pay attention and I don't act impulsively whenever I have a difficult feeling. You might say I grew up and that's true. But my journey into speed addiction and my journey into recovery have been much more. I got out of control in my drive for success; I couldn't stop pushing for more, working harder and longer and never stopping. I've had to question everything I believed, all the principles and values I lived by in order to slow down and stay slowed down. I couldn't just put on the brakes and wait until I could go full speed again.*
>
> *What was it like to be addicted to speed? I grew up a child of opportunity in the eighties and nineties. There was endless possibility ahead with a growing economy and the burgeoning of*

technology. I believed I could have it all and I set out to get it. I came from a loving, supportive family with high expectations and demands. I was pretty smart—smart enough to get on the path of advanced placement and college success. By the eighties and nineties everyone who was on a fast track—a path toward success—expected to go to grad school of some kind. You'd need a business degree, or law, or something professional to catch the wave. Even techies, the engineers and geeks who became the bil-lionaires, needed a skill. Ironically, some of them had to leave college to put it to work, but many of us didn't dare leave. Our degrees would get us in the door somewhere so we could ride a wave. You didn't want to miss this.

Everything was fast and going faster. You learned you had to keep going all the time or you'd get behind. You had to start building your résumé in fourth grade if you wanted to make it into the right high school and college. This was supposed to be a land of equality, yet I knew nothing was equal. I was upper middle class and constantly aware of what my friends had—the latest gadget, the fanciest TV, the games, and the computer. By eighth grade I was online for hours every day. I just loved it— what a high! This was connection! This was belonging.

I got every new gadget and had a buzz going inside of me all the time. I couldn't slow down and I couldn't stop. I hated to log off. I kept it up in high school, though I also went out for sports. Of course, I followed scores and games online, too. I ran for student government, and volunteered for a slew of things, like Big Brothers and Habitat for Humanity. You know, there was that résumé to build. But I was most excited when I was in my tech world.

I began to feel lost without my phone, lost without my com-puter. It got worse as the gadgets could do more. I remember telling my mom, "You're lookin' at number one," as I ran out the door loaded down with my wires and music and then my laptop. When the phones got cameras, I thought we had it all. There was nothing I couldn't do with all this tech power.

Well, you can hear where I was headed. I became arrogant and obnoxious. I thought I was a near-geeky success, on a fast track and destined to make millions. I thought all this would happen automatically. Now I know I felt entitled. I had a swagger and an attitude. I was riding high.

I did go to college and I did well. Then I went to grad school at Yale and got married while I was there. I went to work with a start-up and lived the Silicon Valley breakneck life. We both wanted kids, but our lifestyle got in the way of Maureen's getting pregnant. She also ended up in treatment for alcoholism. She started drinking early every evening to help her unwind and it got away from her. I was too busy to drink and I never wanted to mess up my edge. I've learned since she's been in recovery that my father was an alcoholic and I was afraid of drinking. I remember when I bought that expensive scotch for him. I thought I was giving him the best gift possible.

When Maureen completed treatment, she figured out that she had to slow down, and she convinced me to slow down, too . . . for a while. We had a son by now, but it didn't take me long after that to go back to my frenzied lifestyle.

I didn't know when to sleep, how to sleep without first being exhausted, how to have a live conversation, how to be in a relationship. I didn't know much about life. I knew how to feel agitated and driven and to race to try to get to the goal. Life was nothing but urgency and drive. Move, move, keep going. My behavior was out of control, my thinking was grandiose and my emotions were an intense mix of elation and fear. I needed to

*keep this pace going to keep my mood high. If I slowed down for
an instant, I was full of fear.*

*What happened to me? How did I come to see all this? I had
three car accidents in one month. I just couldn't slow down. I
gunned that gas pedal and raged down the road. On the third
wreck my wife said, "No more"; my doctor said I was a danger
to myself; and my boss said, "Take a break." That was the blow.
I couldn't take time off from work. That made me more anxious. I couldn't sleep, got depressed, and finally saw that I was
out of control. I was racing inside and had no stopping gear. I
had no reverse, no low, no nothing but full speed ahead.*

*I saw a counselor during college when I started having
panic attacks. I got Xanax and went on my way. Didn't change
anything. Now I see that the panic was my fear that I couldn't
keep up. I thought I was going to crash and I was right. It just
took a few years.*

*I had a hard few months of forced leave. I felt alone and
scared. Then I met a guy in the gym who had also burned out.
Raj had been on leave for depression, drinking, and out-of-
control computer use. He couldn't get off-line. Couldn't even come
for dinner. Talk about obsession. He really felt like he'd lost it all
and I guess he did. He was going to AA and learning to live all
over again.*

*We talked, walked, and had coffee. I felt lazy and stupid.
Felt like a failure as a man. But I started to feel better, too. He
told me he had lost control of his drinking and everything else.
He was learning in AA how not to drink and how to live without alcohol. He said he was learning to live one day at a time
and trying not to project into the future. At first I was full of
scorn. One day at a time! What about the dangers ahead? What
about keeping ahead of the game? Ahead of others? You've got to*

stay in the race or you'll lose. He laughed and said I'd get it someday.

And so I did. He was an alcoholic and a speed addict. I was a speed addict. He taught me how to slow down, one step at a time, one day at a time. I followed his advice for behavior changes and began to see how driven I was by my wild emotions—fear and greed especially—and by my crazy beliefs. I really did think I could have it all. I did believe I was privileged and entitled. It was arrogance.

Jack reminds us of the Twenty Questions as he tells his story of becoming addicted to speed. He also moves us into recovery as he outlines what happened to cause him to crash and how he's learned to follow the Twenty Guidelines for Slowing Down.

The Twenty Questions we explored in the first part of the book helped you decide if you're addicted to speed. You thought about your behavior, feelings, and thinking as you pondered each question. You asked yourself "what am I doing?" and now you ask "what will it mean to slow down and how can I do it? How does it work?" You are ready to explore the Twenty Guidelines for Slowing Down which will be your map for change.

The Twenty Guidelines for Slowing Down:
How to Unhook from Speed

YOUR BEHAVIOR:

1. You ask for help; you seek a mentor who believes in slowing down for guidance and support.

2. You develop a recovery action plan.

3. You begin to make small steps toward change.

4. You learn to pause, to reflect on your behavior, feelings, and thinking.

5. You ask yourself, "What am I doing?"

YOUR FEELINGS:

6. You feel the reality of limits and face the feeling of failure.

7. You become aware of feelings, and learn to listen to them.

8. You trust that the high of impulsive action is *not* the feeling you seek.

9. You develop a wider range of new feelings.

10. You come to trust that deep, intimate human "connection" exists in a slowed down, quiet state.

YOUR THINKING:

11. You believe in the reality of limits.

12. You learn to recognize and challenge your belief in entitlement.

13. You challenge your belief in willpower.

14. You believe in the value of small steps and a slower sense of time.

15. You believe in a new definition of success: your best effort within a structure of limits.

16. You believe in the value of delay, endurance, and the concept of "enough."

17. You believe that growth and change are not instant; that "quick fixes" reinforce the thinking of fast and impulsive action.

18. You believe in the value and necessity of reflection as a part of health and success.

19. You challenge your all-or-none thinking.

20. You give new meaning to "service."

How did Jack get to the place where he could take that first step? How does anybody get ready for change?

CHANGE IS A DEVELOPMENTAL PROCESS

Change begins before you know you need it. In the throes of my own drinking, I didn't know anything was wrong so I wasn't thinking about how to change. But when I looked back, after stopping and after some years of recovery, I could see that I was getting ready before I knew I was getting ready. I was making choices that could be seen, in retrospect, as preparation for abstinence. At the time they simply looked responsible.

I declined to join a drinking club in college because I needed to study. I told the young women who issued me this special invitation that I was planning to attend graduate school and therefore needed to get good grades. Undergrad would not be the end for me, so I couldn't spend my time getting drunk with them. I surprised myself when these words came out because I had not yet consciously thought I might go to grad school. What was I saying? At the time I knew subconsciously that I declined because I desperately had to avoid the humiliation of being openly drunk. I had too much shame from my family and needed to believe that my drinking never showed. Somebody saw, of course, since I was being invited to drink with the ladies.

I was only in the earliest glimmers of awareness at this point, not yet ready for fundamental change. After college, when I no longer had to study, I began to worry and to watch myself, thinking, "Oops, I don't think this is normal." So I thought I'd cut back to prove to myself that I was really okay. I wanted to fix the problems of drinking, but not lose the privilege. I was still trying to stay in control so I could keep on drinking. I wasn't ready for actual change yet. For several years I watched myself like a hawk, waiting until I could start drinking each day and anxious about how to stop at the number two or three I'd set as "normal." I knew it would be wrenching to finish my drinking at that so-called normal point. It was never enough for me.

Toward the end of my drinking, I asked myself, "What am I doing?" and came to see clearly that I was an alcoholic, a clarity that propelled me toward a different kind of change, a radical shift, a transformation. I saw deeply and clearly that I had lost control and could not get it back. I began to think about my life *now*, in that present moment, recognizing that I was embarking on something new, and that I had no map for where I was going, no map for what was *next*. What would happen to me in this new world of not drinking?

There was a lot I didn't know about how to make this change. I didn't know what would be different and what would stay the same. I didn't know what I would be able to change and what would be beyond my control. I didn't know what would come easily and what would be a struggle. Yet I knew from the first moments of my own radical change that progress does not move in one direction nor does it move at lightning speed. I learned that my recovery would be a slow step-by-step developmental process.

While development usually means forward growth, the process is fluid, and like eddies in a river, its natural movement is forward and back. It contains inconsistencies, shades of gray, and a mix of growth experiences that occur sometimes through our will and sometimes through the apparent opposite, the relinquishment of our will, to forces outside our control.

None of us has grown up in a straight line, only going forward and only having growth successes. Normal human development is a process of fits and starts; we go up and down normally, and so the process of change for the individual and the culture will include ups and downs, which will be part of long-term successful change.

It can be hard to accept that downs are part of life's process. Many of us identify with Lucy in the old Charles Schulz *Peanuts* cartoon that portrays Charlie telling Lucy with a shrug, "Well, it's just life's ups and downs," as Lucy replies "I refuse to accept the downs." The process of change is messy, often contradictory, unpredictable, and worst of all, uncontrollable. And this is normal. This is one of the reasons change is so hard.

TWO KINDS OF CHANGE

Psychologists Paul Watzlawick, John Weakland, and Richard Fisch described in 1974 two kinds of change: first and second order. First-order change is small, incremental shifts. This is an alteration, a minor tuck or touchup. This is where change usually starts. Second-order change involves conversion or transformation to something different. It is radical, a rupture in the way we see things that can occur slowly over time or suddenly.

The idea of first- and second-order change is analogous to the two change processes that world-renowned cognitive theorist Jean Piaget said are involved in children's normal cognitive development. (Cognition refers to the ability to think and figure things out. It includes an individual's reasoning, remembering, and perception.) He called these two processes assimilation and accommodation. Assimilation is change that occurs by taking in information that fits within the child's current cognitive frame. Accommodation is radical change that disrupts the current frame and helps form an entirely new cognitive system, usually incorporating new skills and new mental operations that change everything. Both are necessary for healthy development, but accommodation almost always causes upheaval that may seem like backward movement until the new system settles into place and becomes the new norm.

For instance, a toddler who has been crawling all over the house may start pulling herself up by a coffee table and fussing because she can't get across the room. It looks like she can't crawl anymore, when in reality she's experiencing a radical change in her awareness. She's on the brink of realizing she can move around the room upright. This is a transitional development stage, what Piaget would call an accommodation rather than assimilation. This interactive process between assimilation and accommodation, between first- and second-order movement, is normal for cognitive development in children and in adults. First-order change is like adding a new orange or two to your pile of oranges; second-order change is like replacing the oranges with apples. The smaller changes influence and build on each other, leading to higher levels of development. Second-order change is usually viewed by the person as sudden, coming in a dream perhaps, but out of awareness until a moment of clarity, even magical or spiritual in its arrival. Or it comes slowly into awareness as a recognizable result of a long, slogging emotional and mental process with terrible fits and starts, usually in an effort to get control of something that is not about to be controlled. Either way, it's often something you couldn't see coming.

Normal cognitive development is an interactive process between first- and second-order movement, between assimilation and accommodation. The smaller changes influence and build on each other, leading to higher levels of development. Sometimes first-order change is all that's needed. If a child understands the concept of an alphabet and has learned A, B, C, and D, she doesn't need accommodation (or second-order change) to learn the rest of the letters. If a teenager experiments with smoking, but decides he is going to smoke only at weekend parties and then never more than two, and if he keeps easily to this decision, he doesn't need second-order change (unless he decides he doesn't want to smoke at all, but can't stop). If a woman who is living an out-of-control lifestyle of frenzied speed decides she is going to cut back and rebalance her life, and if that woman is able to follow through and maintain the difference, she doesn't need second-order change. But if the teenager is addicted to smoking—he decides it's fine to smoke three cigarettes this week, then four, and then no limit, and he begins to smoke on Thursday nights and Fridays—and if the woman is addicted to speed—she decides to change, but can't sustain her slower pace—first-order change will not be enough. Recovery from addiction requires second-order change, a full paradigm shift.

Chances are as you move through the Twenty Guidelines for

Slowing Down, you'll find that the shifts you make and the changes that result will indeed fit a model of second-order change. You will alter your behavior, your feelings will shift from chaos to quiet, and your thinking will be based on a belief in limits and a new value of slow. These are pretty big changes that will usually occur in small, step-by-step, incremental shifts.

STUCK IN FIRST-ORDER CHANGE

In addiction the person keeps circling and re-circling the same territory. You're not sure you want to move from oranges to apples or you don't know how, so you keep adding more oranges and can't figure out why you don't change. Addiction distorts and arrests cognitive processes, interfering with the natural rhythms of movement and change. Addicts and their families, who are bound by primitive defenses, get stuck at primitive levels of thinking. Here's how they often think about change: "I want to stop the problems that come from my drinking, my eating, my time on the computer, but I don't want to give up the privilege. How can I get control so I don't really have to change?" Getting control is what people want, not real change.

The desire to get control—to work harder, faster, smarter so you don't have to slow down—is a first-order idea of change. You want to solve the problem without changing anything. You want to add oranges to oranges or maybe just rearrange your oranges. Perhaps stacking them would work better than lining them up one by one, you reason.

Jack first tried to rearrange his day, believing that a change in his schedule would give him more time and more control. He decided to move his workout to the early morning instead of

8:00 p.m. and to take his son to preschool instead of putting him to bed. He figured this would free him up in the evenings for whatever he needed to finish. He was certain this shift was the answer. He didn't take anything out of his day. He shifted times. But when he didn't have to stop at night he got worse, not better. He thought he was working smarter and could now do more! Ridiculous. He was exhausted, saw his family less, and couldn't understand what had happened.

Jack was locked in the behaviors, feelings, and thinking of active addiction. He was living out the Twenty Questions, still believing he was on the right track! Any problems are the price of success. You just have to figure things out and then it will all be fine.

Next Jack decided he would cut back his schedule and get home to see his son before he went to bed. Maureen was grateful, and Jack began to feel like he had a better handle on how his son was doing. He liked making up knock-knock jokes with him and drawing pictures for him. This worked for a while, but soon he was shifting his work to his computer at home, and he was no more present than when he stayed at the office. His efforts fell in the category of first-order change because his thinking stayed the same. He was working to get control so he would not have to recognize his limits.

Next Jack vowed to slow down by setting limits on his computer use at home. And he vowed to keep the limits. But he almost never did. He was thrilled the one time he looked at his watch, backed up his chair, and stood up from his computer screen, turning it off. But he also felt a pang of loss. He didn't want to stop now. There was so much yet to do and he was on a roll. That was the only time he stopped. After this occasion Jack told himself that he'd proved he could stop so he didn't need to. He jumped right back into unlimited use, believing he could stop anytime. This is similar to the thinking typical of an alcoholic or drug addict. As an alcoholic, you think you just have to exercise control one time and then you've got it. It gives you license to be out of control all you want because you tell yourself you can take control when you need to.

First-order changes, of course, can involve real movement, often toward second-order change. First-order movements are the small, incremental building blocks that do constitute a part of normal, healthy growth. The key is whether these incremental steps are leading to positive change or whether they simply give the illusion of change while allowing the individual to maintain a problematic status quo. So you ask: Do these adjustments involve deception and defense? Am I just rearranging my oranges or have I actually removed one from the plate? Am I really not moving at all?

As Judy focused all her fury on Maya's problems, she maintained her view that she was fine, she was in control. Yet she also began to fiddle with her schedule, almost testing to see if she could let go of some things each day and tolerate the new time and space she would gain. When Judy looked back she could see that she was testing the water, getting ready to see her own addiction to speed. Her small steps gave her a subconscious security that she could take the bigger step of change she always thought Maya needed to make. Judy could acknowledge her limits and ask for help.

It can be easy to fool yourself into thinking you are changing or have changed. You think there has to be change if you're working this hard. You're willing to look on the Internet for information, to read something about the latest diet, and maybe you'll talk with someone. These steps constitute your "effort" to address your "issue." You tell yourself and maybe others that you're working on the problem. Indeed these first steps may be very helpful—they may lead you to change—or they may promote the illusion you're really doing something about your problem while allowing you to do nothing. "Going to therapy" becomes the answer, the fix, rather than the route to actual change. Engaging in "the job search" becomes the end, not the means to finding work. Resolving to start an exercise program next week becomes the act—you resolve and then do nothing, explaining how something—not your fault—got in the way and made it impossible. But you'll start next week.

If you are fooling yourself into believing that you are making changes when you never move past thinking about change or if you make some changes but can't maintain them—if you keep returning to a faster pace despite your desire to slow down—you will need to move to second-order change. Without that, first-order change really becomes no change at all. If you are an addict, you will find all kinds of "reasons" to believe you are changing when you are not. And American culture keeps calling you back to readjust your pile of oranges.

AMERICAN CULTURE AND FIRST-ORDER THINKING

"No change" is the stage where the culture is now. Like the addict who maintains she can control her drinking, the culture believes firmly that we are indeed exceptional: we can have what we want and we can do what we want. We believe we can fix things without making any radical changes in our thinking or behavior. Many cultural, social, and political issues remain in first-order mode of change. Currently issues of climate change and food processing hit all the nerves of our grandiose thinking. Political parties argue whether it is really true that our actions on the environment and on the foods we treat could have an adverse impact on us. We challenge the current evidence about climate change and decide to do another research study, hoping to prove that nothing we're doing is really harmful. Or we agree to a small adjustment, hoping to highlight our efforts to compromise and take the focus off the fact that nothing has changed.

Many people reacted to the economic collapse of the late 1990s and early 2000 with a wait-and-see attitude. Yes, there was a problem, but it was a slowdown of circumstances and events that would soon "return to normal." They would wait for the next new technological discovery to create the next market boom and the next wave of wild expansion and success. Their job was to sit tight. They saw no need to acknowledge limits. They maintained, along with the culture, a false belief in their absolute power or the absolute power of the cultural and economic system. They would wait for the next big thing. Many investors even now are waiting for the next big wave to ride, without limits. These individuals remain within the same belief system, not questioning or recognizing that there is anything wrong. Daniel Gross, a business writer and frequent contributor to the *New York Times*, said: "There's something distinctly American in our propensity to blow bubbles until they pop, spend a few months licking our wounds and then hit replay."[1]

Within American individual and cultural identity there is no model for change that hasn't maintained a fix-it focus with an emphasis on taking charge, taking control, and an attitude that tough, even hostile aggression is perfectly acceptable in the service of winning. American cultural identity is based on power: entitlement, omnipotence, grandiosity, and a rejection of limits. Willpower has been the means to gain and exercise this power. Just do it! Just get a grip! Work harder, work smarter.

Yet our belief in willpower is the great cultural deception that will eventually become the source of our individual depression, anxiety, fury, and self-criticism when we fail. We cannot keep up with society's illusion that everything is possible. We cannot live happily ever after with no limits. And so the reality of our own limits becomes a personal failure. There is something wrong with me that I can't keep up, I can't add one more thing. I can't see that there is a bigger problem than me and my failures. I can't see that society is driving this loss of control.

GETTING READY FOR CHANGE

We need our will and our resolve to stay on a road of difficult change. But the road of change I am proposing is not one of getting more control or regaining control that has been lost by continuing to believe that you just have to work harder. We need a paradigm shift. We need to recognize that we have lost control and we cannot regain it. We cannot work any harder. We need to accept the need for limits and then plan for change. In this process we may make small moves within a model of first-order change and we may make a more radical move to second-order change. Either way, we need a transformation in the way we think. We must accept the reality of limits.

9

A Model for Transformational Change

Jack was typical in his efforts to change. He made his first move before he was even aware he wanted to change. One rainy January day as dusk approached, his employer invited him to a huddle later that night at a nearby bar to brainstorm a new idea. Jack told him Maureen was sick and she was going to cut him off if he didn't get home to help with their son's bedtime that night. Maureen wasn't sick, but she had been increasingly full of rage at Jack's absence. He was aware that he didn't want to face Maureen's anger that night; what he didn't consciously realize was that he missed her, he missed his son, and he wanted to make some changes

Many change theorists outline a process of "getting ready" on the way to change. They often begin with the time before a first awareness of a need for change and the move toward active planning when the individual recognizes a problem and begins to actively get ready. First you do nothing, then you plan what change will look like, and then you make some adjustments—more of the same, only harder, smarter, faster. You add oranges to oranges. Or you decide to "cut back."

The earliest levels of recognition characterize the individual addict who begins to know that the attachment to the substance or behavior has taken on a life of its own, that the person has to have it or has to do it. The first signs of "I can't stop" start the process of thinking about "the day when I will stop" or maybe "when I'll get control." "That's all that's really required here," the addict thinks. "It's not true that I can't stop. I will stop when the time comes. For now I'll just get control." The vision of change is improved control, which may or may not happen; but the attempts may be part of getting ready and thus lead to more profound change later on. Trouble is, you often can't tell. If an addict is relying on willpower, the vision of change will not lead to profound change.

In a recent article entitled "Help Wanted: In the Pursuit of a Healthy Lifestyle, Sheer Grit Takes You Only So Far," author Mary Beckman states: "In the long run, willpower just isn't enough. Not for me. Not for anyone." She quotes Stanford psychologist Keith Humphreys: "There are lots of problems you can solve with just willpower; the problem is, you've already solved them. People who come to a health professional with a weight or drinking problem have already used their willpower to do things like get through school, learn how to drive, become proficient at their jobs. If willpower were enough to solve their current problem, they wouldn't be seeking help from someone else."[1]

There's a reason why willpower fails. The emotional side of the brain can dominate the logical, cognitive decision-making part. Emotions, including deep need, craving, hunger, fear, want or desire, greed, shame, guilt, embarrassment, love, joy, pleasure, contentment, and many others, can win over cognition—not always, but often. We like to believe our intellectual brains are in charge: we can think our way to control, to restraint. But emotion, conscious and unconscious, pushes to impulse and action. It's hard to think your way to no if emotion says, "Go. You deserve it." You start out with the best of intention, but doggone it, something goes wrong. There you are again, picking up that cigarette, having just one little drink or one little bite, one little check of your email or one little text, one more late night or one more hour of World of Warcraft. Jack had revisited this position many times when he finally discovered that the principles of Alcoholics Anonymous could help him in the same way it helped alcoholics, drug addicts, compulsive eaters, and a host of others with one kind of addiction or another.

THE NEW PARADIGM CALLED AA

The birth of Alcoholics Anonymous in 1935 marked the beginning of a new paradigm in thinking, behavior, and emotion about drinking. It was a radical rupture in the longstanding belief in the power of the individual, the power of intellect, and the power of will. Instead of reinforcing the belief in the power of individual will to get control, the founders of AA accepted the reality of loss of control that could not be regained. This paradigm shift in fundamental beliefs about control grew into a new philosophy of human nature that was grounded in an acceptance of human limits and the need for help.

AA was born by chance, not by design. It did not spring from a think tank or a corporate planning retreat. It did not originate in the halls of academic psychology and it was not born from the best of medical science. AA was born as a direct result of two men coming together by chance, drawn by their feelings of desperation and despair to talk about their struggles to control their drinking. From the depths of isolation they started talking. From that first conversation came countless thousands and millions of conversations, with each person pushed to start speaking by deep feelings of desperation, loneliness, despair, and utter hopelessness and helplessness—what they would later describe as experiences of hitting bottom, defeat, and surrender. These discussions continue to this day, almost eighty years later, within the context of what became the organization known as Alcoholics Anonymous.

AA became a culture of sobriety, a safe haven for people who accepted their loss of control, accepted responsibility as individuals to stop drinking, and reached out to others for help in learning how to stop and stay stopped. AA embodies the individual, autonomous and responsible, and the group, comprised of individuals who come together to support their own sobriety and recovery. AA is "alone together."

These men did not know what they were creating in that first conversation, nor did they realize anything more than the fact that talking helped them both not take a drink that day. A seemingly small step. Over the course of the next few days, then weeks and months, they grew to understand and to trust that sharing their deepest feelings and experiences about their compulsion to drink lifted the intensity of their feelings—cravings, urges, impulses— and gave them new direction for their behavior, thinking, and emotions.

These men stayed abstinent by talking about how and what they had felt and what they had always done to cover these feelings or wipe them away. Drink. Their feelings turned into obsession and compulsion and they felt nothing else—just a painful desire to drink and an inability to stop once they started. As they talked about the realities of their loss of control, they changed their behaviors. In more small steps they agreed to call each other instead of taking a drink—to talk through the impulse instead of acting on it. They got together during cocktail hour and talked instead of drinking. They got together at other times to build strength from their conversations of shared experience. They still drank but now it was coffee instead of booze. No white knuckles. They still had the feelings—the cravings, the urges, the impulses—and they still acted on them, but in a different way.

Soon other men, and then women, joined in this radical, wildly counterintuitive idea: they fostered their own sobriety by sharing with others who also could not stop drinking, their experience and acceptance of their deep, total loss of control of their drinking. They did not offer each other suggestions for how to get control. They did not wait together for the day when they could drink again. They had been there before, many times, with new schemes, new hope, and new confidence about how they would get control. This time they shared the futility of their wish to be able to control their drinking. It was the profound, deep acceptance of their loss of control, *and* their inability to ever regain control, that became the cornerstone foundation for the birth and growth of the organization of AA.

In coming together they established another cornerstone: the necessity of "other." The desire to stop drinking could come from the individual alone, in fact *had* to come from the individual alone. No one else could make these people stop drinking; no one could give them the deep motivation to be sober. In that sense they were all alone. They had their autonomy and their freedom, yet they were enslaved to alcohol. The desire to stop drinking had to come from them, but the ability to stay stopped came through the *process* of engagement, and the *result* of engagement, with others who also wished to stop drinking. Thus was AA born from one person sharing with another . . . and another, to become a community of millions joined by one common purpose: a desire to stop drinking and stay stopped.

In this beginning, the founders of AA, Bill W. and Dr. Bob, found each other out of desperation, an emotional hopelessness that started them talking and then changing their behavior. As they felt deeply and identified with the shared experience they both had lived—they had a compulsion to drink and could not stop once they started—they did not pick up the next drink. Thus in their first encounter they combined emotion, thinking, and behavior, the major components of human experience. They did not have to do this on their own, alone. Instead of white-knuckle willpower, they could trade their attachment to alcohol for a new bond with each other. They could grow to depend on their relationship of sharing, and later of working the Twelve Steps, as a substitute for drinking and then as a powerful source of deepening identification and growth in sobriety. They had been through the same awful experience of addiction and so they knew deeply what it was like. They, like millions before and since, always believed they were supposed to get control. No one knew yet that the road to sobriety lay in paradox: you must acknowledge the reality of your loss of control and your inability to regain it before you can change. This is the paradoxical necessity of accepting failure.

Paradox involves a change in level of thinking. It jockeys the basic premises of an idea or rational argument, moving them to a seemingly irrational, but nevertheless true conclusion. Paradox offers the exit for double binds, including the dichotomous thinking that freezes people into captive extremes, such as all success or all failure. If you are addicted to speed, you have to see that indeed you have hit a wall, you have failed to be able to go any faster, produce any more, or add any hours to your twenty-four-hour day. You have to give up and stop trying to get more control. You have to accept your failure. That acceptance can free you from the terrible bind of trying to control what cannot be controlled, lifting you cognitively and emotionally to a different, higher level. You will then be able to make changes in your behavior that were impossible to contemplate or attempt when you were fighting against failure.

It is important to hold this critical change—the paradox of accepting failure—as we explore the process of recovery for the culture. All of the changes I will outline must be viewed from the lens of "both and" instead of "either or." If not, you will likely become defensive and angry, hearing me say that you must give up your desires for success. Not so. As you read the description of letting go and accepting limits, you must remain open to a new way of thinking. I am not suggesting anywhere that we should stop valuing our old ideas of progress, optimism, hard work, and productivity. I just want to place them within a new frame, moving away from our paralyzing dichotomies, which actually create false limits. All-or-none thinking offers the fewest, most rigid possibilities. There is no room for shades of gray, nuance, or complexity for all the aspects of normal behavior, emotion, and thinking, all aspects of healthy living.

APPLYING AA TO THE CULTURE

I have been interpreting AA for many years as a curious student with a mission to bring greater understanding of AA philosophy to the professional world of mental health. Now I want to interpret again. This time I believe that AA philosophy, steps, and principles offer tremendous value to countless individuals and a nation that have lost control. However, let me say: all of the interpretations I make are mine. In no way am I suggesting AA believes what I believe or that AA has any opinion whatsoever about my ideas.[2]

AA demonstrates through its steps for the individual and its traditions for the group how to integrate the individual with other; how to focus on the self in the context of the community; how to live alone together. The same need for integration applies to change for the individual within the culture: how can the individual accept personal loss of control that perhaps originated from and now has spread to the entire culture? Can individuals change if the culture does not? Is it possible to coexist with or pull yourself out of the environments and the social, political, and cultural systems that reinforce and generate the beliefs that constitute addictive thinking and behavioral loss of control? It's a tall order. Let's begin with general principles of recovery for the individual and move to include the individual within the environments and social, political, and cultural systems that reinforce loss of control.

GENERAL RECOVERY PRINCIPLES

Loss of control and a refusal to accept limits are at the heart of this book, the heart of what is desperately wrong for individuals and the culture, so it is loss of control and a need for limits that must be faced. If people are going too fast, they must slow down. That is a limit. That is what Jack came to understand. Of course, going fast is more than physical, behavioral speed. It also involves intensity of emotion and distortions in thinking that we explored earlier. Americans believe in speed. We believe in "more, better, faster." We don't believe in limits. But that's where we're going. What basic principles underlie a developmental process of change based on an acceptance of limits?

Small Steps

As Wendell Berry said in "Faustian Economics," "We have lost the small steps." Nowadays there is only BIG. HUGE. THE BEST EVER! Everything is pointed toward the goal that will save everyone, solve everything, transform life as we know it. This is the "next billion-dollar idea" that keeps many tech people in overdrive. It's hard in real life to value the small steps, though we have evidence of small-step achievements in many areas, such as microfinance in Africa and the building of schools and community services through nonprofit volunteer efforts all over the world. Most people don't want the slower way because it seems too hard. It takes patience, endurance, and a trust in the process, which are hard to sustain in our era of instant results. Plus, most people now think that big ideas are born big or pushed to be big. If there is only success or failure, perfection or failure, colossal billion-dollar ideas or failure, you come to believe that you have to think big. But big doesn't work when it comes to stopping your addiction to these ideas and the fast pace they generate and feed.

Part of thinking big involves a belief that change must start from the top of a hierarchy, a company, government, or culture and move downward. In fact, major change is not a top-down, big pronouncement, big event process, though policy change can sometimes begin with such a radical shift. Top-down thinking contributes to a global sense of helplessness as people think they have no power and, if they try to change, they'll be left behind. The fear of getting off the wild roller coaster of speed and falling behind and failing keeps people locked in the cycle of addiction and loss of control. They believe they will only have power if they keep pushing, yet this pushing drives them to be out of control.

Jack began to go with Raj regularly for coffee after his workouts at the gym. He found a mentor, asked for help, and took the step of meeting with Raj. They talked about recovery, and Jack began to develop a deeper understanding of Raj's words. He asked himself guideline number five, "What am I doing?" (we'll go over all the guidelines shortly) and he began to realize how shortsighted his vision really was. "I always thought I was the top gun, the guy who was destined for the board room and the golf course. I felt very young and naïve though, a sense of myself I tried to hide. I guess I was a prima donna, a big blustery bully trying to impress. It wasn't pretty. I believed in success and that was all there was to it. My poor kid. He was going to have every opportunity and he'd better take advantage. I didn't want it to be like it was with my dad. I loved him and I knew he loved me, but I felt like I was failing all the time. It felt like there was no way to ever get it right. As soon as I finished one goal, it was onto another. There was no stopping, no savoring, and nothing to learn for the next time. It was all producing. All action. I felt stupid. All I wanted was to play catch now and then. But I lived on the top. I couldn't see anything worthwhile in the small things."

Most changes unfold in small steps. One little step at a time in the right direction. These steps have been concretized in AA with slogans such as "put the plug in the jug," "keep it simple, stupid" (also known as KISS), and "a day at a time." These are action guidelines to remind the newly abstinent person to redirect an impulse to a new recovery action and to offer hope: the whole process is only for this day, the one right before you. The *now* of urgent need turns into the *now* of this day only. Nothing more. It puts a limit on how long you have to hold on. It takes out the past and the future. Just deal with now, with a new recovery action. People learn to take one step at a time, to let go of trying to control what can't be controlled, and to slow down. "Easy Does It" has been a familiar bumper sticker for years, alerting other drivers to a friend in front of them or in the next lane. "Easy Does It . . . But Do It" is a slogan that suggests balance. Take it easy, slow it down, but act. Ask yourself: what is the next right step? If you don't know, perhaps you wait until you do, or at least until you know that your next step won't hurt you or anybody else.

In the developmental theory of change, movement is a process of small, incremental steps, coupled with more radical, even bigger moves at points along the way. But despite an understanding of the mix between small and big, many people disparage the small and cannot see it as part of bigger growth. Growth and change accumulate, just like healthy child development.

A New Sense of Time

It seems to be part of human nature to seek immediate results, like the rats in the cage that press the bar for the pellet reward. Speed addicts are focused on the short term, not weighing long-term consequences. Infant time is *now*, which is exactly how speed addicts feel the intensity of their need. For those operating at slightly older cognitive levels, magical thinking jumps in to make consequences, long- or short-term, erasable. You just move ahead and forget it.

In preparing for change, you will be faced with the need to develop and accept a more realistic appraisal of time, number fourteen in the guidelines. This sounds easy, but it is very difficult in practice. Time distortion has served you well. You lose track of time entirely when you are lost in your pursuit of speed, or you are always terrified that you don't have enough time. There is never enough time to finish what can't be finished, to get to the goal that keeps changing in front of you. The reality is that there really never will be enough time to control the uncontrollable.

Instead of pushing against time, you will embrace it as a source of limits. You will come to see: limits = slowed time = progress. You will come to accept that there really are only twenty-four hours in each day, and you can't be awake and on the go for all of them. You will see that the best of success is not one problem solved and then onto another with no end. Success is finding value in the journey as much as in the destination, in process as much as outcome. And seeing that process often leads to a completely different outcome than the one you tried to reach so quickly. Instead of management and control of time, you will also yield to time controlling you. But not in a way that pushes you to go faster, which is what happened when you were caught up in speed and believed you couldn't stop. Paradoxically, the reality of time gives you limits and structure that you now accept. That is how you manage it. You accept limits and work within them, not against them.

Once Judy could really see she, too, had lost control, that she didn't have the power to do everything 24/7, she became able to let the limits of her day actually guide her in making her plans. What a radical concept, she thought! She started her day with a quiet time and then looked at her schedule, adjusted it to fit the actual demands of her day, changed things that needed to be shifted, and canceled what was impossible to fulfill. Yes, you say. What if she couldn't make these adjustments? What if she lost her job? Maybe that could happen. But often, it won't happen. Judy learned she had room to set limits much of the time. She learned to say yes and to say no. She learned to live within her limits and bear the consequences, including the fact that others weren't happy with her.

You see that your belief in no limits—a key in your answers to the Twenty Questions—was driving you out of control. Now you see that your acceptance of limits—a centerpiece for slowing down—is a foundation for your new way of thinking and your new way of life.

You begin to slow down because you know you can't think the way you need to and you can't be receptive to new insights and ideas unless you give yourself space. This is what you've lost: the time and the space for reflection. Now you will get it back.

Following a lecture on speed to educators, a high school creative-writing teacher approached me. "You hit the mark! I am tearing my hair out trying to convince my high school students that they must slow down and cultivate quiet time and space in order to be creative. They can't just spew out a story, with no thought or attachment to the plot or characters. Yes, some things come intuitively and quickly, but the art of creative writing is a process. You can't just push a button."

You also accept that progress and success, like everything else, take time. And practice. You don't inhale knowledge and answers or push a button for your sense of connection. You learn once again by engagement with a task or a person. When you slow down and refocus on reflection, listening and learning from others, you will be on the road again to human connection.

When you learn to live one day at a time, you create a doable frame for slowing down. You simply consider what is important and necessary for you *today* and set about to plan accordingly. This is hard because you are used to thinking that if you're not watching, someone will pass you by. You'll get behind and never catch up. In reality, you cannot see the future even though you try. Paradox is involved again in understanding time: you do need to plan ahead but that plan involves flexibility and options. You will plan, but you won't plan the outcome. This is a key to accepting loss of control. You're ready to interact with whatever happens up ahead. You are not seizing control by planning the outcome now. What a critical difference and how confusing it can be. But it is also liberating.

Jack struggled with this whole idea of time and control. He felt very anxious thinking about just today. He wanted to know he would be okay up ahead. This was a control he couldn't have, but he struggled with the frightening feeling he got when he acknowledged that. It also didn't quite make sense to him. He could see how it might work for Raj in AA, but Jack projects into the future for his business. His company always used to be behind the big innovative leaders, and sometimes he thinks it still is. So of course he has trouble staying slow and calm inside. However, he's reassured when he reminds himself that the deadline in front of him is "just for today."

Jack remembers chuckling as he watched his toddler son repeat aloud: "Don't run with your mouth full. Don't hit. Use your words." Now he applied the same repetition as he murmured to himself: "Just take the next step. Do what's in front of me. Yes, plan. But don't race to grab control. I am unhooking from speed, and I have to remind myself that's what I'm doing and it's a good thing."

Redefining Success as Delay, Endurance, and Enough

As you come to see slow time as progress, you will also redefine success, number sixteen on the guidelines. We can say, paradoxically, "failure is the success" you need now to break the compulsive hold that speed has on you. When you accept that you can't keep going and can't do it all, when you know that you do have limits, you will find new value in delay. Stopping to rest or think before pulling the trigger will now be seen as wise, rather than a stupid loss of competitive edge. You will cultivate an appreciation for endurance, hanging in, and putting the next foot forward instead of demanding instant resolution, instant relief from discomfort and pain, and magical fixes. You will also come to understand and value the idea of "enough."

In addition to becoming aware, you pay attention and listen differently to your inner voice, your emotions, and your needs. You actively work to recognize what and how much you really need. And you learn to push away from your computer and your gadgets, just like you push away from the table or the bottle. As a recent newspaper story noted, "Good enough is the new success."

Jack has come to love the guiding principles of delay, endurance, and enough. When he tells his story to new business associates he is mentoring, he reminds them time and again that most delay is not failure. Delay can be a sign of thoughtfulness, wisdom, and healthy confidence. You learn and you trust that you almost never have to act on impulse or in response to internal anxiety and urgency. You can wait for more information. Learning to wait will help you clarify the times when you must act instantly.

Jack has come to depend on the principle of endurance. He learned from Raj that you know your limits and you follow them, no matter what. That's how Raj has stayed sober in AA, and that's what Jack has learned he has to do with speed. He knows he can endure the anxiety, fear, and even boredom of a slower day. He knows the slower days will accumulate and bring him a fresh perspective and new insights. He tells his staff that enduring a quiet day is the new ropes course. And then you feel a quiet peace, the deep satisfaction of enough.

Repetition

One key to solidifying behavioral change is repetition, a centerpiece of the building block process of cumulative learning. Behavioral repetitions, often interacting with thinking and feeling, move us forward to the next level of knowledge or function, even though we may believe that repetition is stagnant and boring.

This is paradoxical given that compulsive repetition is the heart of addiction. Yet repetition will be a cornerstone of behavioral change. Repetition of new behaviors, *within the context of accepting your loss of control and your need for limits*, will be the groundwork of your new development. You will try on new behaviors and repeat them, over and over, until they become routine and automatic. Even then, you can suddenly return to old out of control behaviors in an instant. The old behaviors, old thinking and emotions can set you off in a panic of fear that you'll never succeed, or you'll never catch up. These moments of doubt and anxiety can drive you back into speed to quiet the fears as you once again try to work harder and smarter. Just like relapse prevention for any addiction, the new behaviors must be practiced intensely and repeatedly in order to work for you through the normal stresses that may not change.

10

Getting Ready for Change

I am always moved when I answer the phone and a person asks me for help. Sometimes it's the first time this individual has ever spoken the word *problem* out loud or the first time he or she has said the word to another person. This is a huge step. I know that this stranger on the other end of the phone is probably frightened and perhaps not hopeful at all. Usually when people call me to ask for help, they do not see it as success. They see it as failure.

How do people get to the point of being ready for change? What moves people from denying a need for change, or from wishing to change without really changing, to a point of recognizing the need for something serious and profound?

First they have to have an idea that something is wrong.

BECOMING AWARE OF A PROBLEM

Shania told me she'd been rehearsing a phone call to me for months, maybe even a year or more. She'd seen a notice that I was speaking at a public forum on the fast pace of life in the culture and, though she didn't attend, she remembered my name and talked with me in her mind over that next year. What did she tell me?

Shania started each imaginary conversation by reassuring me that she was really fine, that she was pretty sure I'd tell her she didn't have a problem and she could go on living at a pace that was just a shade too fast, along with spending that sometimes got a little wild and eating that included a binge or two every week. But these were exceptions, she'd assure me: sometimes she went longer than a week without overspending and overeating. However, she did keep a fast pace every day. This was not something she believed she could change. And she wasn't sure she needed to. Didn't everybody move too fast? Shania couldn't stop racing and she couldn't see any reason to stop.

Shania believed she was on the way up the corporate ladder and needed to keep up her pace in order to succeed. She knew she was good at what she did, and if she worked hard enough, she would rise to the top. Others could see and hear her grandiosity, her arrogance, her entitlement to have whatever she wanted and to be whatever she wanted. They gently suggested that she was riding too high and ought to temper her big-shot comments with her clients. But she was sure her colleagues were just jealous of her success. She'd have to tolerate people who didn't want her to get ahead. But underneath this rationale, she began to worry. She was also exhausted. No matter how many hours she worked, no matter how much she got done, it didn't seem to be enough. That's where the overspending and overeating came in; she needed something to make her feel better. And she did feel better, for a while—until the credit card bills came or the new clothes she bought didn't fit. That's when she read about my lecture and started talking with me in her head. Maybe there *was* something wrong. Maybe she *was* a bit out of control now and then.

As Shania began to think about how to make some changes in her life, she started to get used to the idea of change that would lie ahead. During the year that Shania was talking with me in her head she told herself she had to "cut back," in the same way she does every time she starts a new diet. She looked at her calendar and tried to find one activity, one coffee date, one workout, one appointment to omit. Nothing seemed possible. She looked again and decided she'd just have to push harder and go faster. Cutting back was not an option. She was still trying to get control without changing anything.

Months later she called me. It was time to speak out loud because she hadn't been able to change anything on her own. She was tired of this life, this pace, and had made several serious errors in professional judgment, including missing a critical deadline and forgetting an appointment with important clients. She wondered if I could help her slow down and maybe not spend so much.

Shania had allowed herself to ask, "What am I doing?" after her colleagues challenged her overblown ego. She had unknowingly allowed herself to hear the challenges and to step back and reflect. She was already into the process of unhooking, focused on questions four and five, though she wasn't even sure she had a problem. But as she looked at the questions, she realized she was overdoing her sleep medication, and it wasn't working. She couldn't wake up in the morning and she felt drugged for much of the day.

"What's happening to my edge?" she allowed herself to wonder. And number five grabbed at her: yes, she acts first and thinks later, if she thinks at all. "I've really lost the ability to pause and think about things. I just don't have that reflex anymore. If a thought pops into my mind, I erase it so I can get to action. This knee-jerk way of life is causing me trouble, but I'm more afraid of the anxiety that rises up if I stop a moment to think about things." She mulled that moment of confrontation and tried again to get control on her own. Finally, she came to talk to me, following the path of first-order change with a wish to get control.

Awareness of a problem is a process. Awareness grows and deepens over time, and it isn't until people hit bottom—experience their utter helplessness to effect changes—that real change happens. The process of deepening awareness continued to happen for Shania even after she began therapy.

Shania stayed in the first-order change phase for a while; she rearranged a lot of oranges. She took time off to stabilize her health, joined a yoga class, and continued to see me in therapy. Over several months she began to explore her entitled attitudes. She recognized she couldn't do it all, she had the same human limits as everybody else. These moments, when she knew she wasn't all powerful, gave her a sense of calm and a willingness to slow down. But they didn't last. Shania wasn't quite ready to accept that she couldn't recover her strength and power her way back to the top. If she wasn't the star of her company, she'd be ordinary like everybody else and to her there was no worse fate. So Shania struggled to accept her need for limits was permanent. She'd make changes, but soon return to her old behaviors. She knew she needed limits, but following them was something else. Shania was locked in a repeated struggle to be in control while not having any limits. It just didn't work.

Shania was still in the state of being hooked on fast. She could answer seventeen of the Twenty Questions, but she still thought she could figure out how to get control and everything would be fine. She had all the behaviors, the feelings of buzz and emptiness, and she could even see some of her distorted beliefs and talk about them. But she couldn't feel these realities yet in her gut. She knew, and could tell me, she was holding out against really seeing and feeling her loss of control, but she really didn't embrace that reality. Shania had a ways to go.

She tried to follow the guidelines for getting unhooked, but she'd end up overbooked and overcommitted, while making mistakes in her frantic efforts to multitask. Shania kept saying, "These guidelines don't work," while she also knew she was refusing to acknowledge any limits.

HITTING BOTTOM

Most people don't suddenly see the light. The process of moving toward change we've been exploring involves getting cognitively and emotionally ready to see, feel, and do things in a radically new way. It's getting ready to make a leap of faith or to be catapulted into second-order change. Second-order change doesn't happen until people have experienced deep down that they don't have the willpower to make the changes they want to make. They need to know this in their bones. In AA this is called "hitting bottom."[1]

Jack hit bottom after his third car accident and the directive from his boss to take a break. He reached a point of despair and then of paralysis when he couldn't figure out what else to do. He had tried everything he could think of to slow his pace and rebalance his life, and yet here he was. He had had two car accidents, and while neither of them had caused any injuries, both had caused a lot of property damage and cost a lot of money. Both of them had happened when he had double-scheduled himself and tried to compress two commitments into a single time frame. He knew he had double-booked himself because he was so frantically busy and stressed that he wasn't paying enough attention.

He had tried to slow down but the pull of ambition and the fear of failure defeated him each time. This third accident was much more frightening. Luckily no one was hurt this time, either, but he came within a few inches of hitting a young boy on a bicycle before he sideswiped a truck and totaled his car. Maureen was frantic and furious. His boss was worried and could see the effect stress was having on Jack's performance. This was when he told Jack he had to take time off. Jack didn't know where else to turn, what else to try. "Hitting bottom" is the experience of the end, of no more, no place else to turn. You just can't do it anymore. Jack felt like an abject failure. What Jack did not yet appreciate was that it was in accepting this very failure that he could achieve success.

At this point many people experience a sudden and perhaps fleeting sense of giving up, what they will later call "surrender." The hitting-bottom state of profound demoralization and despair turns into a quiet, unconflicted acceptance of defeat. "This is it. It's over. I can't do this anymore. I can't try harder, push faster, or, once again, try to work smarter. There is nowhere else to go. I have lost the race, I have failed to get control, failed to be able to do everything."

This is at least a four-step process: the individual grows in awareness that there is a problem; hits bottom; accepts defeat at the deepest emotional level—the "gut hit" that Shania resisted; and surrenders to the impossibility of regaining control. This is a key to long-term change. The acceptance of defeat and surrender to the futility of trying to get control become the foundation for a radically new kind of change. We might have called this understanding humility.

An acceptance of your limits, followed by your attention to the guidelines for unhooking, will hopefully bring this deep awareness and the inner peace that results from this depth of change.

THE PARADOXICAL NATURE OF DEEP CHANGE

The processes of deep, radical change (the paradigm shift) that occurred for Bill W. and Dr. Bob and in the birth and growth of AA were based on a paradoxical reality. The deep change that occurred for Jack was also based on a paradoxical reality. So was Shania's eventual deep change. Whether divinely inspired or explainable in retrospect by principles of transformational change, these counterintuitive steps and foundation for change were not intentionally designed.

A paradox is when two apparently conflicting realities are both true. Paradox is a statement that seems opposed to common sense, seems like it shouldn't be true, and yet is true. At first blush a paradox doesn't make logical sense; it feels mysterious, even absurd. But when you look more deeply the contradiction can be reconciled. Here is an example of a paradox: repetitive behaviors are a huge problem for addicts and repeating behaviors is a solution for the problem. Another example: to be free there must be laws to restrict our freedom.

Paradox involves surprise in logic and meaning. The surprise, the incongruity that is a core of paradox, is similar to the mechanisms of humor. The surprise of an incongruous pairing is what makes something funny. We laugh at the incongruity, the connection of opposites and contradictory premises. The punch line catches us off guard and we suddenly see something we couldn't see or predict as we followed logically. But here comes the surprise and it catches us on another level of meaning. With humor, basic premises are altered so you have the shock of the punch line. Or you experience the shock of the impossible, as in the injunction "be spontaneous!"

The change in logical premise that makes something funny is similar to the change in meaning that occurs when people move from active addiction to recovery. Coming into recovery involves shock, the surprise of a fundamental change in premise and a fundamental change in meaning. It's the shock of the aha, the sudden illumination that occurs when a puzzle finally makes sense and you can't believe you couldn't see it before. Individuals will shift from believing "I am not an alcoholic; I can control my drinking" to seeing and believing deeply "I am an alcoholic; I have lost control."

Jack's friend Raj had been through his own struggle to understand that accepting his loss of control over alcohol was not a failure but the beginning of recovery. He had been baffled as he struggled to control his drinking. Each time he had a new plan he *really* believed he'd found the key. He was certain he would be able to drink without problems. But Raj always returned to being out of control. He had the same experience with his pace of life. He just kept moving. Eventually Raj told himself that drinking was his way of controlling his workaholism. "Drinking slows me down! I know I'll stop each day because I have a drink waiting. Look how it helps me regulate my workday." Later he added to his view the idea that working helped him control his drinking. Drinking slowed his overworking down and overworking slowed his drinking down. There's obviously a problem here.

It was only when Raj had accepted his failure to control his drinking that he was able to change. Like many, Raj didn't know how the change came about. This kind of change may come as a sudden leap, a shock; or it may come slowly, methodically, as you hunt for the puzzle pieces and finally find the one that brings everything into focus. Now you see. This same process applies to the problem of speed in a culture that is out of control. In this process of radical change people don't get new glasses, they get new eyes. This is the move from first-order to second-order change.

When you hit bottom, when you realize you don't know how to stop, you also realize you need help. This is how recovery happens. Reaching out for help is key to AA's story of Bill W. and Dr. Bob. They came together by chance to talk about their inability to stop drinking and, paradoxically, were lifted out of the pit of trying harder. Through the process of sharing their loss of control, they didn't have to try anymore to regain control. They shifted their belief in their own power and their own need for self-sufficiency to an acceptance of their total loss of control and a trust in the power of sharing with an "other" to give them strength that they could not muster on their own.

Raj had the same experience. He came to see that he had lost control of his drinking and he had lost control of his time and his pace. He couldn't stop working, couldn't stop his frenzy of speed. As Jack walked the treadmill next to Raj, feeling depressed and hopeless about his forced leave of absence, he tried to get what Raj was saying. Jack just couldn't see the power in powerlessness. He couldn't see how he could win by failing.

It took Jack months, but he got there. It clicked one day, and this time he didn't lose his new awareness. He knew he had lost control. That was it. He really believed he was better than almost everyone (maybe everyone, really) and that he could do and be anything he wanted. He'd learned this as a child. He was privileged, and he was entitled. He worked hard and he could have what he wanted.

Jack ultimately saw that nobody can do it all. That's not what unlimited opportunity means. Everyone has limits in how long, how much, how hard, and how endlessly they can keep going. Jack saw that he never stopped to think about anything anymore. He had become a man of action and nothing else. It was killing him. I'm fond of telling people who are ready to stop drinking about the value of going to AA. Almost everyone balks at the first mention and then they laugh when I say they're no different from anyone else. No one starts out wanting to go to AA. People are not standing in line waiting to get in. But millions of people have found their way and benefited from the help they've found. They have learned how to not drink and, in the process, have also given up their deepest beliefs in the power of self and the power of self-control. By asking for help, they have paradoxically found the power in a new kind of other and in engagement with other as modeled by the two founders of AA. Talking together provided a new way of interrupting their compulsion. Believing in a higher power, whether religious, spiritual, or unknown, confirms an acceptance of the limits of human power.

I have seen that this same process works for people who want to recover from their addiction to speed. But they also must fight the mandates and the madness of our culture.

WHERE ARE WE GOING?

The 1830s were a time of radical growth and change, similar to the radical technological and cultural changes of the twenty-first century. The United States was a "third world country" before the advances of the printing press and the building of the railroads that enabled the westward push of acquisition and enactment of Manifest Destiny. There were anxiety and apprehension in the culture and an erosion of values with such rapid change. Individuals had a hard time adjusting, just like now. Society was threatened with chaos and dissolution, just like now. People could not acknowledge their loss of control at that time. They feared failure if they didn't keep moving.

At a similar place today, we need to recognize the reality of our human limits. In our recent economic crash many people urged the government and its citizens to use this time to radically challenge our thinking and behavior—to fundamentally accept the loss of control and to recognize that it came directly from our beliefs and behavior and the emotions of want turned into need. The culture became addicted to "more" and could not stop its pursuit. Slowed by a financial crisis, many people—some in political, social, and educational circles—see the "solution" to this crisis as simply a matter of waiting it out until it's safe to gear up and start the engines again—the change-without-change model. As I noted in the introduction, this is what happened in the stock market crash of the late 1990s. There was no hitting bottom that would lead to change. People waited for the next big thing, what insiders at speed-driven tech companies now call "the next billion-dollar idea."

Hitting bottom for the culture might bring a state of deep

demoralization and despair, exactly the feelings and state of mind that society fears. Waiting for the next big thing keeps this hitting bottom at bay. The crash of financial markets brought a sense of dismay, a "how could this happen" shock to millions who believed it simply wasn't possible for society to crash. Faulty thinking—addictive thinking—and a sense of infallibility led to downfall.

The era of Manifest Destiny ended with the move toward the Civil War. The nation had to turn its attention from outward expansion to inward preservation, a shift that is equally necessary today. I think of what the fellow I met on the airplane told me: "I asked myself, what am I doing?" These key words and the shift from out-of-control actions of speed to slowed self-reflection become the foundational structure for change.

We need something different now, something greater, something outside of our current focused, compulsive pursuit. Accepting loss of control, reaching out for help and shifting from self-absorption to self-reflection, from externalized blame to personal responsibility, are steps that go against the grain of American greatness. This process of change questions American values and ways of thinking. Like the out-of-control, addicted individual, the out-of-control culture can move from grandiose entitlement to a true sense of one among many and from the chosen "nation of futurity" to the nation of limits and true equality. The paradox of accepting the reality of loss of control and the reality of limits moves us toward transformational change that holds within it a new freedom.

11

Finding Help: The Beginnings of Recovery Development

When Jack was forced to take a leave of absence from his job he felt desperate and lonely and directionless. Anxiety enveloped him. He'd read that exercise helps anxiety, and besides, he needed something to fill up his time or he'd go crazy, so he joined a gym. He went every day at 8:30 a.m. This was when he first met Raj. Some days this short, skinny guy with black hair walked the treadmill next to him. There was something about him that was attractive to Jack—a sense of calm. That and a good sense of humor. They began to chat on their treadmill walks, and Jack soon learned that Raj was a recovering alcoholic. It wasn't until a few days later that Jack understood Raj was also a recovering speed addict.

Jack remembers feeling a mix of admiration and contempt for Raj in their first days of talking together. He could see that Raj was slow and calm, that he was thoughtful and clear thinking. Jack liked how Raj could see the humor in the wild, speeded-up life he used to live, and laugh at himself. But Jack also thought of Raj as a failure, and this made him cringe. He couldn't understand how Raj could accept the label of alcoholic. Jack just kept thinking, "Raj is an alcoholic! He lost control. How can he live with that?"

We know that eventually Jack came to live with his own deep acceptance of loss of control. Jack was not an alcoholic, but he came to think that was only because he didn't use alcohol. When he'd been in his own speed recovery for some months he decided that if he'd found alcohol to quiet down, he probably would have gotten hooked. It works after all. At least at first. And now he has no trouble identifying with the reality of his own loss of control. "Number one on the Twenty Questions was easy to answer," said Jack. "I wanted to slow down, but I could not. This was indeed loss of control. And then I could answer yes to so many of the other questions. It was like the famous shift in figure and ground. One day you can't see, and then the picture is suddenly clear. Now I'm following the guidelines for change, starting with finding my mentor, Raj, and learning to listen to him."

Jack's addiction was just like that of an alcoholic. He was like Raj in his drive to be more, do more, have more, and never stop. As Jack listened to Raj day after day and began to change his own behavior, his admiration for Raj grew and his contempt vanished. Eventually Jack became comfortable telling his own story of being a recovering speed addict.

"My name is Jack and I'm a recovering speed addict. When I found Raj and started talking with him about his program of recovery in AA, I felt like I wasn't alone anymore. It was an incredible feeling of support and safety. I knew inside that I would be okay, something I hadn't felt for years and maybe never. This was a sense that someone else really knew me, knew what it was like to feel so out of control and not be able to stop. Raj knew what I was talking about because he'd been there. He'd lost control, and he'd been able to slow down."

Raj had to stop his drinking before he slowed down, but he quickly learned he also had to slow down if he was going to stay sober. Raj had to shift his attention to himself and his new sobriety, which forced him to stop being so compulsive and frantic about his work. Luckily, he wanted to be sober so badly he followed his boss's advice to take a leave at work, focus on his recovery, and look closely at his work life when he returned.

Raj told Jack he'd been frightened to slow down his pace of life in the first weeks because he still believed he'd lose everything if he didn't keep racing to stay in the game and outperform everyone else. Raj kept repeating to himself, "Focus on yourself, focus on your sobriety, and everything else will fall into line." It did. Raj told Jack: "I actually learned how to do this and it worked. No one was more amazed than I was! Instead of fighting against the idea of failure, I now embraced it. I guess I was becoming one of these recovery geeks." Raj faced the feeling of failure and shockingly realized it wasn't the end of the world. He was opening up to a whole new experience of feelings within himself that he used to disparage.

Raj believed that emotion was for sissies. If you let yourself feel, you'd lose your power focus on success. Raj thought his chronic internal pressure to live fast and act fast was evidence he belonged to the in crowd of high-rolling, running-on-empty winners he lived and worked with. "Fast is what connects me with my world. I hear the beep in my pocket and I get a shot of adrenaline. 'Yes,' I say to myself. 'I'm in the game.' These are the emotions I'm after. It's a high."

"Never thought I'd come to see the power in the very emotions

I'd always belittled. But that's what happened. I do feel deeply about my human limits now, and, instead of scorn, the emotion I feel is acceptance and a peace that comes in knowing I can't do it all and I never could."

In the early days of walking side by side on their treadmills, Jack listened closely to Raj. He heard Raj emphasize the need to take small steps at first, as he adjusted his behavior to support his abstinence from alcohol. He made the same kind of small steps in changing his behaviors online. Just like he made time every day to attend an AA meeting and time to talk with his new friends and sponsor, Raj set new limits on his computer time. Raj explained to Jack that he decided he could work on his recovery online, but he couldn't play games or surf the net the way he used to. He stopped his online poker for a while, replacing his sense of gambling camaraderie with his newfound sense of friendship with AA buddies.

"Didn't you miss it?" Jack asked.

"Yeah, but I was so excited about recovery that it wasn't too bad. And, wow, when I began to see how much time I had wasted getting 'high' online, it was totally worth it."

He continued, "It was really hard at first. I'd felt so many emotions for the first time, and I felt chagrined when I saw how crazy my thinking had been. I really believed I should have control of everything, and I thought I did! I was such a macho driver, pushing myself and everyone around me to constantly do more. Produce, produce! And then those drinks at the end of the day were my salvation. Drinking was the only way I could turn off the compulsive critic in me. People in AA talk about 'the committee,' the voices inside your head that judge and push and tell you to go ahead and drink; go ahead and take what you want. I had a full chorus. But now they're quiet."

Jack shook his head. "I've got a pretty big committee in my head myself."

"It will be okay," Raj reassured him. "As you start making changes in the way you act, your thinking will start to change, too, and you'll see that you don't have all the control you thought you had. Look at the guidelines: half of the twenty are about your thinking. Most people believe if you've got a problem with control, change your behavior. Yes, it's true. But that's not all. You have to challenge your thinking, which is often the biggest hurdle. Learning to live at a slower pace could turn your entire worldview upside down. And guess what? This will be your liberation! I know it's nuts, but seeing your limits is actually a great success." Raj's voice got more excited as he continued. "Now that I live within my limits, I feel so much more."

"I don't know if I like the idea of feeling more," said Jack.

"Yeah, well, it is a mixed bag, but it's so much better than feeling constantly numb. I'm slower; my behavior is no longer impulsive and reactive. I feel like I've become the guy I used to call the old codger. But that's okay. No, it's better than okay. It's good."

So with Jack and Raj as our recovery guides, let's look at what needs to happen for you to slow down. What are the steps of new development?

FORMING A NEW ATTACHMENT

Becoming addicted to a substance or behavior is similar in some ways to an infant becoming attached to a caregiver. You find something—alcohol, other drugs, a behavior like eating or gambling, racking up credit card debt, or getting hooked to the computer—and make an emotional attachment that is similar to early parent-child experiences of emotional bonding and engagement in relationship. The new object initially provides comfort, excitement, fun, reward, even power, or something so positive the newly hooked individual comes back for more. This is oversimplified, but it's right on. Jack used to brag that he'd pulled an all-nighter, flashing his work hours like a badge of honor. Jack didn't know yet that he had to work like this. He didn't know this deep truth: You need something, you find it in a substitute, and you're hooked. So how do you get unhooked?

The process of change involves a move from a belief in self-sufficiency to the possibility of help, to reaching out to "other." You shift attachment from the object of your addiction to a new attachment and engagement with others. This process of change shifts attention back to relationship, back to involvement with others as a route to growth and healthy development.

That's what Jack did with Raj. He took the time to listen to Raj talk about what he had been like as an active alcoholic and speed addict, what had happened to him, and how he had changed. Jack allowed a new kind of information to take hold within him, which in itself was radical. Jack was listening to another man talk about losing control, accepting failure, and finding a new path to slowing down.

Jack allowed himself to open up to another person, who opened up to him. It was the beginning of a new attachment and a new relationship that would give Jack the kind of emotional connection he'd lost so long ago or maybe never even had.

When this shift to a new caregiver occurs the building blocks of new development can move into place with less interference than during the time you were getting ready to see and know but weren't there yet. The new relationship gives you an emotional experience of security that allows you to absorb new truths about yourself and new learning about how to change. When you are still in active addiction glimpses of reality set you off in panic, and you strengthen your defenses of denial, rationalization, and projection. But when you have hit bottom and reached a deep awareness, you are in a vulnerable, infant state—scared yes, but if you've got help, change is really possible. You can see that you have lost control and you want to slow down. Reaching out for help is a behavior, but it's also deeply emotional. Asking for help is almost always a painful move on the uncharted road to change.

At the end of active addiction, emotions are raw and urgent, just like those of a hungry baby. Behavior is dominated by impulse. Individuals act *now*. They're too overwhelmed by the intense emotions of primitive need, anxiety, and the knee-jerk actions of addiction to think. Do it, take it, check it, punch it, eat it, drink it, shoot it, buy it. Then do it all over again. As addicts form new, healthy attachments they become babies in recovery. They are in a state of emotional vulnerability, knowing they have lost control, but not knowing what to do except revert to old behaviors of trying to regain control. In a new relationship in recovery they can be babies, seeking comfort from someone like Raj who's been there, who will teach and model new behaviors to replace the old ones that didn't work.

This is just like infant development that goes well. The baby is protected, emotionally connected, and soothed by attentive caregivers. This emotional attachment forms the foundation for the infant to learn to crawl, walk, talk, and play with others.

As individuals form new attachments they also reclaim the value of being engaged with others, embracing the notion that we all learn through what is essentially an apprenticeship model. Healthy development and healthy living involve engagement with people. Once the principles of interactive learning, including mutuality and reciprocity, are reestablished, the individual can begin to make other small adjustments that will support further slowing down.

A NEW LEARNING PROCESS

In recovery you will begin a new process of learning how to slow down, with the three strands of the addiction necklace now working in a recovery mode. You will learn how to first redirect your impulsive addictive behaviors and emotions that kept you so out of control. You will begin to think more clearly and to look back at what happened. Just like newcomers to AA, you'll start to craft a story of what it was like when you were hooked on speed and out of control, what happened to move you to see it and to stop, and what it is like now that you have changed. Your story will include the emotions, behaviors, and thinking of new recovery—often raw and uncertain—that will later become your grown-up, mature emotions, behaviors, and thinking as a slowed-down recovering speed addict. Just like Raj, you'll have a story, too, brief at first and then deeper and fuller as you grow in your new development. This is the process of recovery in AA. This is what Raj found and shared with Jack. First you shift attachment from your addiction to a new source of help. You reconfirm your new knowledge that you have lost control and that you are a limited human being. Then using the structures of your recovery supports, you redirect your impulses in new ways, taking recovery actions. Recovery supports might include other people in recovery or meetings, if they apply; one of your friends who also wants to slow down; or your spouse or partner. This helper cheers you on and maybe joins you in mutual support, like your colleague at work who helps you protect your new, pared-down schedule, and reminds you of your new attention to slowing down. You might also borrow books from the addiction recovery world, which you translate to slowing down from speed addiction. These are the concrete steps of change, the "how to do its" of slowing down. Jack first decided to actually turn off his computer by 11 p.m. each night no matter what. It was hard. He pushed this limit a few times, and then he settled in to 11 p.m. He changed his bedtime from "somewhere in the middle of the night when I can't see or think anymore" to 11:30. That was a laugh at first, too, and he cheated wildly. But then he settled down. He was going to meet Raj for their workout in the morning and he wanted to be rested. Jack came to see that he listened better, took more in from Raj, and got a better workout if he got more sleep.

You will take clear actions of change while you are also opening to new feelings and challenging your old thinking. You will begin to think more clearly and to talk with others who are on the same path. These are the beginning behavioral, emotional, and cognitive changes of recovery.

Where are these supportive people? You might say there is nobody but you who wants to slow down and change. You may be right, but probably not. Here in my hyped-up bubble of Silicon Valley, I hear sighs of overwork, shrugs of "what can you do," and people everywhere bemoaning the state of frenzy that is now "normal."

When you realize that you are going too fast and you want to slow down, look around and begin to take in who else is in the same boat. If you are ready to find others, you will. They may be just as afraid as you are, but together you may be able to walk and talk like Jack and Raj. You will begin to make small changes, one step at a time. You will look for advice in print and online (articles and books about unplugging are already available) and support each other in your beginning efforts.

Sometimes you will first change your behaviors, opening up your schedule, perhaps allowing time for reflection each day. You may struggle in the beginning, but soon your emotions follow. You like this new space and you settle in to your new, slower pace. Your thinking changes soon, as your anxiety about this vacuum diminishes. Now you begin to see clearly how out of control you were and how confused and chaotic your thinking had become. Now you see what it was like and you have the beginnings of your "story."

This is what Raj did in his first weeks of attending AA. With time he could see that his active addiction had dragged him down to primitive, juvenile levels of development. He was behaving, feeling, and thinking like a child. Recall that the dominance of impulse, along with the distortions of emotion and thinking, has brought the entire culture to a level of three- or four-year-old function. Our belief in no limits and our sense of entitlement to take what we want, when we want it, and to act on impulse or fall behind, keep us in a state of arrested development. We can watch ourselves lose control, say too much, show too much, and then pedal as fast as we can on our tricycles to try to undo the damage.

Raj thought he was a fun-loving guy, not a child in need of a parent. He was spontaneous, a great quality for his tech world, and he could go all night at work or in the bar. Raj had to be called home by his wife, just like a seven-year-old is called off the playground to come home for dinner. Raj had no idea he was immature and out of control.

Addicts feel, think, and behave at the level of infants, or maybe two- and three-year-olds because they are dominated by impulse. At best they may make it to the playground and stretch up the developmental ladder to seven years old. Up to this age children see and interpret the world through magical, concrete thinking. They love fantasy, fairy tales, and the Road Runner that could crash and burn and start all over again. Santa was real, and don't you tell me otherwise.

At about eight years of age reality takes a more prominent place as the child begins to sort out what's real and what's not and to prepare for movement to abstract thinking, which should arrive with adolescence. In our culture many don't make it to this level because dealing with complexity—with its absence of right or wrong answers and the difficulty of determining finite goals or endings—is disparaged. As a culture we prefer to remain at the level of concrete operations; we want certainty. We want to believe we can do anything we want and find a solution to anything we want to solve.

And when we add the dominance of impulse we plunge further down the developmental ladder to infancy and toddlerhood, a time before kids have learned to internalize delay and to use their words instead of their actions. It's scary to think that much of the culture has adjusted to living at such infantile levels and cannot see what's wrong.

Raj believed he was a genius. He was smarter, quicker, and funnier than anyone. Never mind that he was often drunk and out of control. In reality he couldn't remember much of his antics once he had that first drink, which was usually at work since he didn't keep regular hours. Work time faded into cocktail time, and it was hard to come home.

Primitive, addictive thinking keeps people locked in a childhood sense of grandiosity and omnipotence; they believe that things can magically be controlled or reversed. They can rewrite their scenario any way they like. Plus, magic or no magic, they are frozen in dichotomous thinking. There is good and bad, right and wrong, fast and slow, success and failure. Nothing in between. This is normal when you're seven years old, but not for Raj, who was an adult. Raj was on top of the world—his world—and nothing could stop him. He had no appreciation of consequences.

When people are in brand-new recovery they finally know that there are consequences. However, they can also see that their emotions, behaviors, and thinking are the same as they were when they were out of control in their addiction. They can see how out of control they've been, but don't yet know what to do differently. That's when the steps of AA—or the guidelines for slowing down—can help alcohol addicts . . . and people who are troubled by speed.

WHO OR WHAT CAN HELP YOU?

Just like it was for Bill W. and Dr. Bob, and Jack and Raj, alcoholics and addicts of all kinds have been hitting bottom, feeling desperate, resolving to do better, but then doing it all over again, until they really saw the light and knew they couldn't get control. People have been surrendering to the reality of their loss of control and reaching out to AA for decades. They have let go of their addictive attachment to the bottle, the pill, spending, eating, or gambling and allowed themselves to connect with a new "caregiver," a new source of comfort, safety, and guidance. They have made an emotional connection with AA or another twelve-step program, a therapist, their religion, perhaps, or a friend who has been there and can offer support and guidance. Shifting emotional attachment to a new "object" sets the path of recovery and new development in motion.

What, you ask, do you seek that will work like AA but isn't AA? Well, one of the many other twleve-step support groups may help, particularly Debtors Anonymous (DA). A wonderful resource for people who are living in the chaos of out-of-control spending, this program teaches people how to add structure and organization to their financial lives. It is an excellent guide for all issues of loss of control in the culture.

A new twelve-step program is now forming around the country. Called All Addictions, this group is open to anyone with any addiction. It is drawing people from all other twelve-step programs and those who have never belonged to a twelve-step program before. This is a generic program for people who have lost control. It soon may draw speed addicts who have hit bottom and see they've lost control.

You may already belong to social, religious, cultural, or professional groups that value a slow pace and self-reflection. These connections have served you well for many years and they still work. You can strengthen your ties to these groups and use them for support as you detach from your personal addiction to your phone, computer, or your drive for unlimited speed.

FINDING A COMPATRIOT

If you don't have social or professional supports, you can begin with just one "other." You simply need to find one person, a resource who, ideally, has been there, who can guide and support you in holding on to your desire to slow down and to actively help you move toward doing so, as Jack found Raj. Or it can be somebody who wants to slow down as much as you do but is afraid and doesn't know how to do it, either. This might be a peer in the AA frame or any support person who has the same desire. Sure, you say. No problem. You just need one compatriot, one person who sees it like you. However, finding that person may take you some time. Much of the culture will be threatened by your awareness and desire to slow down or to stop, and will resist or actively sabotage your efforts. Your desire to slow down may threaten others who still see your change of pace as a failure.

Your friend says you're not available anymore since you decided you were overbooked and going too fast. Then you unplugged. She wants to talk at 2:00 a.m., but now you don't want to. "What happened to sisterhood?" she wails. You feel a stab of guilt and tell her you'll be back, even though you know you can't go back. But you know you've disappointed your friend. Later on you'll be able to tell her you can't live a life of speed anymore. You won't be back at 2:00 a.m. to talk, but you'll welcome her friendship in a slower, quieter way.

Henri had a similar experience when he began to slow down. His fast-track buddies teased him about becoming a wimp. What's this about paying attention to his limits? When did he ever say no to a high-rolling poker game with the guys, to another hour or four at the investors' dinner, or to adding one more meeting to his already overloaded fourteen-hour day? "Come on, Henri," they joked. "You're bringing up the rear." This was excruciating for Henri to hear. He was always at the front, not the end of the line.

Established cultures and institutions may challenge your desire to slow down. Indeed, all of society may believe in the power of progress without limits to such a degree that your own best judgment, including acceptance of your limits, may ironically lead you to fail in these cultural environments and systems that are airtight in their pursuit of speed and success. A recent example illustrates: A mother with two children in a local high school noted for its fast pace and emphasis on success reported that her children had been instructed to take photos at recess with their cell phones and come back to share with the class. This mother said her kids were embarrassed and scared: they were the only students in class who were not permitted to have cell phones. They were not able to do the assignment and in their view, they weren't being permitted to keep up with their peers. Many everyday tasks we take for granted can only be accessed via computer. You want to use that coupon? You'll need your iPhone to scan it at the checkout. Your favorite shop will no longer take your old-fashioned check? Well, you could carry cash if you don't want to use your credit or debit card. So how do you find a supporter for your wish to slow down when it still goes against the grain?

As I said above, the compatriot will be your new caregiver, coach, and support person, even if you are peers in the process. Just start talking. Talk instead of act. Talk in person if you can. Talk reality. Talk about how fast you are moving. And do talk about your loss of control. Once you have acknowledged the reality, you can start to make a behavioral plan for slowing down. If you start to talk instead of act, you will be slowing down. You will be pausing to reflect and asking yourself, "What am I doing?"—both of which are points in the Twenty Guidelines to getting unhooked from speed. These are actions that move you from your impulsive actions to an inner space for reflection. Scared at first, you will soon catch yourself reaching for your phone and pause right then. Can you put it aside for a few moments? Can you let the urge pass? The answer at some point will be yes.

STICK WITH THE WINNERS

An AA slogan emphasizes "stick with the winners," which means stay close to people who are actively working a positive program of recovery. Or stay close to people who want to slow down but, like you, don't quite know how to do it. A winner accepts loss of control; a winner reaches out for help and accepts guidance. A winner is developing a new capacity for honesty and insight, an ability to see old defenses pop up that will mess with new thinking and behaviors. A winner is developing restraint through new emotional, behavioral, and cognitive development. Importantly, a winner is not someone who has it made, someone who is a success instead of a failure. No, a winner is someone who is on the path of change, of slowing down. Soon, that will be you.

12

Changing Behavior

As we saw in the first part of the book, the Twenty Questions help you identify the behaviors, feelings, and thinking that had you hooked on addiction to speed, a fast pace of life. Now we see what behaviors, feelings, and thinking will be necessary for you to find recovery. Some are clear actions you will need to take and others will be the result of the changes you make. Mostly, recovery will be a combination of self-reflection, action for change, and the results of change over time that are becoming a part of you.

We began looking at these behavioral guidelines in the last two chapters as Jack got ready for change and then approached the challenge of finding help. He found a mentor in Raj and began to make small changes, even though he was skeptical and unsure if he wanted to be a person in recovery. Here, we delve deeper into the process for Jack, focusing on the guidelines for slowing down that will also apply to you.

Twenty Guidelines

YOUR BEHAVIOR:

1. You ask for help; you seek a mentor who believes in slowing down for guidance and support.

2. You develop a recovery action plan.

3. You begin to make small steps toward change.

4. You learn to pause, to reflect on your behavior, feelings, and thinking.

5. You ask yourself, "What am I doing?"

Jack spent some time mulling over his problem and getting ready for change. He tried the trick of tweaking his schedule without really making any fundamental changes, and he hit bottom pretty hard when he had his third car accident and his boss sent him home. During his workout conversations with Raj he began to accept how powerless he was over his compulsive need for speed, and he became open to accept the principles of AA. It was at this point that he began to unravel the three-strand necklace of addiction: behavior, emotion, and thinking. The unraveling involves working with all three strands at the same time; you can't pull out one strand without affecting the others as well. But it's easier to see how the beads on each strand get handled if they are looked at individually. There are a lot of small, concrete steps that go into rearranging or replacing the beads in each strand.

A RECOVERY ACTION PLAN

Behavior is where the action is in new recovery. Behavior is where you learn to do something different and practice over and over again, just like a toddler learning to walk. However, unlike a toddler, an adult in recovery needs a recovery action plan made up of concrete behaviors. You think about your behaviors and outline a new course of action. You substitute a new action for the out-of-control behaviors such as robotically turning on the video game; sliding your mouse and double-clicking your way to Facebook, Pinterest, or some other social media site that sucks you in for hours; checking your smartphone for emails first thing in the morning; or trying to get one more thing done before you leave the office and wind up staying several hours late. You see what the actions are that keep you hooked and out of control.

Stop for a second now and think about the automatic actions you take everyday—actions that feed your speed addiction and steal your time. List some of them here:

1. ....

2. ....

3. ....

4. ....

5. ....

Of course once you recognize these actions you're confronted with the emotion strand at the same time. You begin to make the connections between these robotic behaviors and the emotions that drive them. You see that you wake up scared and anxious. You dampen that feeling immediately as you turn on the computer, getting into repetitive action that makes that feeling go away. You begin to see how you rationalize escaping into your computer even though you know you need time to exercise or you know your child wants time with you.

Think about the five actions you listed previously. Now I want you to spend some time trying to figure out the emotions that drive them. Why do you check your email constantly? Why do you spend hours surfing the Web? What feeling do you get when you engage in these activities? What feelings are you trying to avoid?

1. ....

2. ....

3. ....

4. ....

5. ....

As you recognize your primitive emotions and the behaviors that blunt them, you also correctly see how hard it will be to suddenly stop it all. So you start with little chunks of change, small steps that do make a difference. The changes you make for yourself will have an impact on your environment and your bigger family and the cultural system. In just a bit, I will ask you to list some small steps you can take, but first, let's start with guideline number two.

Okay, so let's make a recovery action plan.

1. Ask yourself, "What am I doing?" Look at the list of automatic actions you wrote and select one to focus on right now. Write down exactly what it is you do. Perhaps you listed your vigilance to your iPhone as your number one action. So now you expand: "I keep my iPhone on and in my pocket or my hand at all times. I check it constantly, even if it hasn't vibrated. I am never out of contact."

....

....

....

....

....

2. Next write down the positive and the negative effects of this action. You might write: "I make a lot of money for my family. I'm the most successful salesperson on the team." Or on the negative side: "I am so stressed that I can't sleep at night. I rarely see my family." What are the benefits and what are the problems for you? For your family? Start here, but you may want to come back to this question later. You'll likely have more answers as you begin to reflect and to make changes.

Positives:

....

....

....

....

....

Negatives:

....

....

....

....

....

3. Examine your schedule. In response to your question "What am I doing?" write out the schedule for your day *as it really is* on page 221. Fill in fifteen-minute intervals. You should do this with your entire day. For this exercise I'm just giving you a twelve-hour period of 8:00 a.m. to 8:00 p.m., but adjust it to the hours that apply to your life.

4. Next, write another schedule on page 222 with these same intervals with the new behavior you will substitute. You can delay turning on the computer for five minutes (maybe you can make it ten minutes tomorrow). You can put a cup of coffee or breakfast in between you and your morning run. If you wake up with anxiety, you can immediately read a recovery book of daily meditations, take a walk, or write your dream or first reflection for the day. This is redirecting your impulsive behavior. You decide to do something else. Soon you begin a shift from immediate action on a negative, rote behavior to quiet and self-reflection.

Schedule

8:00 a.m.	2:15
8:15	2:30
8:30	2:45
8:45	3:00
9:00	3:15
9:15	3:30
9:30	3:45
9:45	4:00
10:00	4:15
10:15	4:30
10:30	4:45
10:45	5:00
11:00	5:15
11:15	5:30
11:30	5:45
11:45	6:00
12:00 p.m.	6:15
12:15	6:30
12:30	6:45
12:45	7:00
1:00	7:15
1:15	7:30
1:30	7:45
1:45	8:00
2:00	

Schedule

8:00 a.m.	2:15 ....
8:15	2:30 ....
8:30	2:45 ....
8:45	3:00 ....
9:00	3:15 ....
9:15	3:30 ....
9:30	3:45 ....
9:45	4:00 ....
10:00	4:15 ....
10:15	4:30 ....
10:30	4:45 ....
10:45	5:00 ....
11:00	5:15 ....
11:15	5:30 ....
11:30	5:45 ....
11:45	6:00 ....
12:00 p.m.	6:15 ....
12:15	6:30 ....
12:30	6:45 ....
12:45	7:00 ....
1:00	7:15 ....
1:15	7:30 ....
1:30	7:45 ....
1:45	8:00 ....
2:00	

Jack was puzzled about how he was going to make radical schedule changes. He was sure his boss would not be happy if he left work at 5:00 p.m. when he had a 6:00 p.m. meeting scheduled. Raj advised him that he could not make these changes all at once. "You need to keep your job, and you'll be going against the tide, dealing with bosses, customers, parents, and friends who do not want to slow down and don't want you to slow down, either. It's small steps," Raj told Jack.

5. Remember small steps. One of the main slogans of AA practice is "keep it simple." Another is "one step at a time." Jack started with a small request. He could stay most days of the week until 6:00 p.m. and some days he would stay much later. But how would it be if he left by 5:00 one day a week, which would enable him to be with his family for dinner and the evening? There was a huge difference in everybody's experience of family time when he was home for dinner. Jack started small, hoping he would be able to add a second day as the first one worked out. Jack was careful not to challenge anybody else's work habits or the norms of his office. Jack focused on himself and what he needed to change without disturbing anybody else's speedy life. Jack was going to see if he could be a recovering speed addict in an environment that still pushed for long hours and nonstop action from its employees.

6. Examine your environments. The environment is context, what's all around us—background, foreground, or center stage. It's the air we breathe, the sounds of silence or noise, the sounds of cheering for a win or screaming in fear, the color of a partner's mood, the smell of the Thanksgiving turkey, or the smell of alcohol after a binge. Most of the time we're not terribly aware of our surroundings, unless they're a cause for heightened pleasure or concern. A very hot day gets us all talking about how hot it is. Oppressive, perhaps, or a good reason to head for the beach.

The environment touches directly on the senses, the earliest infantile experiences that shape first perceptions and interactions. These sensate memories, many without words or before words, bring us immediately back to a young age. We notice a wafting smell of something and—oh, I'm six years old. It's the smell of chocolate chip cookies baking in the oven, which I grabbed hot off the tray. I can taste the gooey chocolate. Or the sound of the phone ringing in the middle of the night forever puts me back in the startled state of hearing about my father's death.

Researcher Cynthia Castro described the power of the environment: "For most Americans, the environment emphasizes abundance, convenience, urgency. We want things fast. We want things cheap. We want them right now."[1] Abundance, convenience, and urgency are conditions that can stimulate a desire for more. Abundance means there is no limit to what's available, convenience means it's easy to get, and a feeling of urgency pushes us to action.

Think about the environments that create the most stimulation for you and thus the most frenzy, the most rushed thinking, feeling, and behavior, the environments that make you a speed addict and keep it going. Make a list of the five that push you the most.

1. ....

2. ....

3. ....

4. ....

5. ....

What is it about each of these environments that hits your speed nerve? Be as specific as you can.

1. ....

2. ....

3. ....

4. ....

5. ....

7. Change your environments. Environmental manipulation can help restructure your behavior and thinking to find a balance. For instance, many experts recommend manipulating the environment to limit bad food choices and make good food choices available. Some suggest using smaller plates, an excellent behavioral and cognitive intervention. Behavioral nutritionist Brian Wansink said, "It's a lot easier to change your environment than to change your mind. The best diet is the diet you don't know you're on."[2]

People who are newly abstinent from alcohol learn to keep alcohol out of the home. They know that an alcohol-free home environment adds to their feelings of safety. If, by chance, they suddenly feel an urge to drink, they will have to do some work to get to alcohol. They can't just open the cupboard and take a swig.

Think about the five environments you listed above and what small change you can make in each one. You might be stymied at first, so let the notion sink in. What can you do to alter each over-stimulating environment? Look at the answers you wrote for why these environments are a problem and use them as a guide to begin making small changes.

1. ....

2. ....

3. ....

4. ....

5. ....

Clarice recalled how tech gadgets had taken over her family's entire living space, almost like a storm of grasshoppers invading the plains. Not only did everyone have a cell phone in hand or pocket, tech wizardry could be found on end tables, the coffee table, on top of the TV in the family room, and by the bedside. There was even a phone sitting by the coffeemaker to check messages first thing in the morning so no one would have to wait for the first hit of caffeine.

"Enough," declared Clarice one day when four out of five people at the dinner table had their phones in hand and eyes turned down to the screens at the same time. "What are we doing?" she asked. Clarice established a new policy for tech gadgets within the home. She recalled the mudroom from her childhood home in Oregon, the place where you left shoes and coats when you entered the house in rainy weather. She set up a tech room on the same principle. When you enter the house you leave your tech gear in a similar designated space.

This is just like using smaller plates to reduce the amount you eat. Clarice set up specific times of the day when everyone could retrieve their tech gadgets and be wired. She also established tech-free times, with grudging agreement from all family members. The tech room became the hub of action for a brief time as family members experienced withdrawal and snuck in to peek at their iPhones. But soon everyone quieted and settled into a calmer home environment. They began to talk again at dinner and to read printed papers, magazines, and books in the evening. Changing the structure of their relationship to their tech gadgets by creating a separate space with limits radically changed their inner experience of intense drive and need to be connected online. It was a dramatic but relatively easy environmental shift. If you weather the pangs and anxieties of first withdrawal, you will find these small changes really work. Clarice was able to reinstate an old, quiet tone that facilitated conversation; you, too, will be able to find your way back. Or you will discover the quiet that is inside of you, waiting to have room to meet you for the first time. Many of our children do not have a relationship with themselves, or others, except through technology. They will be learning about quiet for the first time.

Many people are coming together now to form sub-communities in school and work environments in support of environmental change. Teachers and school boards are actively working to bring back islands of calm within a chronically stressed and often out-of-control educational environment.

A recent article described the "homework center" established for all students at Jordan Middle School in Palo Alto, California. Kids need a quiet place, which is no longer provided in the home. As sixth-grader Cleneisha said: "I'd spend hours on homework at home and not get anything done." Eighth-grader Mario agreed: "At home you got sports, church. You're busy with things to do." Mario reported that since he has been able to concentrate more, his grades have improved dramatically.[3]

In creating a recovery environment you will carefully assess your daily activities and plan for what is possible within your new limits. You may determine that you can do soccer or music, but not both. You can have computer playtime one hour a day, but not three hours. You will eat dinner with the family four nights a week without television or other distractions. These behavioral changes within the framework of new limits will alter the structure of your day and contribute to a new calmer environment.

Once again we are wrapping around the other strands in the addiction necklace. Even though you accept that you cannot do it all and you begin to live within this new reality, you won't feel the calm until you really accept the truth of your limits. If you try to slow down without accepting the need for limits, you will likely feel like you're failing, just like always, and continue to look for ways to speed yourself up and do more. You really have to face the truth of your need for limits before you'll reap the rewards.

8. Identify high-risk people. Who drags you down? Make a list: Who are your supporters? Who are your saboteurs? Seek out your supporters as you begin to make changes. Steer clear of the saboteurs, the toxic people, for the moment. Their anxiety, their own rush for the high of speed, and their warnings to you about the dangers of slowing down can pull you under.

Supporters:

....

....

....

....

....

Saboteurs:

....

....

....

....

....

As Jack could identify more of his out-of-control behaviors, he also began to see what set him in motion. It was a combination of anxiety he felt at any time-out from constant action. But it was also his sense that the people around him—his wife, his boss, some friends—wanted him to go faster. His wife wanted that new weekend cottage, his boss wanted the new account, and his friends pushed him to join their daily morning runs at 5:00 a.m. so they could have more time to talk business. Jack needed to create new space for quiet reflection and he needed to take time away from all of these people who believed as he used to: you can never have too much, do too much, or go too fast. You'll only get behind.

9. List the activities or places where you can feel calm and quiet. If such a thing no longer exists, see if you can remember what used to calm you down and give you pleasure. A walk? Working out? Playing catch with your son? Dinner and a movie with your husband? Reading for pleasure? Reading for depth? Meditation in the morning or before bed? Quiet for ten minutes at midday? You just took the time back then. You came back to work alert and clearheaded, the chronic buzz of internal chaos now quiet.

List those activities and places on the next page.

....

....

....

....

....

10. Identify the triggers that will set you off on a new chase for speed. A trigger is the emotional experience of sudden craving, set off by all kinds of environmental cues like the smell of chocolate chip cookies baking in the oven. The person passes a bar on the way to work and recalls the feeling of the first shot of the day. Suddenly he can taste the bourbon. Another hears the sound of a cell phone in the audience and can't resist the urge to look down and check her own phone. She is suddenly off and running in her thoughts about her own calls and no longer can concentrate on the lecture she's attending. She suddenly feels anxious with a sense that she must get going or be terribly behind by the end of the day. Your child brings home a B-plus, and you're frantic she won't get into college. You yell at her to study more, while she wonders where she'll find the time for more. Plus, she feels like a failure.

People in recovery develop a behavioral plan to avoid situations that may invoke the trigger and to actively substitute alternative actions when they feel the need to get a drink or check the phone. If your phone distracts you when you are reading a bedtime story to your child, put it out of sight in another room. The change in environment will help you avoid temptation.

There are other kinds of triggers besides the environment.

Emotion is a powerful trigger. You can suddenly feel anxiety, fear, sorrow—any feeling at all can do it. You activate your inner speed-up button to push away the feeling. All kinds of memories—happy, sad, painful, fun, loving—can be triggers, too.

List some other triggers that feed your addiction.

....

....

....

....

....

As you begin to make your small changes, you'll find triggers everywhere. It seems like everything sparks you to check your phone, check your email, open Facebook, tap your foot with impatience because you have to wait. Each time you feel the spark and the automatic impulse and action to start your rush, see if you can pause. That's it. Just pause and take note. Just this one small move, a delay, has you on the road of change.

You are taking recovery actions, numbers one through five, and you probably don't even realize it much of the time. You are unhooking from speed.

Some triggers are so problematic you must avoid them altogether. Just like newly abstinent alcoholics, you need to stay away from the people, places, and things that kick-start your drive to speed up. Your running buddy revs you up with his rapid speech and panicked certainty that he's about to be fired. No wonder you're anxious when you round the bend for home. You know you should be just as worried and now you are. Realizing this is a trigger, you decide to gently suggest a different topic for discussion or you take a break from running with him.

In many regions of our country it's next to impossible to screen out the chaos and buzz. Everywhere you go you see people rushing, talking on the phone, working on their laptop or iPad. Commuter trains and buses, coffee shops, and even parks have become places of excessive action and buzz. Perhaps you can't escape, but all you have to do is recognize it and see if you can back up, move aside, or shut it out for a short time. You take the slow road home. It's longer, but you're not shouting at the driver in front of you. You hear of another great after-school activity for your sixth-grader, which you now know is a trigger. You finally really see that it's you who doesn't want her to miss out on anything. That fear gets you going. Revved at the chance for her to learn even more, and not to miss out, you're off and running to sign her up. Then you remember your plan and tell yourself you must accept that your daughter can't do it all. She will be just fine and she will get into college. Now see if you can remind yourself that she is not a failure. If you can't believe that she's not a failure, think of guideline number one: ask for help; check with your mentor: "Please remind me that my daughter will still get into college if she doesn't sign up for soccer. I can't believe it at this moment and all I want to do is push her." The new success lies in accepting limits and saying no. Your daughter can't do it all and neither can you.

11. Develop your support system. You need that compatriot, the partner or friend who wants to slow down, too. Just like Bill W. and Dr. Bob, you can talk about what's real. You can acknowledge how frightened and out of control you are. Together you support each other and strengthen your ability to set new limits, just like Raj and Jack talking on the treadmill. If your family, your neighborhood, and your job are all high stress, you may have to start with just one compatriot who wants to get off the bandwagon, too. You may have to actively look for others who can now acknowledge the realities and problems of the fast pace of life. Think about whom you can turn to. Don't worry if no one comes to mind immediately; as you begin to speak honestly, others will realize they can speak out, too. You will find your compatriot.

12. Create, evaluate, and adjust your structures of recovery. Structure is a container that is essential to change, a container that sets limits, gives direction, and provides a sense of safety and grounding. AA provides this kind of container. AA provides external structure that you will begin to internalize when you participate regularly. The individual attaches to AA, engages in the process, and experiences an interaction with others that produces a new experience of security. Control is not coming from an exercise of will. It is coming from the process of engagement and interaction with others.

Raj was describing the AA structure to Jack when he talked about how a meeting works to provide safety and reassurance. "There's predictability in the schedule. Meetings start on time, end on time, and follow a specific format. No surprises. The meeting will not lose its focus or get out of control. It's safer when you know what's coming."

Structures also exist in the AA literature and in the format of a meeting. They exist in the informal connections people make: talking on the phone, meeting for coffee. In all of these actions people are learning how to live in new, slower ways and how to look inward to see how and where they became addicted. Structure is all about limits, and limits are exactly what you need and what you fight. Paradoxically, instead of robbing you of your freedom, structures and limits give you freedom. By accepting that you have lost control, and that you also lost structures and limits to contain you, your program of recovery from speed addiction will give you the tools to establish the structures and the limits you always thought you didn't need. These changes are encompassed in the behavioral guidelines and they are reinforced by your growing capacity to accept your feelings and your new thinking.

If you are not involved in a twelve-step program, how can you create supportive structures? Think about who is in your life now: family, friends, your work, your organizations, and your religious community, if you belong to one. Who in each of these worlds can hear you, listen to you, and support you for slowing down? Just like you listed your supporters and your saboteurs, list those who can function as new scaffolding, holding you almost like the beams that support a building under construction.

There's nobody out there ahead of me, you say. We're all in the same mess with speed. Then get together and form a group of supporters, feeling your way step by step. Remind yourselves that you all want to change, and when you're stuck or you stumble, look back at the Twenty Questions and the Guidelines for Slowing Down. Focus on one that stands out now and think about a small step. Remember that pausing to reflect is a first step toward change, even if you can't see what to do next or where you're going.

13. Assess and create other structures: rules, rituals, and boundaries.

Rules. People in recovery usually tell of their disdain for rules when they were actively addicted. Many were proud to be rule breakers, seeing themselves as special and unique and therefore not required to follow anybody else's authority. Others broke rules by default; they simply couldn't manage to stay within the limits or structures of their families and work lives. People living in a chaotic world of speed have minimized the need for rules and forfeited a lifestyle that provided them.

It's automatic for you to apologize first, no matter what rule you've broken. You arrive late at work because you overslept after staying late at work last night to finish a project. Or you park in the visitor spot because you don't want to walk the extra block from the employee parking lot. You work harder than most people in the office, so you deserve a reserved parking spot. You tell yourself there aren't many visitors, so you'll just claim the space.

In recovery individuals will find that rules help. Rules can reestablish authority in the home, the school, and the workplace, an authority that has been abandoned in the service of total freedom and the loss of control it has bred. Sherrie's experience illustrates how rules help. She was in early recovery and realized as she tried to slow down that she no longer paid attention to people, including her husband. Her mind was always somewhere else. She and her husband both worked hard at listening to each other and getting back in the mode of opening up to each other. They made a new rule that they would devote one weekend a month to each other and not work. It was a hard rule to follow. The first Saturday they looked at each other and almost tossed it out. They wanted to open their work email so much it hurt. But they stuck it out and now they're on the way to a relationship again.

Rituals. People need rituals. An important part of life, rituals add structure with their repetition, predictability, and their symbolic meaning that strengthens attachments and transmits identity and social and cultural heritage and mores. Rituals can be positive or negative. They can foster and strengthen healthy individual development and relationships or they can undermine both, strengthening unhealthy adjustment. Active addiction, which is obsessive and compulsive repetition, is usually full of rituals that will have to be redirected or rewritten, just like other behaviors. Instead of a cocktail with your spouse at 5:00 p.m., you now take a walk together. Instead of checking your email first thing each day, you spend your waking minutes in quiet meditation.

Many rituals have also been positive and can be maintained or reinstated in recovery. You always ate dinner together until speed took over and you couldn't manage it anymore. Now you reestablish that custom. You drove the kids to school because it was the best time for talking. This was the time they spontaneously opened up, but you farmed out the driving to have more time for business emails. Now you drive them again and you leave your cell phone at home. No glancing up and down at your screen.

As they become increasingly lost in their addiction to speed, people give up many attachments and pursuits that had been nourishing, such as friends, clubs, sports, dinners, church, or synagogue—all the relationships and activities of a healthy life. Reestablishing old positive connections and rituals or creating new ones can be very helpful if they are supportive of a slower pace and lifestyle. Obviously, introducing anything that will add to your loss of control will not work.

Every meeting of AA begins and ends with rituals that reestablish the common purpose, the reason people come together: a desire to stop drinking. Many meetings also begin or end with the Serenity Prayer, an acknowledgment of limits to control by Reinhold Niebuhr: "God, grant me the serenity to accept the things I cannot change, the courage to change the things I can, and the wisdom to know the difference." These rituals reinforce the reason people are together and connect them as they remember the horrors of their loss of control and register the awe of their recoveries.

List some of the rituals of your addiction such as checking

email first thing in the morning, reading the newspaper online as you eat your lunch at your desk, answering phone calls when you're in the car commuting home or running errands. Next to these rituals, list a new ritual you can substitute:

Old Ritual	New Ritual
1.	1. ....
2.	2. ....
3.	3. ....
4.	4. ....

Now think about those healthy rituals you have abandoned in pursuit of your addiction: the book club you became too busy for, the morning meditation time replaced by getting in early to work, or the check-in each night at dinner.

1. ....

2. ....

3. ....

4. ....

5. ....

As you engage in positive rituals, you automatically reinforce the human connection, the emotional bond that is bedrock for a healthy self and a healthy life. You didn't believe this was true until you found it again or for the first time. You were getting this false sense of connection from speed and your gadgets. Now you know there is something else.

Boundaries. Addiction is a loss of boundary. You merge with your object of desire—your alcohol, other drugs, gambling, eating, or technology. You no longer exist separately from your action to use or to keep moving, to keep going as fast as you can. You and your addiction become one. Alcohol becomes your best friend. Your iPod, Twitter feed, and Facebook become extensions of you. Forgot your iPhone? You feel anxious and lost, searching frantically for the umbilical cord of high tech to keep you grounded.

When you slow down, you will separate from your drugs of choice. You will feel a new boundary between you and your tech gadgets as you become quiet and reflective. As you move from all action to new thinking and feeling, you become available for deeper human interactions. Sherrie found that when she and her husband set a boundary between themselves and work for that weekend a month, they were shocked to see how intertwined their lives were with work. They had lost a sense of themselves that was separate from their work and their gadgets, and they'd lost an intimate connection with each other. The new boundary gave them time for themselves and their relationship.

An understanding of boundaries is important for healthy human relationship. Recovery boundaries will give you a new sense of you, your space, and your place in relation to yourself and others. If you begin to live in reality, you will soon grow boundaries.

Think about the idea of boundary. What comes to mind for you? Who and what are you so tied to that there is no separation, no air between you? It could be your iPhone, it could be your craving or urge for instant action. It might be your partner or your child. Your addictions don't have boundaries. They become part of you. But maybe you feel the same lack of boundary in your work. Many new companies provide everything you'll ever need—your food, your gym, your friends—so you never need to separate by going home.

Many people in recovery feel stumped at first by the notion of boundary but then they get it. "Holy cow, I have no sense of myself as separate from anybody or anything! I don't even know what separate is. Isn't it all about connection? Isn't that what I'm after? Sometimes I think I'm separate with my tech gadgets, but that's an illusion. I'm hooked."

14. Pump your motivation. There are many ways to sustain your desire to stay the course in recovery. Addiction authors Patrick Fanning and John O'Neill offered one very effective technique.[4] They created the exercise for alcohol and drug addicts, but it is easily translatable for other addictions, including speed.

This is an exercise called the Decision Box, which I have adapted. On a piece of blank paper, draw a table similar to the one at the bottom of the page.

Now begin filling in the boxes. What are the good things about slowing down and what are the bad things? What are the good things about going faster and what are the bad? Keep adding to these lists day by day and tally your results. This box is a great way to see the changes in your thinking and feeling about your behaviors. As you progress in your lists, you will likely become more open and honest as you become better able to face the truth about how fast you go and how much you deny and rationalize your behavior.

	Slowing Down	Going Fast
Good Things		
Bad Things		

Jack's Decision Box at First

	Slowing Down	Going Fast
Good Things	More aware More present for my family	Feel the high Think I'm more productive
Bad Things	Fear I'll be fired Feel the vacuum inside More anxiety	Can't listen or pay attention Become a robot Can't stop

Jack's Decision Box at Six Months

	Slowing Down	Going Fast
Good Things	New feelings of joy, pleasure, trust, and love Less driven to be in motion New thoughts: I do have limits; this will be okay Have close relationships again I see and feel reality	I still idealize the high Can feel like I'm in charge until I crash
Bad Things	Still have cravings to get in motion and ride the high Still can feel like a loser but not too often	I'm out of control I think I don't have limits I believe I can go 24/7 without stopping I feel numb I'm turned off and tuned out from my life

The Decision Box was useful for Jack very early in his recovery. On the "good" side of the ledger for slowing down, Jack wrote: "I'll be more aware and more present for my family." On the "bad" side of slowing down, Jack noted: "I'll get fired." Jack kept these pages and added to his columns as the days and weeks passed. Soon the "good" column of slowing down grew, and Jack had fewer negatives to add to the bad. (See Jack's Decision Box on p. 240.) When Jack looked back six months after he first created his Decision Box, it became very clear how much he had changed. It provided not only a reality check for Jack, but great motivation to stay in recovery. His increasing comfort and joy in life were captured in black and white on the page. Jack could see the changes he had made in his behavior, feelings, and thinking. It was striking how much more in control he felt, how clear he was, and how much he enjoyed his new and old relationships. All this from slowing down. He marveled at how out of control he had become and that he couldn't see it.

15. Prepare for relapse. Relapse is harder to define with speed addiction than with alcohol and drug addiction, where you are either using or you are not using. With speed addiction you're looking for a middle ground, so it may be very hard to determine whether you're in recovery or not. Think about it: in this particular mood or situation I'm troubled by or find confusing, am I responding to a trigger for speed or am I behaving within my new limits? You will identify cravings, cues, and behaviors that are either triggers for you to speed up or that indicate you are already out of control. Then you watch carefully. The compulsive overeater knows that nibbling is an addictive behavior. Just one little bite, just one little taste, can set off the overeating compulsion. The compulsive overeater knows that structure is essential. You cannot trust yourself to know that you are full and you cannot nibble away all day long, believing you're not really eating.

With relapse prevention you need to pay attention to all three strands of the addiction necklace. You must focus on recovery behaviors and work to identify your faulty, addictive thinking and the emotions that will drive you back to being out of control. Keep those Twenty Guidelines handy. Remember: behavior, thinking, and emotion work together. You recognize that behavior can have a positive effect on thinking and feeling, particularly mood. Within a few weeks of minor behavioral changes Jack's mood improved radically. He wasn't as hyper or anxious as he had been. Slowing down even slightly quieted his mood.

You assess your methods of relaxation, if you've had any, and begin to include physical exercise, meditation, or relaxation tapes. You take time to sit or lie quietly for even a few minutes; you turn off your gadgets and darken the room. You actively arrange your environment to facilitate quiet and slowing down. As you recognize feelings of fear creeping in, you substitute a pleasant memory, go to a movie, think about positive people or events coming up, and tell yourself it's just one day at a time. Fear can drag you down. You actively work to channel it positively.

Here you are, beginning on the steps of small behavior change in your journey of recovery from speed addiction. At the beginning of this chapter you laughed, thinking "this is a snap," and then you saw that it's not so easy. We can glibly say we're going to make a change, but we don't do it. Now you've done it. You've seen how Jack's experience applies to you, you've completed the exercises, and you may even have your own Decision Box. Watch. You can change, one step at a time.

13

Feeling Emotion

You just looked closely at your behaviors of speed and to the environments and emotional triggers that set you off on a path of frenzy and loss of control. Now let's look at the emotions that can fuel impulsive behavior, and the new feelings you will come to experience and eventually to know as normal. These are the feelings that come with slowing down, not by force, not by reluctant will, but by an acceptance that slowing down is what you want and need.

Twenty Guidelines

YOUR FEELINGS:

6. You feel the reality of limits and face the feeling of failure.

7. You become aware of feelings and learn to listen to them.

8. You trust that the high of impulsive action is *not* the feeling you seek.

9. You develop a wider range of new feelings.

10. You come to trust that deep, intimate human "connection" exists in a slowed down, quiet state.

The first time people who are struggling with addiction walk into my office they are usually not feeling much at all, or at least they are not aware of feeling much. They often can't put a name to what they do feel. Others are feeling intensely, but usually they, too, can't put a name to these wild, painful emotions. During active addiction people are like infants emotionally, unable to reflect, driven by impulses that are responding to their bodies' sensations. An infant roots around desperately looking for milk because he feels the sensation of hunger intensely. An addict looks desperately for alcohol or heroin because he intensely feels the sensation of a different kind of hunger. Addiction brings front and center the primitive feelings of a baby and the quick, impulsive actions to satisfy the felt experiences of instinctual urgency, or craving.

So it is with the speed addict. The intense internal pressure to act, to move, to check your email, to text, to keep going, to work harder and longer is just like the infantile pressure the addict feels to get a drink or that piece of cake waiting in the fridge. You feel a hunger so desperate, so urgent that you can't stand it. Your muscles twitch, you even shake as you push away from your computer for the night. You can't stop because you'll be flooded with feelings—the worry you won't finish, the worry you can't keep up. So you take another look at your screen. You need to act to quiet the craving you feel all the time; rush, rush, rush. Get it done and on to the next task.

Addicts use impulsive and compulsive actions to avoid painful feelings: deep need, hunger, longing, envy, fear of loss, fear of not keeping up and falling behind, deprivation, anxiety—focused or floating, raw and shaking. These are frightening feelings, and addicts struggle to keep them from surfacing. This is what Jack was doing when he tried to cut back, to tweak his schedule in ways that would allow him to basically go at the same pace he had been going all along. He was very frightened of what he might see and feel if he really slowed down, so he cut back without making any fundamental change. This is what's going on when people get stuck in first-order change.

FACING THE REALITY OF YOUR LIMITS AND YOUR FAILURE

You have tried and tried and now you can't try any harder or any longer. You reach a point when you know—in your heart and in your gut—that you can't do it all and you never could. You come face-to-face with the reality of your human limits. At first you're not sure you can survive this shocking truth. It feels like ice water across your face, waking you up to a reality you've avoided recognizing forever. You can't do it all. That means you are a failure. You have worried for years that you couldn't keep up. That you couldn't be a player. That you wouldn't be chosen for the high-stakes team of fast living. Well, now it's true. You look at the guidelines in your lap and you focus in on number six: "You feel the reality of your limits and face the feeling of failure." You have a moment of clarity, a moment you are open to deep emotional truth: "Oh, this is it. This is hitting bottom. I can't do this anymore."

Have you been to this place? Have you felt the reality of your limits? Have you felt that you've failed as you always believed you would? Let yourself settle into a quiet state and think about the times in your life, in the past and now, when you've known deeply that you had limits and you'd reached them. Think about failure. Was that what you felt? What did you do? Did you ask for help? Did you change anything at that point? Did you push this feeling away and determine to keep going, to try harder? See if you can list these moments of clarity and what happened as you recognized your limits.

1. ....

2. ....

3. ....

4. ....

5. ....

THE EMOTIONS OF RECOVERY

When people hit bottom and hover on the edge of recovery, they feel all kinds of emotions. They generally feel anxious about changing their behavior. They may feel depressed at losing their closest companions—their gadgets, computer games, junk foods, drink, speed, the constant motion that they've known so long. They become jumpy, anxious without constant motion, without an incoming call. The emotions of active addiction—tension, agitation, vigilance, active craving, and withdrawal that comes with too long a pause—are omnipresent, and internal anxiety may dominate around the clock. Jack was sure he'd find himself revving up and getting wild again. His emotions felt out of control. Suddenly he had highs and lows of elation and despair—feelings he'd never let in before. He thought he was a pretty mellow guy. No feelings actually, which he thought was a plus. Then his impulses would take over; wham, do something, get online, keep going. Jack was living numbers seven through eleven of the Twenty Questions: Yes, he felt pressure to live fast and act fast. Yes, he felt empty if he wasn't in constant action. Yes, he felt nervous without his tech gear in his hand or pocket. Yes, he felt the beep of his phone as a comfort and an adrenaline rush. Yes, of course he felt he belonged when he was rushing, stressed, and in action. He had all the emotions of "hooked on fast." And yet he thought: "But isn't this normal? Isn't this what everyone feels?"

Emotion immediately connects with behavior and thinking. Individuals may first recognize their loss of control as a thought, a musing about the need for more, or awareness that their thumbs are moving automatically, waiting to receive the next text. They may push the thought away or chuckle at the knowledge of their thumbs standing by for action. They may begin to worry, to feel the panic that resides within.

In the beginning of recovery addicts often feel overwhelmed by emotion that they see as negative. They feel withdrawal and craving in their bodies. The extra time and space they have, which might be positive for some, scare them. Plus, they're not used to thinking or spending time in contemplation. They aren't numb anymore, so some won't feel empty inside, which opens up a whole jumble of feelings—welcome and unwelcome—as they come alive again. This is the time when numbers seven and eight of the Twenty Guidelines come into play. New recovery is a time of new feelings and of feeling for the first time. You become aware of what a feeling is and that you have some. If you let them be and don't push them all away in panic, you'll learn that you have lots of feelings. As you feel safer, you learn to listen to them.

Soon you begin to see the extraordinary value of slowing down. You have a big life going on inside of you that you've never known. You begin to look forward to quiet time so you can pay attention to your feelings and begin to give them names. You begin to believe and to trust that the high of impulsive action is not the feeling you seek anymore. You even come to see that impulse pulls you down and drives you away from your most important connection: yourself.

With your newfound emotional space, you begin to develop a wider range of feeling that doesn't send you into panic, even if these new emotions don't feel so good. You strengthen your behaviors of recovery, which now serve as a safety net for new feeling. If you feel a twinge of panic, a rush to get into motion, to binge on a texting spree, you pause and take a recovery action to stabilize yourself. You may even need a brief time-out. Your new feelings set off anxiety. Then when you're calm you can open up to feeling again. This is guideline number nine. You are expanding emotionally.

Have you had this experience yet? Think about your emotional world—what did you feel, if anything, in the throes of your high-stress, impulsive action? And what did you feel when you slowed down? What do you feel now in new recovery? Can you translate a body twitch that used to drive you crazy into a feeling? "You mean that ache in my neck was a sign of stress? I was overwhelmed and knew I couldn't do it all, but I kept going?" Now you know you are sad, happy, relieved, scared, or any one of many possible new feelings. Make a list of the old feelings you remember before you got lost in your speed addiction, then the feelings you had when

Feelings Before Speed	Feelings During Speed	Feelings in Recovery

you were caught up in speed, and third list the new feelings you have discovered since you slowed down.

Some of the common emotions you can expect in early recovery include heightened anxiety, shame at seeing how you lost control, and guilt about what you did or lost in your race for speed. Jack had trouble getting out of bed in the mornings when his boss first sent him home. The first time he and Maureen had friends over for dinner after his leave of absence started they asked what prompted him to take his leave. He was so embarrassed he found himself unable to tell them the truth. He mumbled something about always having wanted to explore some other options, and then he changed the subject. He also felt guilty when he couldn't afford to fly his parents out to see him or get his son all the new things he was used to buying for him. He felt like he had let them down. In a vicious circle this increased his anxiety and depression.

Raj had felt shame in his early recovery at least as intensely as Jack did. On one of the many nights he'd stayed late at work and drunk too much before heading home, he got in a fistfight. He took a swing at one of his colleagues and broke the colleague's nose. His co-worker came in to work the next day with a bandage, and Raj got a lot of funny sideways looks. He was able to avoid thinking about it by grabbing an early afternoon scotch, but when he began recovery there was no avoiding it. The memory of that incident was searingly present for him. Shame, guilt, and anxiety are frequent companions in early recovery.

In the first days you may feel frustration and anger as well when you can't stay in motion. You are developing a recovery action plan that gives you limits, and it's now your job to maintain them. It's understandable that you'll feel angry. You didn't want limits and you believed you didn't need them. What a rough reality to face your need for limits and your difficulty in meeting them. "These are the new feelings you get when you slow down? Who asked for these?"

Jack felt tremendous anger during his early recovery. He felt like an exploding bomb. He'd run on the treadmill at the gym and talk to himself. "What am I doing? Am I an idiot? Why did I think I had to slow down? Was I crazy? There's nothing wrong with me!" He'd find himself yelling at Maureen, blaming her for his out-of-control frenzied lifestyle. He'd accuse her: "You were one big interference, pushing me and demanding more and more. I'd be okay if you weren't such a nag." It was easier for him to be furious with her than to feel guilty about letting her down or to see that he was out of control and that was his problem.

You may also feel grief at the loss of the actions that you believed saved you, the speed that numbed your worry and desperation, even if this pace eventually took you under. As time passes you may also experience mourning as you accept the reality of the loss and your commitment to slowing down. You are not waiting until you can run fast and high again. You are not taking a time-out from speed. You are saying good-bye.

The good news is that you will probably experience a welcome feeling of relief that you saw the reality and you are facing it. Once you know, you know. The fight is over. With time your sense of relief will likely grow. What does it feel like to slow down? Hard at first, but if you shift your attention to yourself, your family, community, or the other things you used to love, you may find that you reclaim an inner calm and quiet that you lost in your chase for speed. Maybe you never realized you lost it until you got it back. You may begin to feel a deep and unwavering sense of grounding, a new connection to yourself and to others that you remember from the past, or that you are feeling for the first time. You recognize you've found number ten in the guidelines: you do feel like you belong, but this connection comes from within you, and it only exists within a slowed-down way of life. You can only feel this deep bond with yourself, others, and humanity when you can be quiet, reflective, and focused within.

This is what Jack says about his experience. "I've come to accept and value my feelings and to know what they are. I can actually name them and appreciate what a range of emotion we all have. I've worked to allow my feelings to come up and to let them be. Then I get to see what's behind them. Feelings really tell you a lot and it's not always good. But it's being able to feel that has given me a whole new sense of myself."

Over time adjusted recovery will mean a balance between emotion, behavior, and thinking. You will have more internal space for thought and contemplation, both of yourself and your life—relationships, work, and intellectual, social, and physical pursuits. When you are less driven to action you will have more space for both emotion and thinking. Initially threatening, your developing capacity for a greater range of emotion and thinking will ultimately put you back on the normal developmental path you left behind or put aside with your focus on speed.

CORE OF CONNECTION

Importantly, emotion is not just feeling. It is also the core of your connection with yourself and your deepest link to others, as you noted above in guideline number ten. You had felt alone and lonely, missing a connection with others that you knew must exist, must be possible. You'd seen others who looked engaged. But you believed it would never happen for you. Even when you got hooked on speed, chasing a feeling of human connection, you didn't find it. Sometimes you convinced yourself you had it. And sometimes you did, as you participated in deeper conversations with people online. But this connection faded. It was illusive and almost always caused you disappointment. You long to feel part of the human race.

This felt experience of being emotionally in tune with others provides the necessary base for healthy individual development. It's paradoxical, too. We grow our healthiest selves through connection and interaction with others. The individual cannot grow without relationship, yet the pressures for speed are dramatically interrupting and changing the kind and depth of what is possible and acceptable in relationship. The biggest danger—what makes chasing speed an addiction—is the shift in core emotional attachment from people to pods, from mutual interdependent relationships to a primary attachment to technology for connection, and the fast pace to control it.

In new recovery you will put the emotions of speed into second or third place as you direct the same intense feelings into new behaviors and soon into new thinking. The fear will subside as you begin to slow down and learn how to sustain a slower pace and stay away from speed. You will no longer feel yourself hooked on an

Connection Before Speed	Connection During Speed	Connection in Recovery

intense emotional reaction, fueled by strong feelings of inadequacy and fear or the opposite feelings of defensive entitlement and superiority. These extremes of emotion will find a middle ground, tempered by the emotional containment you now experience. Your new behaviors and thinking lead to emotional restraint and emotional moderation. You will no longer be driven by the impulses of a four-year-old. You will be developing a capacity to engage with people beyond the parallel play of toddlers and preschoolers. You will learn or relearn the give and take of conversation and you will experience empathy for others. That, too—the ability to feel what others are feeling—is a basis for true connection.

What are you feeling as you read about emotion and especially connection? Is this you? Have you lost true connection and have you now found it again as you slowed down? Think about times you felt deeply connected to others in your past, before speed. What was your sense of connection like during speed, and what is connection like for you now?

COPING WITH UNPREDICTABLE EMOTIONS

How do you deal with emotion early on? Redirect it to new recovery behaviors. First is action. More of the same, only now you have a new object. If you can't stop twitching, moving toward your computer, or turning your gaze downward in search of your smartphone, put something else in its place. Roll a ball or a stone in your fingers, and keep a pen and paper close by to doodle furiously until your craving subsides.

Put that emotion on paper! Write what you're feeling. Let it pour out, even if it scares you. Get it down and out of you. You can read it or not. Keep it or not. It's the shift in focus to new action that counts now. As action absorbs the intensity, you will begin to feel safer and calmer. Shania used this technique a lot when she first came to see me. She wrote down all the conversations she had been having with me in her mind during the year she contemplated beginning therapy. Sometimes she would bring these sheets of paper with her to help her remember the overwhelming array of feelings she had experienced between our sessions. And sometimes she just threw them out. Either way, the writing helped her cope with the intensity of emotion.

Reach out, talk with another. Talk about what is real, how fast you have been going, and how out of control you became. The experience of sharing with another is calming. It also gives you a compatriot in developing new behavioral strategies to slow down.

People lose themselves in addiction, merged as they are with the object or behavior of their desire. Part of what they lose is the ability to feel. Or to know what they are feeling. As they enter recovery and let go of the addictive object or behavior, a plethora of emotions rushes into the newly emptied space. This is frightening, so frightening that it stalls many people temporarily and some permanently. But the possibility of welcome emotions waits for them on the other side of the tumult. As they recover, as they have the time and ability to reflect, they can experience relief, contentment, even joy—a very different emotion than feeling high. Though they may have consequences to deal with such as job struggles, relationships that need attention and repair, and neglected physical well-being that will bring worry, they also have the grounding to deal with them. The emotional breadth and depth makes it easier to sustain the behavior changes they are working on, and along with the bigger emotional repertoire comes the ability to think more clearly. They know that, having started with number six—feeling the reality of their limits and the failure that meant, they moved to numbers seven, eight, nine, and ten, and as a result they are no longer out of control of their feelings, and no longer frightened of their emotions.

14

New Ways of Thinking

We've looked at two strands of our addiction recovery neck-lace, challenging and changing our behavior in recovery, and growing into accepting our feelings and expanding the range of emotion we can know and experience. Now it's time for think-ing, the strand of the necklace that often gets overlooked in under-standing and treating addiction. We still think we just have to focus on our behavior and, bingo, that will be it. "Just do it," we keep coaching ourselves. But then we remember that there's more to it.

We saw that thinking is a major part of active addiction and it's a major part of recovery. We will come to change our deepest beliefs and values about the way we are and the way we think we should be. Let's look at our big list of nine guidelines for thinking in recovery.

Twenty Guidelines

YOUR THINKING:

11. You believe in the reality of limits.

12. You learn to recognize and challenge your belief in entitlement.

13. You challenge your belief in willpower.

14. You believe in the value of small steps and a slower sense of time.

15. You believe in a new definition of success: your best effort within a structure of limits.

16. You believe in the value of delay, endurance, and the concept of "enough."

17. You believe that growth and change are not instant; that "quick fixes" reinforce the thinking of fast and impulsive action.

18. You believe in the value and necessity of reflection as a part of health and success.

19. You challenge your all-or-none thinking.

When Raj stopped drinking, opened up to his feelings, and started in AA, his thinking began to change. He began to see how much he had distorted his thinking into strange channels in order to justify his drinking. Raj laughs as he recalls telling his wife that the extra shots he had before bed were good for his sleep. He said the true meaning of *nightcap* is to knock yourself out. If you're too speedy, too wired and driven, how can you expect to say good night and trundle off to bed for a blissful sleep? Raj decided his extra drinks also helped his thinking. By the end of a day, he felt overwhelmed with the day's information. "Have a drink, relax, and clear your mind," he'd say. Well, if the before-dinner (at 9:00 or 10:00 p.m.) drinks were good, that nightcap would seal the deal. He'd wake up clearheaded and ready to go once again. Raj convinced himself that drinking helped his thinking.

AA calls this "stinkin' thinkin'." As Raj progressed in AA and became clearer in his thinking he began to see that he was using the same kind of stinkin' thinkin' to justify the perverse pace of his life and work. Raj hadn't believed he had limits in anything. There was nothing he couldn't do. He was a wild, raging success. Wild and raging, yes. Success? Raj didn't think so anymore. As he became healthier and clearer in his thinking, success began to mean something different to him. Number fifteen he could readily quote: "I do my best within my limits."

He began to see that for him success had been money and status. Rather than being motivated by passion and drive to stand for something, he saw that he had been motivated by greed. It drove him, but it didn't lead to any satisfaction. As his thinking became clearer he saw that success included other dimensions such as his relationships with his family and friends. That's what really fed him, unlike chasing money, which never fed him at all. It was an addiction. Many things take on different meanings as you break the choke hold of the addiction necklace. As with changing behavior and emotion, changing thinking is a process that takes time. In recovery, thinking will deepen and grow clearer in the context of new awareness and new beliefs. It will grow within the paradox of having accepted loss of control and failure as the foundation for a new definition of success.

COGNITION

The third component of human function—the third strand of the addiction necklace—is cognition. Sometimes cognition, or thinking, dominates human experience, preceding behavior and emotion, and sometimes thinking comes last because intense feeling and impulsive actions overwhelm the ability to think. In recovery, thinking becomes integrated with feeling and action.

When primitive feeling and impulse become the dominant force for an individual, thinking becomes confused, distorted, or submerged in the emotion and out-of-control behaviors. Who can think straight under these circumstances? Because the addict needs to explain to himself what is happening, he uses faulty reasoning to rationalize the need to drink, use drugs, or work eighteen-hour days. His thinking has become distorted in the service of maintaining an out-of-control lifestyle.

CHANGING YOUR THINKING

Recovery both requires and results in new ways of thinking. It involves accepting the value of limits and structure, appreciating the value of slowing down behaviorally, and moderating emotion instead of living with wild extremes of emptiness or elation and the impulsive actions that follow. As we know, our culture mitigates against this. Taking time to think things through is often referred to in political, social, and business realms as "dithering" or is even seen as high-risk behavior. The cultural norm still highlights the need for speed. "You don't want to stop to think for too long or you'll lose out." Taking time to think sends a message that you're uncertain, ambivalent, not a strong leader. These feelings or states of mind are still viewed as negative, rather than normal parts of a complex experience or state of affairs. In recovery you will be going against the direction of the culture as you come to see traits such as delay, endurance, patience, and restraint as positive, something to be sought, rather than evidence of failure or loss of competitive edge. "Look at those guidelines!" Jack says now. "My thinking has changed so much, but it didn't happen overnight. I couldn't buy an app and plug it in. No instant anything. But now numbers eleven through nineteen are all true for me most of the time." Jack means he has been through a process of radical change and new development and now he likes it a lot. When he first met Raj, Jack could say yes to most of the Twenty Questions and be proud of his drive for success. Now he can say yes to most, or even all, of the Twenty Guidelines for Slowing Down and marvel at how he used to think and what it cost him. Jack thought all he ever needed was the next new thing, the next gadget, the next app to answer every question he ever had and to solve every problem. Jack felt sad as he realized he kept giving away any need for his intelligence, his ability to think things through. Jack had outsourced his thinking. Now he would take it back. Jack came to see that he had made faith in technology his higher power. Now he saw that technology could be a great tool, but not his god or even his driver. As Jack changed his thinking to match the guidelines, he saw that the problems he'd had with speed and the solutions he'd found were within him not with his technology. Jack learned that technology is neutral, neither good nor bad on its own. He's got the responsibility, not his iPhone, his datebook, or his iPad.

Not long ago an organizational consultant who works with speedy corporate executives told me that I couldn't propose slowing down because the executives wouldn't hear it. They wouldn't like it so they would reject my suggestions. They would say, "Tell me how to get my people to work faster, harder, smarter. That's what we've hired you for!" At some point even, and especially, corporate executives must ask, "What am I doing?" Until then we focus on ourselves and the small steps we can take each day that will help us become slower, thoughtful, reflective people who can listen and engage in old-fashioned conversation. We might even identify as speed addicts in recovery who, like Jack, now embrace numbers eleven through nineteen of the guidelines.

WHAT IT'S LIKE NOW: EMBRACING THE GUIDELINES OF THINKING IN RECOVERY

You, like Jack, are a speed addict in recovery. You look at the list about thinking and start with number eleven. Yes, it's true, you say. Just like I felt the reality of my limits when I hit bottom, I now believe in the reality of my limits and think of the reality of my limits as a deep part of me. I've got limits on my behavior, and I've got limits in my heart. My soul and my brain matter. Now when I'm thinking big I remind myself that I've got limits. Maybe I can see them now, or maybe they'll come to splash at me like ice water down the road. But I've got to know that there are limits, and I've got to accept them as I can see them.

What about you? Do you believe in limits? Do you have limits? What are they? Spend some time on this exercise. Keep a pad close by or a file on your iPhone to list your limits as you come to recognize them. Keep it simple.

What Are My Limits?

1. ....

2. ....

3. ....

4. ....

5. ....

What Can I Do to Accept and Live Within My Limits?

1. ....

2. ....

3. ....

4. ....

5. ....

Next you go to number twelve. "Do I really think I'm entitled? I never would have signed on for this guideline when I was wildly out of control with speed. I would have been pissed off with you for even thinking that. But now it's so clear. I really did, and sometimes still do, think I'm entitled. It comes out in subtle ways, but it's there. I shouldn't have to stand in line like everybody else. I should have first dibs for the new computers at work. After all I'm important. I cringe to say that, but it's how I'm thinking. Why do I have to do the mundane things of life? Okay, so I pay somebody, but I can't pay someone to tie my shoes. I have to do some things for myself, but I really do have disdain for it. It doesn't feel good to see this. I'm beginning to understand why parents in my kid's playgroup said I'm arrogant. I can see it and I can see I need to work hard to challenge it."

What about you? Have you believed you were entitled? Where did that belief come from and how did it work for you? In recovery, when you recognize your limits, you might feel chagrined. It's painful to see that you are arrogant and entitled and you couldn't recognize it. Turn to your notepad, then write how you thought you were entitled and special, and explore ways to challenge these beliefs. Take your time and keep it simple.

How Was I Entitled and Special?

1. ....

2. ....

3. ....

4. ....

5. ....

What Do I Do Now to Recognize and Challenge This Belief?

1. ....

2. ....

3. ....

4. ....

5. ....

You move down the list to number thirteen. This is really tough and continues to be hard as you slow down. You have always believed that it was your force of will that got you where you are, or your failure of will that stopped you. Now you're coming to grips with a new way of thinking. You accept that you do have willpower and you need it to help you slow down, but you don't have *all* the power you need to stay slowed down, just like you haven't had the willpower to stay on your diet or to cut down on your spending. So now you accept that you have limits and you begin to live and work within them. You won't use your willpower or your defenses to overcome them. No doubt this is hard and tricky. It's a huge source of conflict in the culture. So start with a list again and take it in small doses.

Do I Believe in Willpower Without Limits? Do I Think I Can Use Willpower to Conquer Anything?

....

....

....

....

....

How Do I Remember and Remind Myself That I Don't Have All the Power?

....

....

....

....

....

How Do I Accept That I Need Help?

....

....

....

....

Now you look at number fourteen. These guidelines were hard to comprehend as you began to change, but now you're saying yes. You have changed. Now you know that it is small steps that accumulate to bigger change and that these small steps unfold within a slower sense of time. You're quiet inside, taking time to reflect and move away from your action-only mode. Everything is not *now*. Everything is not already late. Slow time creates calm internally and surprisingly lets you think clearly again. How does this fit for you?

List Three Reasons or Experiences You've Had That Convinced You Change Unfolds in Small Steps:

1. ....

2. ....

3. ....

List Three Reasons or Experiences You've Had That Helped You Value a Slower Sense of Time:

1. ....

2. ....

3. ....

So, success is no longer full speed ahead? Number fifteen in the guidelines gives you a new definition of success. It took you a while after you faced your limits to see the paradoxes in this whole business of change. Success is no longer power-drive until you drop and you still have more to do. You now define success as your best effort within your limits. This is a view of success, and progress, too, that doesn't defy limits, but rather embraces them.

Try this one out:

Can you give your very best, your all, and can you stop when you can't go any faster or any further and you can't take any short-cuts? You begin to know your limits.

Have you faced your limits like this? When? What happened? Have you come to value your limits?

"Oh no, here comes number sixteen," you say. "I have come to believe in the value of delay, that everything should not be instant, and I've learned to endure, which mostly means I can't have it all, this minute, when I want it, and how I want it. I am not two years old, after all. I've learned to wait. And then there's the concept of enough. Not so long ago I would have said, 'Are you kidding?!?' There's never enough. There's always more—more money to make, more things to buy, more to explore and experience." Yes, it's true.

There is more, but now the pursuit of more is not what drives you. You have a deep sense that you have what you need. You have enough. It may rarely feel that way to you as you're pushing deadlines and trying to get everything done, but as you've accepted your limits and a slower sense of time, you begin to recognize that catching up and pursuit of more are not the passions that drive you anymore. You have learned to pause, and even to stop and to know that you've done enough, you've had enough, or you've spent enough. It's a new feeling and a good feeling now.

What do you think about delay, endurance, and the concept of enough? Does my description of these traits and beliefs resonate or are you laughing at the foolishness of such ideas?

List some recent experiences when you've had to wait. How did you respond? What did you feel and what did you think? If you had trouble seeing yourself as entitled in number twelve, this guideline might get you there.

1. ....

2. ....

3. ....

Now, what about "enough?" "Reeeally," you say. "Maybe time could slow down, but there still won't be enough of it." See if you can remember a moment, an hour, a day when you were slow, time was slow, and you felt at peace. In that moment, you had enough. That's what I'm talking about. You will never think you have enough if you are always catching up, always going fast and faster. You'll just run out of gas and feel like you've failed.

List Three Memories, Even Years Ago, When You Felt You Had Enough, That You Were Enough:

1. ....

2. ....

3. ....

This is a long list, you want to say to me. I know. Getting to number seventeen was a huge challenge. You just couldn't slow down, wait, endure as you worked to face your addiction to speed. Everything is instant, was all you could think. Progress is problem solving and quick fixes. But that thinking just led you to move faster and resort to more impulsive actions. You had to be leveled many times in order to really get that growth, change, progress, and success are not all quickies. Life is not a checklist.

List Three Times You Faced the Truth That Change Is Slow:

1. ....

2. ....

3. ....

You come to number eighteen only when you've faced number seventeen. You can't deeply believe in the value of reflection if you're still chasing instant everything. In seeing the value of reflection, you embrace the paradox that slowing down, focusing inward, and reflecting are not part of failure, but rather part of a new success. You are calm, quiet, thoughtful instead of knee-jerk impulsive. Can you check off as many things to do as you used to?

No. But paradoxically, what you do, you may do better, with more depth and greater understanding. Is there a time for fast? Yes, but not always.

Now think about—reflect—on why you value reflection as a part of health and success. What happened?

List Three Examples of How Reflection Resulted in Something Good, Important, or Vastly Different For You Than a Quick Fix Would Have Yielded:

1. ....

2. ....

3. ....

Here we are at number nineteen, the last of our thinking changes. It's back to that old problem of all-or-none thinking. In the old days, when you were speeded up and chasing fast, you believed that yes or no was the highest form of thinking. Decide and then you know. Decide and then get moving. There's nothing but dithering around when you can't make a decision or come to an answer. Not anymore. Now you feel liberated by the flexibility of many different points of view and many yeses as well as maybes. If you now embrace complexity, you will slow down. You simply can't jump to an answer if you're going to understand the ins and outs and shades of gray on a particular matter. The old you would have said this was a waste of precious time, a filibuster on constant action. Now you say it's your default. You don't want to jump to quick, uninformed answers. You want time to think it over.

**List Three More Examples of When You Found That
Reflection Helped You:**

1. ....

2. ....

3. ....

There is one more guideline of our twenty, which we'll meet in chapter fifteen. Now let's look at how you'll resist these changes and how some of the people we've met in the book overcame their best efforts at defense.

UNDERSTANDING YOUR DEFENSES

Defense mechanism is the psychological label for the hierarchy of cognitive mechanisms, or ways of thinking and reasoning, that we all use to help us achieve internal peace in a complex world. These are the same defense mechanisms we outlined in chapter six to help us understand how reality gets erased, distorted, or re-written to help us cope or just survive. These defenses can work for or against us in recovery as well. We use defenses to explain difficult things to ourselves. They are normal and useful—until we use them to override or circumvent realities we need to face. This is what addicts do. When you're actively addicted, you're not paying much attention to your defenses. How you think is how you think, and don't mess with it. But understanding your defenses is part of what you will do as you change your thinking in recovery.

You'll recall that repression and denial are two common defense mechanisms. They are primitive in the sense they blot out

reality. Repression is simply blocking something out of your awareness. You don't see or hear the danger of something. Denial is
similar, though you can register a reality—you just don't pay attention to it or give it any credence. You smoke knowing it can cause
cancer, but you deny it could happen to you. It simply doesn't alarm
you enough to get you to change your behavior. You deny your fear
or you tell yourself the danger doesn't apply to you.

We can see these defenses at work in Gina, the fashion designer and buyer from New York who started a business as a personal organizer and consultant when she moved to San Francisco.
If you will remember, she became clinically depressed, went back
to her speedy lifestyle after treatment, and then ended up addicted
to alcohol and diagnosed with chronic fatigue syndrome. As she
recovered from alcoholism she finally recognized her addiction to
speed as well. It was then that she saw the way she had been living
with denial. She knew deep inside that her frantic lifestyle was so
stressful it was driving her to drink and making her sick, but she
wanted the American definition of success so badly she chose to
ignore how miserable she felt. When she finally entered recovery,
she noticed how constantly she used denial. Gina told herself day
after day she was pursuing her dream and her eighteen-hour workdays were not taking a toll on her. She was not tired, not grumpy,
and not stressed! This is what it takes for success, she'd tell her
husband. So she ignored the mistakes she was making in her bill-
ing and that she was behind in every aspect of her life. Gina told
herself this is what successful people have to deal with! You never
get it all done!

Once in recovery she began to respect the reality of her limits.
If she took on one task too many, or two or three tasks too many,
and she started to feel her stomach tighten and wanted to reach for
a drink, she would stop and think. She no longer told herself she

could handle one more day like this, that she was tough and it wouldn't get to her. Gina says now, "I have limits."

Rationalization is a particularly strong defense in staying on a path of speed. You say you have no choice, you can't stop because you need the money. Who can argue? You must work ninety hours to stay on the corporate ladder or get the big bonus. This is what Anita did when she and Felipe returned from the vacation when she felt unbearably agitated by the slowed-down pace. She dove full-scale into work again, but she rationalized she had no choice if she wanted to feed her family. Jack did the same thing until his enforced leave became the wall he hit.

In recovery you remind yourself slowing down is good for you as it keeps you from being out of control. Ironically, others who don't want you to slow your pace, set limits, or abandon the chase, may see you as rationalizing your "laziness." Unless you are strong in your resolve and you've got that compatriot to back you up, you may land in a funk, suddenly uncertain about the wisdom of slowing down since it looks like you're a lazy quitter. It's very difficult to step off a bandwagon in a culture that sees any slowdown as a betrayal and a failure.

Projection is when you are feeling something uncomfortable and you attribute it to somebody else. You are cold so you tell your child to put a sweater on. Not long after Sherrie and her husband decided to spend a weekend a month without technology, focused on their relationship, she began to feel angry at him. She was having a tough time staying away from her computer and she lashed out at him for making unreasonable demands on her, even though she had readily entered the agreement. As time went on Sherrie was able to short-circuit this defense. She stopped to think and was able to identify her own feeling, her fear of the emptiness she was finding as she slowed down. With recovery you will learn to identify and accept your own thoughts and feelings. You are afraid of stopping and you know it. You learn what you think and feel, and you learn to deal with it all.

Isolation, automatism, and selective inattention are mechanisms that have been viewed as psychological defenses, which help people deal with internal anxieties, conflicts, and interpersonal difficulties. With speed these defenses become so constant they become part of a person's character. People living a frenzied lifestyle are more isolated, focused on automatic, rote, and robotic thinking and behaviors, and reflexively selective in attention. People stop listening to others. They skim for width of information rather than depth. They pick out bytes of information rather than integrating a whole.

When Jack began to accept limits he challenged his defensive isolation. As part of his recovery plan Jack started making time at work to talk to others in person. Jack used to believe that reducing the need for human contact was progress, so of course he felt anxious in person and was sure that people were annoyed that they had to talk to him directly. Surely they felt that human interaction was a waste of time, not a positive use of it. It was so much more efficient to push a button and press a key. Still, Jack made it a priority to speak directly to people, and it got easier as Jack practiced making one personal contact a day. Seemingly a small step, this one personal contact felt like climbing Mount Everest. What difference could one contact make? But as Jack did take that first step, stopping to chat with just one person, he redefined personal contact as value added. Jack followed guideline number three—he took the small steps—and his thinking changed.

One phone call moves you away from isolation back into personal connection. An interaction or a project that involves you in dialogue or exchange requires you to listen more carefully. You must turn on your attention, activating your thinking and your feelings. You will work to modify your selective inattention. First, as soon as you recognize you've drifted away from listening, you jolt yourself back to the present reality of interaction. You keep pulling yourself out of your personal reverie, where you may be thinking ahead to what you'll say, or planning the menu for the next week. You want to listen, so you interrupt yourself at the first sign and get back into engagement. At the same time you learn to screen out a lot of noise—the constant buzz of your gadgets and the beeps that interrupt your focus. You learn to concentrate on your own internal thoughts and feelings, to read longer passages or engage in dialogue that deepens as you talk. These two changes may seem contradictory, but they're not. You pull yourself out of the defenses of inattention to enable you to pay closer and longer attention to another person or your own internal process. You're moving yourself away from a norm of interruption and distraction either way.

This is so retro, you say! Nobody sits down to talk in depth anymore. Precisely. This is a big part of what is wrong and a big part of what needs to change.

The change in thinking doesn't happen all at once. The change in thinking progresses over time and maintaining it is a lifelong process. Jack is aware that he still has to be watchful because he knows he still readily distorts or twists his reasoning to fit his needs of the moment. Jack laughed as he caught himself suddenly zooming into high energy and high emotion the minute his late meeting was canceled. Jack's internal *go* alarm sounded, and he was off in instant-speed gear to cram as many tasks into this unexpected gift of time as he could. Jack was on supercharge, telling himself that he had to seize this moment or be a slacker. Then Jack laughed. "Look at me! Look how quickly I grabbed the speed mentality and shot myself out of the cannon. That impulse is still there, just waiting for the trigger to set me off. Luckily I paused and laughed. I was only on the high for ten minutes and that was enough to prove to me that I don't want this speedy life anymore."

Jack can pause when his wife gently suggests he is not seeing himself clearly, that maybe he has a vested interest in staying confused about what is a reasonable time frame for slowing down. Sometimes Jack knows exactly what *reasonable* means and sometimes he hasn't a clue. As he tries to justify adding back work hours, he gets muddled and confused about what slowing down really looks like. Jack often tells himself he's cut back too much, that he really could reinstate a few more tasks and meetings. He could add back the hour online he cut out when he first started talking with Raj. Jack has to watch his automatic urge to get back into fast action.

Jack knows Maureen is usually on to him and he quickly asks himself, "What am I doing?" Jack has gotten good at recognizing his "conflicts of interest"—he wants to be a slowed-down speed addict in recovery and he wants to jump on the bandwagon as fast as he can so he won't be left out and miss the deal—and the defenses he still uses to deny any problem. But now he can laugh when he recognizes his denial and rationalization working away.

"I know that internal conflict is normal, but I struggle when I want too many things at once or when I want opposites I can't have. I see how I used to rationalize staying on the computer till the wee hours, believing I had to finish the work and that I was enjoying it. Neither was true. I wanted to be a success in my company and yet I could never work as hard or as long as I thought was necessary to be a success. I need to watch my thinking all the time. I want to know that I'm rationalizing and to think about whether it's harmful to me or not. I know I'll deny—we all do, and sometimes it's very helpful—and that I'll reason my way into a position that suits me, and I'll project, too. Sometimes it's funny and sometimes I'm embarrassed. But now that I am aware of my defenses, I can make a truly honest decision and be responsible for it."

SEEING SHADES OF GRAY

Throughout this book I have emphasized dichotomous thinking as a core feature of addiction. The belief that you are either a success or a failure, a winner or a loser, will drive you to stay in motion. If you are caught in dichotomous thinking, you might think you are being asked to embrace the opposite of frenzied speed with no limits. You tried to do everything before so now you'll do nothing. This thinking, often believed to be the way smart people operate, is actually false and dangerous when you're a grown-up living in a complex world. Very few complicated decisions can be boiled down to yes or no without careful thought to the multiple factors involved and the potential costs. Yes, we all must make quick decisions everyday, but we also should be considering the complexities, the plusses and minuses of many other decisions we must make. Yes, pausing to think things through takes time, and you'll likely fight the wisdom of waiting. But, in fact, all-or-none thinking often stimulates fear that you'll be out on the street. If there are only two alternatives to outcome, you'll believe you must keep going, trying harder and harder, or face the threat of losing everything. Dichotomous thinking doesn't allow for the possibility that there is something in the middle. The all-or-none thinker lives on the extremes. You've got it right or wrong. You're a winner or a loser. A woman in treatment said she always feared she'd be a bag lady if she gave up trying so hard.

Pay attention to what you say to yourself and others. Be conscious of falling victim to all-or-none thinking. "Wait," you say. "I just think the way I think. How can I recognize I'm into my right-or-wrong mode? When I'm there it's right or I'm looking for right—just one way, one answer, and that's it." Well, how about watching yourself closely this week, and if you're comfortable, ask your partner or a friend to watch with you. Together you're going to see if you can begin to bring your rigid thinking into your awareness. So ask yourself: "When am I in the mode of all or none? What was I thinking—and what did I say?" It's the same as the mantra you've learned throughout the book, the key to becoming aware: you pause and ask yourself, "What am I doing?" As you begin to find examples of your all-or-none thinking, list them below. The more you see, the better able you'll become to interrupt your rigid way of seeing the world. Never mind that this preference for certainty and false simplicity is the main mode of thinking all around you.

Examples of All-or-None Thinking:

1. ....

2. ....

3. ....

4. ....

5. ....

As you become consciously aware of your most common dichotomies, ask yourself what will happen if you loosen your grip on these either-or choices? "When I'm feeling so terrified, I do believe I have to keep working my eighteen-hour days or I'll be on the street, a bag lady who's lost it all." Now begin to rewrite other possibilities in between. See if you can chip away at the extremes by filling out a middle ground of gray. Yes, you might not get the promotion you're after next year, but you won't lose your job, you won't lose your salary, and your husband and kids will be so happy to have you home on the weekends. Can you settle into this new alternative as a viable option?

It might be easy if we only had to deal with thinking. Of course, you tell yourself, just be realistic. But we have those pesky emotions and old beliefs that won't yield to reason. So we also look at our emotions and deep beliefs at the same time. It's the deeper fears that may keep us stuck in the all-or-none bind. See if you can write a new scenario for your worst binds and then add the emotions that keep you from trying out a middle ground. This is tough to do and takes time. Ideally, this kind of reflection will become a practice you'll value and use forever.

What New Scenarios That Diffuse the Extremes of All-or-None Can I Try Out?

1. ....

2. ....

3. ....

As touched upon earlier, dichotomous thinking is the normal stage for children between eight and twelve years of age. It is concrete, a way of thinking and seeing the world that gives certainty, or at least an illusion of certainty. So for kids there are good people and bad people, and you stay away from the bad people. For many adolescents it's the new extreme that you're either on the advanced track, working toward success, or you're goofing off, destined to be turned down at the best schools. For adults you're either solving a problem or you're making one. It's the old "you're either with us or against us," even if no such extreme exists.

The highest level of thinking, abstract, begins to develop in children at about the same time as puberty—ten, eleven, or twelve years of age. Abstract thinking allows for complexity, for shades of gray and uncertainty. This expansion and deepening of cognitive abilities also deepens emotion as the adolescent faces new feelings and impulses arising from the hormonal changes of puberty. Many of these new thoughts and feelings are frightening. The adolescent and the adult may move to rapid motion and out-of-control actions to temper these threatening experiences. Growing into a capacity to embrace and live in complexity of thought and feeling, without containing them through impulsive and compulsive actions, is a cornerstone of maturity.

With your new acceptance of limits and your reliance on your new environments and structures that support and reinforce slowing down and containment, you will find a new interest in contemplating alternatives, mixed possibilities, feelings, or ways of seeing things. The new safety you feel in not having instant answers lets you open to nuance and richness of meanings you could not allow yourself to think about before. The world truly is bigger, wider, deeper, and safer when you are not out of control.

Ambivalence is not a dirty word. When people are thinking clearly, they see things from several vantage points and may feel positively and negatively about the same thing. Internal conflict is not a sign of immaturity or lack of resolve or strength. As you progress in recovery this becomes more obvious to you. You do not have to figure out what you think or take a stand on everything.

You do not have to live by the mantra "you're either with us or against us." That level of decisiveness is not necessary or desirable for many areas of life. Taking time to understand complexities will lead you to much more thoughtful and realistic answers. Impulsive action to prove you're not a wuss will often cost you now and later on.

Shania, who was climbing the corporate ladder and couldn't stop her pressured rise to the top, eventually got to recovery and, over time, to a whole new way of thinking. It took her a year of mulling it over to ask for help, and even when she called me for therapy, it took a long time for her to accept that she had limits and had to slow down. But she eventually understood deeply her addiction to speed and her thinking became more complex. She used to demean her colleagues who took breaks, who chatted with each other in the halls, or who went home to dinner. Shania used to say, "It's all or none. You're either working hard on the road to success or you're falling behind and you're a loser. There was just one direction for me: up. I had an image of myself high in the clouds, flying and passing all you schmucks.

"I was devastated when I began to make professional mistakes and my colleagues challenged me. I tried slowing down, but it took me a long time to really get it that I was addicted. As I progressed in recovery, I slowed down for real. I saw that I didn't have to be the star of the company to be a good-enough person or to be happy. As a result I felt much more energized at work and I quit making the mistakes that were sabotaging me. I used to laugh at the guidelines, but there's so much I now believe. Entitlement? No, I'm not special and that's wonderful. Willpower? Right. There are limits to what I can control, how long I can work, and how much I can power-on. Delay? You mean pause to reflect, to give something time? Delay because it was prudent, smart? Never! But now I pause first, and it's a great help. The action I do take is less likely to be impulsive and driven by instinct and emotion."

MAKING NEW MEANINGS

As Jack understood his defenses and was able to think in new ways, many things in his life took on new meanings. When Jack decided to take time for making one personal contact each day at work, over time he came to see that his thinking had been distorted. He had long believed that talking with people was a waste of precious time—the more time he could spend with his computer, the more productive he would be. The more he practiced his new behavior, the more value he assigned to relationships. He began to see that he needed to redefine what a workday should be, and would be for him, so he would have periods of quiet and time for interaction with his wife, child, and his peers at work.

He decided that his feelings of intense internal emotional pressure and speed were no longer a sign of progress and success, but rather evidence that he'd become out of control and was actually failing on every front. Jack realized that talking with people in person had slowed him down, a terrible flaw in the race for speed. But he also saw the paradox: while talking with people slowed him down, really listening instead of rushing to get to the point also calmed him down. Speaking live reawakened an old feeling of connection based on an experience of mutual understanding, an experience of *engagement* that filled him with satisfaction. Though at first he felt antsy making these slower connections, he came to see that he could think, feel, and behave in a clearer and more productive way than he ever could when he was so driven by internal pressure, fear, and speed, even when these conversations were difficult or negative. Jack, like so many, soon saw that he had stopped listening to people on the Internet or in person. He was always preoccupied with his next move, so he missed the benefits of connected interaction.

Jack also redefined his relationship to time, deciding that time was not out to get him. Jack used to believe that he was in a race *against* time. He bet himself about how long a call would take and how much time he could shave off before he could say good-bye and rush back to his real work. Jack smugly gave himself a thumbs-up when he hung up minutes ahead of his estimate. "I'm a winner again," he'd say, not realizing he'd barely made contact with the person he'd been talking with. Months later, when he was practicing listening to his clients, he felt a wave of embarrassment—he hadn't been a winner at all in beating the clock. He'd been a loser for not making good client connections.

Jack thought time was the big hulk, an oppressor out to get him. In fact, time is neutral. In moments of clarity Jack knows he has all the time he needs, a truth he cannot see or feel when he is driven. Under pressure time becomes the grim reaper or the coach who is ready to throw him out of the game if he can't keep up. There is never enough time, and no matter how fast you go, you can't catch up. Time is the enemy, an opponent he must outsmart.

As Jack settled into recovery and began to challenge his all-or-none thinking, he could also challenge his worldview that everything is a contest. You are always out to win. Nothing is neutral, everything will get you if you let down your guard. This oppositional attitude comes directly from dichotomous thinking. If you are right, somebody's got to be wrong.

But when you slow down, and begin to loosen your rigid thinking, you can finally see that time isn't doing anything to you. You're setting up time as your enemy.

As Jack began to feel secure at a slower pace, he grew clearer about his race against time. There was no such thing. Jack came to see that time is neutral, and that it could be a source of support, giving him structure to set realistic limits. Instead of fighting time as the enemy, Jack embraced time as a friend that would remind him of his limits and his need to honor them. Time could help him structure his day and help him stop at a reasonable hour. He had to adjust his relationship to time, a radical shift of his figure and ground that was only possible when he recognized his limits.

You may be wondering if Jack could now accomplish all that he couldn't before. Somehow, by magic, could he do it all just by changing his attitude? No, it didn't work that way. Jack was never able to do it all. He just had to face that reality and stop trying.

Human beings have limits and will always fail in a race to control cyberspace, which is supposedly unlimited. We will also fail in our efforts to control whatever is uncontrollable. You cannot keep the sun from coming up because you need more uninterrupted nighttime to finish your project. You cannot make your speedy husband slow down until he wants to. You can nag, you can threaten, but only he can make the changes, even grudgingly.

A new kind of success comes when you see you don't have all the power you used to think you had. Accepting your lack of power used to be your automatic definition of failure. But here's another paradox: you give up your belief in unlimited power and you gain a new kind of freedom. You no longer have to push to do the impossible and you're not failing.

Your evolving healthy behavior and emotion will reinforce your evolving thinking. For instance, Jack sometimes feels panic when he can't hold on to his new belief. Then he tries to act as if it were true, and his recovery actions hold him until his cognitive clarity returns. An emotion of panic can drive the thought that time is pressing in and trigger the behaviors of moving faster, re-starting the addictive cycle. Instead, acting as if time really is neutral, your rhythmic behaviors will lead you to calm and your thinking will soon be back to your new normal. You do have limits and time is not out to get you.

Can you imagine trying this out? List three distorted thoughts you have when you are racing against time—"there's just not enough time" starts you off and running, behaviorally and cognitively. Panic distorts your thoughts: "I have to stay late and write this email or they'll think I'm a slacker. If I don't get this presentation finished tonight, I will get fired. If my son doesn't finish his science project tonight, and if it's not perfect, he'll never get into a good college."

Examples of My Distorted Thoughts When I'm Racing the Clock:

1. ....

2. ....

3. ....

Take a look at your list and then, for just a moment, act as if you do have enough time. No, you can't stay up, you can't do it all, but this project will come together. You will be able to do what is necessary. You have to trust.

Changes in attitude, belief, and thinking must come from within. First you have slowed down. You lightened your defenses and see more clearly. But that doesn't mean old ways of thinking won't creep in. You start to panic, knowing there isn't enough time to finish the project. But then you pause. You acknowledge that you've done all you can do. You've done your best. And even if the fear or guilt starts to rise within you, you proceed to follow your new limit, even if it doesn't feel like yours yet.

You are better able to act "as if" and to really change when you are not locked into a win-or-lose mentality. When you move out of the dichotomous frame, you will change the meaning of things to embrace complexity. When you understand shades of gray, you can give new meaning to the ideas of delay, patience, endurance, and tolerance. You used to disparage these character traits as loser excuses, defenses just like denial and rationalization that would help you explain away your failures. Now with your acceptance of limits, you strive to develop these traits as part of your new, slower self.

Judy came to see that what used to be definitions of failure have become anchors in her new thoughtful, quiet inner experience. Judy says she automatically pauses now before any major decision, and even the small ones. She knows that a bit of delay improves her thinking and her judgment. It's the same with patience. She pays attention to herself, making sure she's done what she can and letting others do their best as well. Even though she sometimes wants to shout at Maya to get a grip, she chuckles at herself instead. Judy is not a saint, by any stretch. She feels upset, angry, and wants to gear up to push her speed limits again. But mostly she doesn't. She calls up her new, growing ability to endure the uncertainty of the future and to resist trying to control anyone else. And, not a small thing, she tolerates the human limits in others, just like she's learned to accept her own.

Instead of searching for the airtight, perfect answer, you become able to contemplate "fine lines." Judy never thought she'd value waiting as a smart strategy. But as she loosened up and grew into much more complex thoughts and feelings, she became able to recognize and embrace the unknown and the complex: the day she felt both love and hate at the same time for Maya, she saw the new power she had gained. She sits on the fence about many daily decisions. "Should I make that call, confront the anger on the team, or should I not make that call and let it be for a while to see what happens?" There's no right answer. And there are fine lines convincing her back and forth. She can wait for her gut to kick in and guide her, she can sit in the unknown and let it shape her and her responses as time passes, or she can decide when she can't stand it anymore and jump in.

You can work with the dilemma of hard choices and conflicts of interest; you pick this particular path and give up the other one. You accept that you have failed in your quest to "have it all," but no longer see this as failure. Success means something else; it means accepting realistic limits and learning to live within them.

When you stumble—and you will—and you suddenly find yourself in that old bind of yes or no, right or wrong, stop for a moment. Just recognizing this thinking shifts you to pause—that momentary break in your speed focus—and then you look for the shades of gray that are no doubt present and you murmur to yourself, "Slow down, try a little patience and see what comes." You've shifted from a belief in instant action to your new value of reflection. Now the question "What am I doing?" is always part of your conscious awareness.

For many this path to a reduced speed zone in life will be a process of fits and starts. They will cut one activity for today and bring it back tomorrow. They will decide to stop watching their smartphone and immediately grab it for a quick scan. But soon they do get the picture. You must go through withdrawal; you must endure the pangs of craving, of need, and of anxiety about what you may be missing and how you will surely fail. Then one day you don't look, you don't scan. You are quiet and it feels good. You reach for the phone or you email your friend suggesting you go for a walk, ready to talk again. You return from your hike with a feeling of connection, quiet, and well-being rather than a heightened fear and urgent need to check your messages. "What if I missed an important call?" is not your first thought anymore.

YOUR STORY

Like everything else in recovery, your creation of a "story," what is still often referred to in AA as a "drunkalogue," is a process that is both active on your part and a result of being in recovery. Your story is your history, a narrative you create that tells what it was like for you when you were living in your loss of control with speed, what happened to start you questioning "What am I doing?" and what it is like now that you have accepted your limits, slowed down, and are in recovery.

When you hit bottom, you had your awareness that you were out of control with speed and couldn't stop. You began to look back, to reflect on what you were doing, how you raced around, bent on success. You took in the realities of your behavior as you were able, and you made small changes. Then you paused and let your feelings rise in you. "Ah," you sighed, "I was such a jumble of nerves, such a mass of intensity. All I felt was pressure, pressure, pressure. It often turned into anger and I was off on a rage.

"And then I slowed down, I began to think again. I could pause, listen, consider, ponder, and give some thought to almost everything. As my thinking cleared, the realities of my loss of control and my crazy race to go fast and faster became so sharp. Now I had a story. I had a before and after."

Jack had his first opportunity to tell his story at the gym. Raj was away and Jack was pacing on the treadmill, quietly reflecting on where he'd been and what had happened to him in the last eighteen months since he'd recognized his addiction to speed by listening and talking with Raj, and he had learned to slow down. A racy, frantic guy got on the treadmill next to him, pounding his feet in his drive to set a quick pace. "Uh-oh," Jack mused. "This guy looks like me not so long ago."

They began to talk. Anwar was in a hurry. He was always behind, but his doctor had urged him to get some exercise. "Well, at least I can look at my iPhone as I do my paces."

It wasn't long before they were chatting and Jack mentioned he'd made some big changes in his life. Anwar wondered what and Jack began to tell him: "I used to be such a racehorse and live in such a frenzy. I thought I was a wild success, but I was actually ruining myself and my life. I wrecked my car, had trouble with my wife and my work, and I had no idea what was wrong. If all these bozos in my life would have let me be, things would be fine. But the bozo jerks wouldn't leave me alone. My boss ordered me to take a leave of absence to pay attention to my health. I started on the treadmill, just like you're doing, and I met Raj. That was the beginning of a new life for me. He had stopped drinking, and then he slowed down, and he was a new person."

Jack never thought he'd be sharing his story with a guy on the treadmill who was just like he used to be. Anwar listened and grew curious. Maybe Jack had something. He sure seemed to understand what Anwar was doing. He seemed to understand it better than Anwar did himself. This was weird.

Jack became a mentor for someone else who was out of control with speed but didn't yet know it. Together they walked and talked and became a threesome when Raj returned. This is how it works—one person at a time.

Gina had a story, too. As she settled into her recovery from her drinking and her fast pace she told me how much her thinking had changed. The longer she was away from alcohol, and the more time she gave herself to develop an open inner space and deepening reflection, the more she grasped how essential it was to her to hold on to her new sober, slower self. "Every day I feel the pulls to get back in the race, to compete for power and so-called influence. My husband is supportive, but his idea of help is to fix every problem, every uncertainty I've got. He wants answers and fixes so we can slap our hands together for a job well done. Then we'll get to the next problem. This constant problem solving wears me out now. I want to sit in my newfound experience of uncertainty, tolerate the shades of gray and the fine lines where all points of view are right. This is what life is really about. And since I stopped drinking, I've changed my behavior to support my sobriety and to support slowing down. Now I'm aware of so many more deep feelings and I live with the joys of complexity in my thinking. I feel like I'm just opening up to a new identity of myself as a woman with a voice who doesn't have to know everything, who values taking time and letting things unfold. Not everything, but I've come to value a process in life, rather than nothing but outcome."

Here we are at the end of our Twenty Guidelines for Slowing Down—or almost at the end, as we'll let number twenty—the importance of service—cap our journey in the final chapter. But now, we pause and reflect. We think about what we've learned about limits and about change. We think about where we've been in learning new behaviors, opening up to our emotions, and expanding a greater range of feeling that we now value, and we think about thinking. Can it really be that slowing down is not a failure? Can it be that slowing down is actually the path to freedom? Can it be that as you learn to pause, take quiet time, and reflect, your thinking will grow sharper rather than more frantic? Now your thinking helps you pause before instant, impulsive action, and you feel calmer and more contained from morning to night. Jack says: "This is better. This is radical and it's lifesaving. I think, feel, and act like the grown-up I am."

15

Living a New Kind of Life

We've faced our addiction to speed, our addiction to fast and faster. We've looked at how it happens and how it works as a three-strand necklace that begins to choke us when we can't go any faster and we can't slow down. Then we looked at recovery, what happens, and what it's like when you face the reality of your loss of control and your human limits. You faced your fear and you have slowed down. Now we come to the last pages of our story, to focus on number twenty of the Twenty Guidelines. Then we can step back, looking at our own stories, to see the gifts we've gained.

Twenty Guidelines

20. You give new meaning to "service."

After a three-month leave of absence, Jack went back to his old job, but with a healthy respect for limits. He had unhooked from speed and now often felt the guidelines as part of himself, natural and even obvious. He separated his home life from his work life. He came home in time for dinner with his family and enjoyed reading to his son at bedtime. He became less self-absorbed and consequently was able to notice the people around him, the community he lived in, and the needs of other people. One Saturday he volunteered to help work on a house that Habitat for Humanity was building for a low-income family. Jack brought his son along; even though he was young, he was able to fetch nails and help Jack stack bricks. His son loved the experience, and Jack loved doing it with him. He also felt great about contributing to his community. Over the next few years it became a regular activity for Jack and his son to share, an activity that enriched their relationship and enriched them individually. It also connected them to a larger community, an interdependence that is critical to health.

All the changes in individual behavior, emotion, and thinking in recovery lead people to a different kind of focus on the self, a growing capacity for self-reflection; it also frees them to look outward toward the power of interdependence. As part of the focus on others as well as on yourself, AA emphasizes service. It is an effective way to make interdependence a reality. It grounds people and helps them maintain sobriety. Service is number twenty on the guidelines. Let's explore it now.

THE VALUE OF SERVICE

Service was a new idea for Jack the first time he went to AA as a visitor with Raj. One of the participants was talking about the importance of service, and after the meeting Jack and Raj went for a walk. Jack protested to Raj, "It seems pretty weird to me: everyone is saying I need to slow down, and now I'm hearing I have to fit more work into my life."

Raj felt very strongly about the value of service, and he launched into a mini lecture. "Service doesn't have to add a lot of work, although at some point you may choose to do that. Service is an attitude, a sense that you need to get out of yourself. Yes, you pay attention to you and your recovery, but you also turn outward to give. I used to turn outward to *get* something. If I was talking with somebody, I'd think about how I could finesse the conversation to get what I wanted. If I was going to give money to an organization, I'd think about which one would give me the best visibility so others would know I cared. I'd think about where I could volunteer to increase my exposure to big players. Now I just show up at AA, work on myself, and share my experience with others who can be helped by it. That's service.

"Service works against greed, selfishness, and that awful pride when you really believe you don't have limits. Service keeps me in check. When I'm in a lot of inner conflict, struggling with my cravings for fame but also really happy about my sobriety and my slower pace, I reach out and it calms me down in a heartbeat. Talk about instant gratification! I start to rev up and think I can go faster, and suddenly I remind myself to take a breath and slow down."

Raj chuckled as he caught himself in lecture mode. He put his hand on Jack's shoulder. "It's not all about you, man."

Your service may be as simple as really listening to your spouse, taking time to play with your child, or to chat with a neighbor down the block. Your service may evolve to something bigger than you and bigger than the other in your now-small world. As it was for Bill W. and Dr. Bob, your close connection with another may grow into active service outside of your immediate self-interest.

You work one step at a time in helping others. This is not a hollow "Do good" that you check off your list. This is service that comes back to you as a greater sense of fulfillment and inner peace. This is a core premise of twelve-step programs: you give to get. You "carry a message" of hope by sharing your experience.

When Raj first went to AA he didn't think he had a single thing to give. The focus he needed to put on himself was a huge struggle. But when a new guy came into AA a week after Raj did and wanted to know how Raj had managed to not drink for a week, Raj told him, "You just don't drink, you go to meetings, and you make a call. Stay connected." When he heard the words come out of his mouth, he realized that he did have something to share. We really do help each other. People told him he was the most important person in the room because he was the closest to drinking. He showed everybody else what it's like out there when you're out of control. The guy coming in right behind him let Raj see that he did have something to give: his own experience.

You may become the "compatriot" for a friend who can't slow down but sees that you can, that you have cut back. You now can tell her how you did it and what it takes to keep your new pace: about hitting bottom, accepting the reality of limits, living day by day as you change your behavior, feel your emotions, and discover new ways of thinking and staying connected with other people.

SPIRITUALITY

AA is the individual within community. AA provides the context and structures to facilitate and maintain interaction between the individual, fundamentally responsible for self, and the community of "other," who become the supporters of new development and a new way of life. Individual freedom and autonomy will be found and expressed within the context of the AA group—the community that holds and passes on its values, norms, and standards of behavior. The individual exists in relation to a safe, calm, and containing recovery environment and to a cultural system of recovery. The individual is separate, but in connection and not alone. AA is "alone together."

Bill W. and Dr. Bob found relief and rescue from the compulsion to drink through reaching out to "other." Through the efforts of these two people, many more people came to provide support for more and more newcomers. The founders and early members of AA credited the power of their mutual support and they also credited a spiritual higher power many called God. Even so, AA and its program of recovery are not religious. There is no external dogma for the person to adapt to or serve. The Twelve Steps are a "suggested" guide for self-development and the identification of shared experience rests solely with the individual. Initially people focus on themselves as they are learning from others. This new interdependence will grow to include a reliance on a higher authority—something greater than the individual or the other person—that will be defined by the individual. This can be tricky.

This process of giving over the power of self to "other" is paradoxical like so much of AA. The individual relinquishes the belief in the power of self, forms a new attachment to something outside the self, and establishes a mutual dependency relationship with others who have also accepted their loss of personal control and power. Power does not exist in the other person. It exists in the bond between them and the process of change that emerges as a result.

As people come to accept the reality that they do not have the power they have always believed they had, and that, in fact, they have limits, they can begin to recognize and feel just like anybody else. At first this may not be a welcome truth, but over time it becomes another source of freedom. They are not a higher power for themselves or anyone else.

Over time many members of AA will transfer their initial strong dependence on people to a strong dependence on the higher power they have defined. A personal and concrete experience for many, and symbolic for others, the externalization of authority frees the individual from an emotional need to return to a belief in the power of self, a belief that will send him or her slowly or quickly back into loss of control.

American culture is a mix of complicated and sometimes antagonistic beliefs and practices of religion. Many in the culture want no part of anything higher than the individual and thus reject the need for dependence on or even engagement with "other." Many people reject AA because they believe or fear it is religious. Ironically, in my view, there is probably no organization or philosophy in the world that is more devoted to individual freedom and autonomy without religious dogma or practice. Individuals within AA may be religious, and find links between their religion and AA, but their religious faith is outside the domain of AA. Religion is not a requirement for change. However, individuals may be religious and call on their religions for support.

Many people in AA and many in the culture look toward spirituality as their source of connection with "other." While there is a wide range of definitions for spirituality and no clear agreement, in the context of cultural loss of control and change, I define spirituality as the relinquishment in the belief in the ultimate power of the self, of the individual, and the recognition of something higher than the self. Spirituality is an acceptance of dependence. I suggest we think of a "secular spirituality," the acceptance of human limits and an experience of connection with "other."

I believe we cannot free ourselves from addiction to speed unless and until we recognize our loss of control and accept the need for help. I propose that the "other" we can turn to involves a dramatic shift from our primary focus on the self to a reemphasis on the deep importance of community. I propose that cultural recovery can be facilitated by elevating our values of community, service, and altruism.

CULTURAL RECOVERY

Francis Fukuyama writes about the Great Disruption, an upheaval in social values, norms, and behavior over the last fifty years, which he attributes to multiple factors.[1] Most important is the increase in intensity of focus on individual rights and choice and a "miniaturization" of community. There has been a greater emphasis on the individual in a way that has likely strengthened feelings of entitlement and grandiosity, and a fear of yielding to anybody on anything. In our either-or thinking, the individual wins and the community, based on compromise and a willingness to yield, loses. We stand ready to see when something is being taken from us, especially if it demands giving something up or yielding control.

The emphasis on individual freedom leads to increasing chaos with the elimination of rules and constraints. Without a sense of goals or purpose, and without societal structures to establish containment, individuals get lost. When we act like infants we need crib bumpers to keep us safe from our impulse disorders, and when we think we're above the rules we need stop signs to remind us we don't own the road. Cultural boundaries give us structure and identity as an individual and as a group. Fukuyama stresses the focus on individualism above community and the cost to society. "A society dedicated to the constant upending of norms and rules in the name of expanding individual freedom of choice will find itself increasingly disorganized, atomized, isolated, and incapable of carrying out common goals and tasks. The same society that wants no limits on its technological innovation also sees no limits on many forms of personal behavior, and the consequence is a rise in crime, broken families, parents' failure to fulfill obligations to children, neighbors' refusal to take responsibility for one another, and opting out of public life." We see this focus on individual freedom in our insistent denial of limits, including our "right" to go as fast as we want for as long as we want at work, on our computers at home, in our cars, in how much we eat, or how much we drink. We are on the lookout for anyone who might stop us or slow us down.

As Fukuyama noted, our focus on individual rights has led us to chaos. We are out of control in our race against time and our race simply to go faster and be faster. We claim our individual right to do what we want in the pursuit of progress and success. Attention to the well-being or the rights of our communities slows us down. We have abandoned our commitment to the community in favor of reinforcing a belief in the ultimate power of the individual.

I am advocating a shift in emphasis, not a dichotomous replacement of the self with the power now granted to the community, which is what so many people fear. We must challenge our belief in dichotomous thinking. We must work to move ourselves up the developmental ladder as a culture, to appreciate shades of gray and complexities in how we think and what we do. If we continue to insist on success as a win-or-lose contest, we will be stuck in a younger, all-or-none way of seeing the world. We'll stay back at ten years old, dueling for first place in one video game after another, with no clue that there's anything wrong except how empty and unsatisfied we feel.

American society has become the individual versus the community. It is individual freedom versus group or government restraint. It is individual freedom versus rules of any kind. Our polarized, dichotomous thinking is embedded in the cultural system. It is in our beliefs and values. You keep working, or you'll lose. You go faster or you'll fall behind. You go for the top, or nothing matters. You fight for your right to be out of control, and never mind the others. Despite our political differences, we are living out the belief that individual freedom flourishes without limits or restraints. Even without structures. But this kind of individual freedom without rules or constraints leads to chaos. It leads to loss of control and addiction.

It is our belief in limits and the reality that we have limits that gives us freedom. Without limits, our grandiosity and omnipotence— a belief in our ultimate power—leads us directly to loss of control and addiction. We keep trying to reinforce self-power by proving that we can't and won't be limited. Yet we gain self-regulation, self-restraint, and containment of our behavior, emotions and our thinking in the context of learning to live with others in relationship. Maturity is not a free-for-all. Boundaries, limits, rules, and structures provide scaffolding and direction to hold and guide us. Can they be overdone? Yes. Can we do without them? No.

The culture needs an acknowledgment of a higher purpose and a greater good than individual power. We need to move away from dichotomous, adversarial positions—the individual versus the community—to a way of thinking that allows us to focus on the individual *in* community. We will move to the individual *within* the culture, the individual *and* the culture. It will be "both-and" not "either-or."

The intense pace of life, driven by technology advances, pushes against rules and boundaries. There seems to be an unspoken rule that if something can be expressed, you should express it. We see this particularly in revelations about the private lives of public figures or celebrities. We operate as if there is no longer a valid line between public and private. Don't stop to think, don't invoke limits on behavior, feeling, or thinking. Just do it. Rituals now evolve around constant and chronic technological "connection." Many of these connections serve people well. But many others have crossed the line into speed addiction. People measure their popularity by the number of "friends" they have on social media sites. Adding a number to the list serves to boost a person's self-esteem for a moment, but it often doesn't lead to an emotional connection. The numbers, the "likes," and the process of getting a response become speed addiction, which ends up with a loss of connection.

We saw earlier that many students believe they must answer their phones at any time and any place to prove their friendship and their loyalty. This is a new kind of dependence, and codependence, as people sacrifice their autonomy to acknowledge limits because they fear they will lose a friend. This is the same kind of submissive, self-sacrificing attitude that characterizes many unhealthy relationships, personal and professional. The employee believes she can't have a voice because she'll lose her job if she speaks up.

The culture must instill a new value of turning off and slowing down, a new idea that is moving toward a tipping point in American culture. As I've been writing this book, alarmed for years by a fast pace and no acknowledgment of limits, I've often been a lone voice, with people curious but not the least bit concerned. In the last few years people are worried and voices are rising. It happened with smoking and it happened with drunk driving. What had been socially acceptable became unacceptable. We need to begin to speak and to challenge beliefs and values we have held for hundreds of years about American grandiosity. We need to move from an outward-driven focus to inward attention and a return to live, personal interaction. One step at a time, you decide to make the call instead of the text. It's not going to be all-or-none. Technology is important and vital. We just don't want it to replace all live human interaction. You remind yourself that open, honest, engaged, mutual conversation is a key to a healthy self. The changes in your thinking, in the guidelines numbered eleven to nineteen, reinforce your new values, or your return to old values, which are reinforced by your new behaviors and emotions.

This will only happen if individuals lead the way. The culture will follow individual change that includes a return to human interaction. Communities can begin to restructure neighborhoods, schools, and businesses to support slower time and pace. It is not an easy change. This pace is not good for us or our children. But individual people have to say, "We're going too fast." And again, paradoxically, individuals have to lead the way, but not alone.

Jack was very clear that he did not find his new, happier life in recovery by himself. He says, "I met Raj and I stuck around to hear what he had done. He shared his experience, strength, and hope with me on that treadmill for days, and I let him in. At first I wanted to walk out. As we chatted I knew something was different about him. I was intrigued and put off. I saw he had a deep quiet and a spark of life that I wanted and thought I could get by chasing speed. I soon learned that he got it by giving up on speed. How could that be?

"I was drawn even more to hear what had happened to him

and I wanted to run away. I was full of envy and disparagement. As he told me about his life in AA and how he had used that knowledge to slow down, I knew he'd found an answer. But I hated him, too. He had it and I didn't. I was still thinking that I had to be faster and smarter and then I'd be successful. So he also looked like a loser to me. But he didn't sound like a loser. This guy had something very special. He was content and he wasn't waiting to chase the next big idea. He was still a big tech guy, but he was quiet.

"I saw how much I had lost and began to get it back. But it did mean stepping outside of the people and the places that thought I shouldn't slow down. Sometimes even Maureen, who knows I need to slow down, will press me to fill up the calendar, but I insist on open spaces for quiet time." Jack has been in recovery from his speed addiction for four years. By following the guidelines for slowing down, he feels like a different person and he is a different person. He likes the new Jack. With a quiet smile, he added: "I've been growing through slowing."

SLOWING DOWN: THE NEW SUCCESS

For many years women and men in recovery from alcoholism and other drug addiction have been finding that their acceptance of powerlessness, which is loss of control, and their acceptance of responsibility for it sets the path for change. Only by accepting their limits are they able to grow a new, healthy self. People addicted to speed can use the same path for change. That's what this book is about: accepting your limits and your responsibility for change. Then asking for help so you don't have to do it alone. You are not looking for ways to get control, to "fix the problem" of your human limits. No. You are accepting that you can't go any faster, work any harder, or drive yourself one more hour. And it is in this acceptance you find success. When you are in recovery you will find the same successes that women and men in recovery from other addictions have attained. What are they?

YOU'RE PRESENT IN YOUR LIFE

You're different in every way. You've been on a new developmental path, slowing down and becoming the new you, the person who is no longer an active speed addict, no longer living in a constant, chronic state of being overwhelmed. You have new behaviors to slow you down, new thinking to support these moves, and new emotion that you love and hate because at first it makes you feel too out of control. But you're adjusting to feeling and you grow to value emotion. You are present for whatever is happening; you pay attention rather than distract yourself. You have a different relationship to time; you believe there is enough of it. You've got what you need.

A NEW SOURCE OF STRENGTH

Rather than power over others, strength becomes an internal sense of solidity and confidence. You have the confidence that you can meet the personal challenges that come your way and make decisions that are in the best interests of yourself and others. When Henri stepped off the rat's wheel, stopped juggling his multiple plates in the air, and began to recover from his addiction to speed, he understood strength in a new way. He says, "I discovered a new definition of male macho. I feel a deep strength from within. It's a contented strength, not driven by self-power or force. It's shaped by acceptance." He notes that he never thought he could sit quietly, reflect, and listen intently to others without feeling like a wimp.

Now these experiences infuse his sense of inner strength. "Slow down; follow guidelines. These are my mantras."

A SENSE OF MASTERY

Mastery is not about control. Mastery is an internal sense of competence, grown from within. You feel like you "get it." You know yourself and you know what you need to do to stay quiet, calm, and in that sense, in control. You don't get this mastery by grabbing for more, holding on ever tighter, and trying to go faster. Mastery is the experience you get when you stop fighting for control, accept your limits, slow down, and begin to live in connection with others. Just like kids used to feel when they understood the steps to solve a math problem, you also understand the steps. You're not winging it anymore, without any idea where you are or where you're going. Your sense of yourself does not come from your BlackBerry, no longer fused to you as the source of your brainpower.

When Shania was still obsessed with being the star of her company, mastery meant being in control of other people. She was an entry-level manager and felt like she was the smartest person there; she was ready to be on top with her next promotion. But she didn't get the promotion. Instead, she ended up in personnel, discussing her people problems. She wielded her BlackBerry like a weapon and intimidated others; she wasn't doing well in the interpersonal sphere. When she had entered recovery, learned to slow down and rebalanced her life, she learned how to be in relationships and her people skills increased. Paradoxically, when she was less driven, she was more successful, both in personal terms and in corporate terms. Most important, she experienced mastery in her own development.

CONNECTION

You have a new sense of belonging. You've reconnected with people and understand that the inner peace and comfort you feel is a direct result of your new sense of shared humanity. You see yourself as one of many, one of the ordinary living, breathing limited people of the planet. Before, this meaning of connection was equal to failure. You couldn't be the same as everybody else. This was death. Now this is freedom.

You no longer see the world as one big contest. You no longer have to size up every person and every situation to determine who's ahead, who's behind, who's winning, and who's the big loser. It is not you against the world. You no longer fear that you'll lose your competitive edge if you listen or cooperate. It's fine to take time to deal with complexities and it's fine to compromise. Moving away from dichotomous thinking will not cause you failure.

BALANCE AND INNER PEACE

Just like people in recovery from all kinds of other addictions, the person who is recovering from speed addiction gains a sense of balance and inner peace. You may occasionally miss the high of chasing speed, but you know the rewards of a calmer pace of life. You have limits, you recognize them, and you live your life with your limits guiding you. It now seems so simple, but it wasn't so long ago that you couldn't imagine slowing down. There was just too much to lose. Jack tells us what healthy means to him.

"It's pretty simple really. I have balance in my life. I know I can't do it all, and mostly I live by that truth. I have time for myself and my family, and I work hard. Sometimes I push too much, but I'm never far from home base and slowing back down. It's that recognition of limits that grounds me now. And I do see the paradoxes of life all the time. I laugh when I think there are no limits to what my new start-up can do and yet I am limited in how fast I can develop it. What a lesson. So many things are faster than I am. That's all right as long as I don't try to keep up. I remind myself to stay in the moment, to stay in this day, and there will be plenty of time. It works. Now my excitement and my highs are based on reality. What a concept."

SELF-RESPECT

You always thought you had self-respect, but now you know it in a new way. You see that you really lost yourself to your race for more, so now you redefine what self-respect means. You no longer look to others for what you should do, how you should feel, and how fast you should go. You don't let others push you to do more and go faster. You really can get off the train that's moving too fast. You make your own choices now, realistic and within your limits, so they're healthy.

YOU FIND PEACE IN THE PROCESS AND CREATIVITY FLOURISHES

You don't just throw your life to the wind. You do have goals, but now they are goals that fit within your acceptance of your limits. You plan carefully, but you don't plan the outcome. You set your goals based on a more realistic assessment of your abilities and the time you can and want to give. You recognize that the path to your goal is not instant. It's a process with small steps that you learn to define or to trust if you can't see clearly. Creativity involves a trust in the process, a trust in your intuitive knowledge. You're headed somewhere but you're not controlling every step; fits and starts are a part of the journey. Anxiety falls away when you don't have to be producing or winning a contest every minute, when you are not constantly measuring your distance from the "goal" and worrying about how far you still have to go. Sometimes the outcome still matters—you have to finish your paper before the class final, so you block out time, far enough ahead of the due date, to do the work. As the deadline approaches, you carefully hold on to this time, no longer giving it away with a belief you can squeeze in the paper someplace else. You can't and now you accept it. Or your daughter has a role in the school play, but the opening night conflicts with an important business dinner. What will you do? You look at your options, you look for ways to do both, and you decide. At other times you can open up to discovery and to the unknown path of creativity. It's not all or none. You plan but you don't control the process.

Does this compromising stance work in the business world? In labor? Industry? Does it work in education? Can we take our focus off of the end result long enough to see what's happening on the way to the end? It worked for Jack. He's in charge of a new start-up now, and his healthier, more balanced life—time for relationships, exercise, nutritious food, service, solitude—has given him more creative energy for his work when he is there. As a result he's generated some ideas for marketing the start-up that have worked surprisingly well. His increased empathy has also made him a better listener, which has paid off in better collaborations at work. In recovery from speed addiction, goals and aspirations guide us rather than drive us. They no longer exist as the empty end of wild pursuit. Jack says he sometimes feels pulled back into old thinking and a fear that he's falling behind. But he stops short of revving up his behavioral engines. Jack pauses and reminds himself: "the guidelines, Jack, the guidelines; pay attention." Just that pause can get him back on track.

COMING HOME

Running the rat's wheel in the corporate cage, or any other driven and pressured environment, can become an addiction as surely as alcohol, drugs, sex, gambling, and eating can. The key to getting out of that cage is the same key as recovering from other addictions. You become aware of having a problem and ask, "What am I doing?" You let yourself stay aware of the problem as you get ready to change. You enter first-order change, that is, you start to change some behaviors. Many will get stuck in this first stage, making adjustments, but always from the perspective of trying to get control. Then you hit bottom and know deeply that you cannot maintain a lifestyle of frenzy and pressure, that there are limits you cannot deny. You accept the paradox that you must accept being a failure in maintaining a lifestyle of speed if you are to succeed in having a fulfilling healthy life. And then you reach out for help. You look to a power other than yourself, a friend and compatriot who can lead the way, a Twelve Step group, a community you can be part of, learn from, and contribute to. You begin to see your world as it really is and you see it in new ways. Changes in your behavior, emotion, and thinking will follow, some automatically and some with directed focus. Some will be easy and many will be hard, even painful. But change is possible. You learn new ways of behaving, one small change at a time. You allow yourself to notice, identify, and feel your feelings so you don't have to flee from them into addiction. Your thinking changes, becoming clearer as you assign new meaning to concepts such as time and success. You remind yourself to think about the guidelines and to follow them. One moment you catch yourself in old behaviors—you've crossed the limit you set for computer time and it's now more than an hour past your bedtime, for example. You pause and see that you felt anxious at leaving some emails unread, so you simply continued. You see that you brushed aside the voice inside that said, "Turn it off. You will have time tomorrow." But now you do turn it off and head for bed. Suddenly you remember there really is enough time for all you need to do. Suddenly, you're calm again.

Finally, you get the gifts of internal peace, new relationships, strength, stamina, confidence, quiet, joy.

Now you are on your way. You fretted at the Twenty Questions, sure somebody made a mistake when you answered yes to fifteen of them. Then you laughed, and after some months, you saw it was true. You were addicted to fast and faster. You had become a speed addict.

You spent time reading the book and reflecting, page by page, one exercise at a time. You looked at your own addiction necklace of behavior, feeling, and thinking and began to see how you distorted it all in order to keep going, to keep working for success. You've been unraveling the strands that almost choked you, and now you've reached a new understanding of yourself and a new you.

You no longer act first and think later. You no longer reach for your iPhone first thing and last. You have a deeper, wider range of feelings that you never knew existed. Sometimes you long for the old days of feeling numb, but mostly you value the richness of your life that has come from opening yourself to more feelings.

Finally, you think so differently! How could this have happened? How could you have gotten off the racing rat's wheel and feel like a success? You've slowed down and it's not a failure. You no longer need to rely on denial, rationalization, and a host of other psychological defenses to protect your addiction to speed. You value slowed thinking and reflection. Your relationships are stronger and healthier. They are real.

Do you relapse? Yes. You feel the constant pull from all around you—your family, your work, your friends—to get back on, to join the wild ride again. Maybe you do. But you're vigilant now to be sure you catch yourself slipping back. You use your supports to reinforce your slower pace.

You remember the mantra: One step at a time. In tough moments that you'll surely encounter you remind yourself: "Pause. Take a breath. Reflect." This is great progress. It's a new skill that has given you back your life. Day by day, you know how and when to ask yourself: "What am I doing?" This is facing addiction. This is slowing down.

NOTES

CHAPTER 3: ADDICTION TO SPEED

1. David Denby, "The Quarter of Living Dangerously," *New Yorker*, April 24 and May 1, 2000, 190–200.
2. Matt Richtel, "It Don't Mean a Thing if You Ain't Got That Ping," *New York Times*, Week in Review, April 22, 2007.
3. Judith Warner, "Majoring in Stress," *New York Times*, Opinion Pages, April 23, 2009.
4. Ginny Graves, "The Ragged Edge," *Vogue*, December 2009, 182.
5. The Stressed-Out Students Project became a major research and educational training program called Challenge Success. According to the Web site, "Our current educational system and parenting practices are out of alignment with the well-documented need of children. As a result, we are seeing rising and debilitating levels of emotional problems and educational distress. Experts are documenting high levels of anxiety disorders, depression, stress, disengagement from learning, cheating and boredom. This is as true for the student struggling to pass the high school exit exam, as it is for the student who is overloaded with AP courses and extracurricular activities."

The researchers suggest that our culture's configuration of success is too narrow, focused on a limited range of academic skills that doesn't match the wide diversity of children's abilities and talents. This narrow definition of success is pushing kids to massive stress disorders and disengagement from an educational system that doesn't match their needs. The Challenge Success training program works with educators to change schools from within. These conferences are usually oversold as educators, parents, and the general public recognize that the current school pressures are causing serious problems for children.

6. Vannevar Bush, "As We May Think," in *From Memex to Hypertext: Vannevar Bush and the Mind's Machine*, edited by J.M. Nyce and P. Kahn (Boston: Academic Press, 1991), 85–107.

7. David Levy, "No Time to Think: Reflections on Information Technology and Contemplative Scholarship," *Ethics and Information Technology* (2007): 1–13.

8. Nicholas Carr, "Is Google Making Us Stupid?" *Atlantic Monthly*, July-August, 2008, 55–63.

CHAPTER 6: THINKING LIKE AN ADDICT

1. Anthony (Tony) Lavia, "U.S. Must Change Ways or Fall Behind," *San Jose Mercury News*, Readers' Letters, November 28, 2009.

CHAPTER 8: STEPPING OFF THE RAT'S WHEEL

1. Daniel Gross, review of Panic: *The Story of Modern Financial Insanity*, edited by Michael Lewis. "Boom, Bust, Repeat." *New York Times*, Sunday Book Review, December 28, 2008.

CHAPTER 9: A MODEL FOR TRANSFORMATIONAL CHANGE

1. Mary Beckman, "Help Wanted: In the Pursuit of a Healthy Lifestyle, Sheer Grit Takes You Only So Far," *Stanford Medicine* 24: 3 (2007): 8–13.

2. Alcoholics Anonymous takes good care of itself. In its early development members crafted the Twelve Steps and the Twelve Traditions to clarify the key elements and focus of what this group should be. The steps provide guidance for individuals who want to stop drinking and stay stopped. The traditions offer the same guidance for the group. Both the steps and the traditions hold the wisdom that grew in the founders as they took their individual journeys step by step.

Tradition number six says that AA does not endorse or lend its name to anything outside of its own province. It makes no partnerships and sponsors nothing. Tradition number ten makes clear that AA has no opinion on outside issues. Thus AA is not making public pronouncements on the problem of speed or anything else in the sociopolitical world. AA is not jumping up to promote its program. These traditions are important to AA's survival. But other people can and do borrow and interpret for themselves the wisdom from the founders.

CHAPTER 10: GETTING READY FOR CHANGE

1. There is a school of addiction treatment called "harm reduction" that focuses on diminishing the damage of alcohol and drug use rather than setting a goal of total abstinence within the AA frame. It is based on accepting the need for limits while maintaining the behavior. You recognize problems with your control of your drinking, eating, spending, or your obsession with technology, and you determine that you do need limits. In this paradigm you do not recognize that you've lost control and cannot get it back. You have not hit bottom; in fact, you are working hard not to hit bottom, but to gain some control by reducing the damage. You see that you've lost control or are on the way to losing control and your job is to take back control. Your job is to set your own limits and regain the control you've let slip. This way of thinking often maintains the deep belief in the power of the individual to be in control that we explored in earlier chapters. Harm reduction allows you to set the limits and to work toward reducing the damages of your excesses without moving to the second-order premise of accepting your total, permanent loss of control—that you are a limited person and you cannot ever return to life without limits—and seeking help to deal with it. This is the starting point for most people who are beginning to grapple with behaviors that are causing problems.

Does harm reduction work? This is a huge controversy within the addictions field. Accepted professional wisdom sees harm reduction for chemical use as "change without changing"—you are working on change, but that's as far as you ever get—a plan that keeps people stuck in first-order efforts at control, or perhaps it might be a step in a process that will lead people to total abstinence. Many people try to set limits, and try to keep them, in the process of "getting ready." The controversy centers on whether people have control. Clearly there are Twelve Step programs for addictions that cannot follow a recovery program of total abstinence, such as food and spending. The key difference is in views about where the power lies. Harm reduction sees that control can be restored through individual will. Twelve Step philosophy rests on an acceptance of the loss of human power and the need to look outside the self for help in achieving abstinence, whether total, such as drugs and alcohol, or limited, as with food and spending.

There are premises that must be embraced for harm reduction to be helpful. You must recognize the need for limits and accept that the need for limits applies to you, a condition for change that is rarely welcome and often not acceptable. You will struggle with harm reduction if you still believe deeply that you shouldn't need limits, that you are entitled to all you want—a core belief Shania finally had to relinquish. You will actively or unconsciously resist and even sabotage your decision to "get control." The changes you make will be temporary. The underlying belief in no limits, or anger at the need for limits, keeps many people cycling between their efforts to take control and the reality of being out of control.

Shania chuckled as she remembered how many times she'd decided to slow down and how many times she'd given up trying when she couldn't hold to her new limits. "I felt so sure I could change, that I could set a limit on my computer use and hold it. What could be so hard about this? But just as soon as I'd had my limit for the day I'd think of all the things I had to do on the computer that couldn't possibly wait. Each one was urgent. So I'd add some time and go to work. I don't think my limits lasted more than a day or two each time I tried. I told myself this was the price of being important. Lots of people wanted me and I loved it. I didn't want to slow down."

You can see that Shania's underlying need to be important, and the power she gave to her computer to confirm her importance, made it impossible for her to shut it down. Shania had developed a dependence on her computer to prop up her faltering self-esteem.

Many programs of weight control, budget control, and drinking control offer people behavioral plans that help them recalibrate their relationship to their behaviors of eating, spending, and drinking. In some cases, such as food, there is no such thing as total abstinence. If you eat too much, you have to learn to eat less. The same is true with spending. Most people have to deal with money. But we have to budget. In fact, the culture lost sight of the need for financial limits in the last twenty years with the expansion of unlimited credit. We are now living with the consequences of this denial of limits and the cultural loss of control of spending that followed.

Some people recognize they need limits, set them, and reduce the harm. "I am going to eat less" translates to eating less. "I am going to exercise two times a week" becomes a new workout twice a week. But many people also fail. They keep trying again and again to institute change that never lasts. Why does the dieter become the chronic dieter? Why does a decision to eat less translate to no change, or even eating more? Why is the person who intends to "improve control" often not successful?

CHAPTER 12: CHANGING BEHAVIOR

1. Mary Beckman, "Help Wanted: In the Pursuit of a Healthy Lifestyle, Sheer Grit Takes You Only So Far," *Stanford Medicine*, 24:3 (2007): 8–13.
2. Brian Wansink, *Mindless Eating: Why We Eat More Than We Think* (New York: Bantam, 2006), 12.
3. Chris Kenrick Chandler, "A Wired, Distracted Generation of Students," *Palo Alto Weekly*, April 9, 2008, 24.
4. Patrick Fanning and John O'Neill, *The Addiction Workbook: A Step-by-Step Guide to Quitting Alcohol and Drugs* (Oakland, CA: New Harbinger Publications, 1996).

CHAPTER 15: LIVING A NEW KIND OF LIFE

1. Francis Fukuyama, "The Great Disruption: Human Nature and the Reconstitution of the Social Order," *Atlantic Monthly*, May 1999, 50–80.

BIBLIOGRAPHY

Aboujaoude, Elias. *Virtually You: The Dangerous Powers of the E Personality.* New York: W. W. Norton, 2011.

Andersen, Kurt. "The End of Excess." *Time.* April 4, 2009, 32–50.

Ball, Aimee Lee. "A Life Unplugged." *New York Times,* Sunday Styles, November 11, 2012.

Beckman, Mary. "Help Wanted: In the Pursuit of a Healthy Lifestyle, Sheer Grit Takes You Only So Far." *Stanford Medicine* (Fall 2007): 8–13.

Begley, Sharon. "Your Brain Online: Does the Web Change How We Think?" *Newsweek,* January 18, 2010, 28.

Begley, Sharon, with Jean Chatsky. "Stop: You Can't Afford It!" *Newsweek,* November 7 and 14, 2011, 52–54.

Bergeson, Samantha. "Our So-called Lives: Is Techno-Chatter Replacing Relationships?" *The Almanac,* March 3, 2010, 18–19.

Berry, Wendell. "Faustian Economics: Hell Hath No Limits." *Harper's Magazine,* May 2008, 35–42.

Bosman, Julie. "In E-Book Era, Rule for Writers Is Type Faster." *New York Times,* May 13, 2012.

Brown, Janelle. "The Unplugged Home." *Sunset Magazine,* January 2013, 75–80.

Brown, Stephanie. *A Place Called Self: Women, Sobriety and Radical Transformation.* Center City, MN: Hazelden Books, 2004.

Brown, Stephanie. *Treating Adult Children of Alcoholics: A Developmental Perspective.* New York: Wiley, 1988.

Brown, Stephanie. *Treating the Alcoholic: A Developmental Model of Recovery.* New York: Wiley, 1985.

Brown, Stephanie, and Virginia Lewis. *The Alcoholic Family in Recovery: A Developmental Model.* New York: Guilford Publications, 1999.

Brown, Stephanie, and William Miller. "Transformational Change." In *Judeo-Christian Perspectives on Psychology: Human Nature, Motivation and Change,* edited by William R. Miller and Harold Delaney, 167–183. Washington: American Psychological Association, 2005.

Brown, Stephanie, Virginia Lewis, and Andrew Liotta. *The Family Recovery Guide: A Map for Healthy Growth.* Oakland, CA: New Harbinger Publications, 2000.

Bruni, Frank. "The Land of the Binge: From Bacon to Politics, America Could Use Some Moderation." *New York Times,* Sunday Review, February 10, 2013.

Burrough, Bryan. Review of *iDisorder: Understanding Our Obsession with Technology and Overcoming Its Hold on Us,* by Larry Rosen. New York: Palgrave Macmillan, 2012. "When You Text till You Drop." *New York Times,* Business Day, May 13, 2012.

Cain, Susan. "The Rise of the New Groupthink." *New York Times,* Sunday Review, January 15, 2012.

Carr, Nicholas. "Is Google Making Us Stupid?" *Atlantic Monthly,* July-August 2008, 55–63.

Carr, Nicholas. *The Shallows: What the Internet Is Doing to Our Brains.* New York: W. W. Norton, 2011.

Clay, Rebecca. "Mini-Multitaskers." *Monitor on Psychology* (February 2009): 38–40.

Coleman, Jonathan. "Is Technology Making Us Intimate Strangers?" *Newsweek,* March 27, 2000, 12.

Deangelis, Tori. "America: A Toxic Lifestyle?" *Monitor on Psychology* (April 2007): 50–52.

Denby, David. "The Quarter of Living Dangerously." *New Yorker,* April 24 and May 1, 2000, 190–200.

Dukoupil, Tony. "Is the Onslaught Making Us Crazy?" *Newsweek*, July 16, 2012, 24–30.

Evangelista, Benny. "Attention Loss Feared as High-Tech Rewires Brain." *San Francisco Chronicle*, SFGate.com, November 15, 2009.

Fanning, Patrick, and John O'Neill. *The Addiction Workbook: A Step-by-Step Guide to Quitting Alcohol and Drugs.* Oakland, CA: New Harbinger Publications, 1996.

Feiler, Bruce. "The Stories That Bind Us." *New York Times,* Sunday Styles, March 17, 2013.

Foer, Jonathan Safran. "How Not to Be Alone." *New York Times*, Sunday Review, June 9, 2013.

Freeman, John. "Not So Fast: Sending and Receiving at Breakneck Speed Can Make Life Queasy: A Manifesto for Slow Communication." *Wall Street Journal*, sec. W, August 22–23, 2009.

Fukuyama, Francis. "The Great Disruption: Human Nature and the Reconstitution of the Social Order." *Atlantic Monthly*, May 1999, 55–80.

Gladwell, Malcolm. *The Tipping Point.* Boston: Little, Brown, 2000.

Goleman, Daniel. *Vital Lies and Simple Truths: The Psychology of Self-Deception.* New York: Simon & Schuster, 1985.

Gomes, Lee. "Why We're Powerless to Resist Grazing on Endless Web Data." *Wall Street Journal*, Portals, March 12, 2008.

Gorlick, Adam. "Media Multitaskers Pay Mental Price, Stanford Study Shows." *Stanford Report*, http://news.stanford.edu/news/2009/august 24, August 24, 2009.

Gross, Daniel. Review of *Panic: The Story of Modern Financial Insanity*, edited by Michael Lewis. "Boom, Bust, Repeat." *New York Times*, Sunday Book Review, December 28, 2008.

Grossman, Lev. "The Hyperconnected: We're Addicted to Data, and New Inventions Like Twitter and the iPhone Will Only Make It Worse." *Time*, April 16, 2007, 54; 56.

Haber, Matt. "Coming Clean at Camp." *New York Times*, Sunday Styles, July 7, 2013.

Hafner, Katie. "Driven to Distraction, Some Unfriend Facebook." *New York Times*, sec. A, December 21, 2009.

Hamilton, Joan O'C. "Separation Anxiety." *The Stanford Magazine*, January–February, 2011, 55–59.

Heffernan, Virginia. "Miss G: A Case of Internet Addiction." *New York Times*, Sunday Opinion, April 10, 2011.

Homayoun, Ana. "Digital Learning Complicates Girls' Social Lives." *San Jose Mercury News*. sec. A, May 28, 2013.

Israel, Betsy. "The Overconnecteds." *New York Times*, Education Life, November 5, 2005.

Kenrick, Chris. "How to Capitalize on Failure." *Palo Alto Weekly*, August 10, 2012.

Klass, Perri. "When Technology Means Never Learning to Let Go." *New York Times*, sec. D, July 10, 2012.

Kolbasuk McGee, Marianne, Diane Rezendes Khirallah, and Michelle Lodge. "Backlash." *Information Week*, September 25, 2000, 50–70.

Kolbert, Elizabeth. "Spoiled Rotten: Why Do Kids Rule the Roost?" *New Yorker*, July 2, 2012, 76–79.

Kramer, Jane. "The Politics of Memory." *New Yorker*, August 14, 1995, 47–65.

Kreider, Tim. "The 'Busy' Trap." *New York Times*, Sunday Review, July 1, 2012.

Kumar, Reshma. "Internet Addiction Deemed a Clinical Disorder." WebGuild, http://www.webguild.org/20080620/internet-addiction-deemed-a-clinical-disorder, June 20, 2008.

Lavia, Anthony (Tony). "U.S. Must Change Ways or Fall Behind." *San Jose Mercury News*, Readers' Letters, November 28, 2009.

Levy, David. "No Time to Think: Reflections on Information Technology and Contemplative Scholarship." *Ethics and Information Technology* (2007): 1–13.

Lobdell, Terry. "Do High Schools Squash the Joy of Learning? Parents, Youth Experts Argue Against 'Busy Work' and Emphasis on College Admissions." *Palo Alto Weekly*, November 18, 2011.

Lobdell, Terry. "Finding Purpose: A Bigger Job Than Before. Previous Generations Actually Benefitted from Fewer Choices, Societal Turmoil." *Palo Alto Weekly*, November 18, 2011.

Lobdell, Terry. "Getting off the Treadmill: Finding Purpose Can Help Youth Discover Their Own Path to Success, Professor Says." *Palo Alto Weekly*, November 18, 2011.

Lobdell, Terry. "Teens, School Staff Unite Against Stress: Gunn's New Peer-Network Support Program Promotes Healthy, Supportive Community." *Palo Alto Weekly*, November 18, 2011.

Maslin, Janet. Review of *Elsewhere, U.S.A.: How We Got from the Company Man, Family Dinners, and the Affluent Society to the Home Office, BlackBerry Moms, and Economic Anxiety*. New York: Pantheon, 2009, by Dalton Conley. "So Plugged In, Yet So Disconnected: Field Notes from Wired America." *New York Times Book Review*, January 12, 2009.

Mendoza, Martha. "Tech Firms Plan Perk-ier Offices." *San Jose Mercury News*, sec. B, April 6, 2013.

Morozov, Evgeny. "The Perils of Perfection." *New York Times*, Sunday Review, March 3, 2013.

Nass, Clifford, and Corina Yen. *The Man Who Lied to His Laptop: What Machines Teach Us About Human Relationships*. New York: Current, 2010.

New York Times, "Bless the Blackout," April 21, 2007.

Novotney, Amy. "Dangerous Distraction." *Monitor on Psychology* (February 2009): 32–36.

Orenstein, Peggy. "Stop Your Search Engines: Forcing Ourselves Offline May Be the Path to True Knowledge." *New York Times Magazine*, October 25, 2009. P. 11-12.

Packer, George. "Change the World: Silicon Valley Transfers Its Slogans— and Its Money—to the Realm of Politics." *New Yorker*, May 27, 2013, 11 55.

Parker-Pope, Tara. "Cellphone Use Tied to Changes in Brain Activity." *New York Times*, NYTimes.com, February 22, 2011.

Paul, Pamela. "Cyberparenting and the Risk of T.M.I." *New York Times*, May 5, 2013.

Peters, Jeremy. "In a World of Online News, Burnout Starts Younger." *New York Times*, NYTimes.com, July 18, 2010.

Richtel, Matt. "Growing Up Digital, Wired for Distraction: In Flood of Texting and Technology, Schools Fight to Keep Students Focused." *New York Times*, November 21, 2010.

Singer, Natasha. "Slowing Down to Savor the Data." *New York Times*, Bright Ideas, July 24, 2011.

Slater, Dan. "A Million First Dates: How Online Dating Is Threatening Monogamy." *Atlantic Monthly*, January–February 2012, 41–46.

Stross, Randall. "I'm Losing Money, So Why Do I Feel So Good?" *New York Times*, Business Day, January 13, 2013.

Sullivan, Bob, and Hugh Thompson. "Brain Interrupted: How Distractions Make Us Dumber." *New York Times*, May 5, 2013.

Turkle, Sherry. "The Flight from Conversation." *New York Times*, Sunday Review, April 22, 2012.

Wansink, Brian. *Mindless Eating: Why We Eat More Than We Think*. New York: Bantam Books, 2006.

Warner, Judith. "Dysregulation Nation: Is Our Inability to Control Ourselves the Defining Feature of Our Time?" *New York Times*, Sunday Magazine, June 20, 2010.

Warner, Judith. "Majoring in Stress." *New York Times*, Opinion Pages, April 26, 2009.

Watzlawick, Paul, John Weakland, and Richard Fisch. *Change*. Palo Alto, CA: Science and Behavior Books, 1974.

Wayne, Teddy. "The No-Limits Job." *New York Times*, Fashion & Style, March 3, 2013.

Weinerman, Lea. "What Draws Us to Facebook?" *Monitor on Psychology* (March 2013): 56–58.

Wortham, Jenna. "Facebook Made Me Do It." *New York Times*, Sunday Review, June 16, 2013.

Yadegaran, Jessica. "The Loss of a Smartphone Was a Blessing in Disguise: A New Life Offline Brings Freedom, Solitude, Peace." *San Jose Mercury News*, sec. D, May 6, 2012.

Young, Kimberly. "Treating Internet Addiction." RecoveryView.com, http://www.recoveryview.com/2010/04/treating-internet-addiction/, April 10, 2010.